The Pollyanna Principles

Reinventing
"Nonprofit Organizations"
to Create the Future
of Our World

by
Hildy Gottlieb

Published by:

Renaissance Press

4433 E. Broadway Blvd. Suite 202
Tucson, Arizona 85711   U.S.A.

Orders@Help4NonProfits.com
http://www.Help4NonProfits.com
1-888-787-4433
or 1-520-321-4433

Book Design and Artwork by Dimitri Petropolis

ISBN: 978-0-9878928-0-1

To Martin Luther King, Jr.,
who taught me what can happen
when one's eyes are set on what is possible

To Bill Clements,
who taught a much younger version of me
what humility looks like in action

To Steve Cortopassi,
who has taught me what grace looks like
when we walk our talk

To Dimitri Petropolis,
who teaches me about building upon strength by
unfailingly and joyfully encouraging
my own strength and potential

And to my father,
Walter Gottlieb,
who taught me how to see

I am honored and humbled to learn from each of you,
wherever you are.

Table of Contents

"The Twentieth Century will be chiefly remembered by future generations not as an era of political conflicts or technical inventions, but as an age in which human society dared to think of the welfare of the whole human race as a practical objective."

Arnold J. Toynbee

Part 1

The Path So Far

Chapter 1:
Future, Present and Past

We are creating the future, right now, with every action we take.

Today's reality is the result of thousands of actions and decisions and occurrences that happened in the unchangeable past.

We cannot change the past, and we cannot change the present. The present - this very moment - is gone the minute we take a breath in and out. That in-breath is in the past, and soon the out-breath will join it.

As organizations and as individuals, however, we can indeed change the future.

In my own life, I can change what will happen five minutes from now by taking a different route to the office, by writing a different word on this page.

I can create the future. We can all create the future.

And we are doing so, right now, whether we do so consciously or not.

The future I want to create:

A future where my home, this planet earth, is at peace. Where all peoples share this global home, perhaps first in an awkward truce, and then in true harmony.

A future where our planet is physically healthy, where rivers run clear and clean, where air is pure, where the animals that inhabit this planet (including we human animals) and the physical environment are living in balance.

A future where we value our collective potential and responsibility as much as we value our individual potential and responsibility. A future where the true meaning of humanity, in all its ability, is present.

The list runs on and on. It is not much different from the list of what most people want for the future of our planet, our country, our community, our family.

To those who say, "Get real," there is nothing more real than this:

> We are creating the future, right now, with every decision we make, with every word we speak, with every action we take.

To date, as a global people, we have based our decisions on what we could see - what we knew from the past, and what we knew (and usually, what we did not like) about the present. We have made our decisions as if the only possible future was the one we could envision based on what we already know about the past and the present.

What if it were instead possible to create the future we want, for our kids, our grandkids, and their grandkids? What if our decisions and actions were all aimed at that future? What if we had tools and systems that helped us bring that future about?

Assuming we can use today's actions and decisions to create the extraordinary future we all want for our communities, what will it take for the work of individuals and organizations to accomplish that?

First it will require that we understand the path that has led us to today - not just seeing the path for what it is, but also understanding the assumptions and expectations that created that path.

From there, creating a different future will require that we consciously create a different path - a path that will lead us to the future we want for ourselves and for generations to come.

That is what this book is about.

It is first about identifying the assumptions we have come to accept as "reality," to see how those assumptions have led to the systems we currently use to do community work. Before we can create effective systems change, we must understand those systems.

The book will then share a new set of assumptions and expectations, aligned behind the goal of creating a healthy, vibrant, humane world - The Pollyanna Principles.

And from there, the book will share practical systems built upon those principles, showing how a new set of assumptions and expectations can not only transform the path we have been walking, but can indeed create the future we want.

By changing the assumptions at the root of planning, program development, funding, governance, resource development and other systems, and by developing new systems to align behind the future we want to create for our world, we will be taking the first steps along that new path.

Simply by creating and using those new systems, we will begin consciously creating the future of our communities and our world.

Chapter 2:
The Path We've Trod

Our present was created by the multiple layers of our past - a past that includes yesterday, last year, and a millennium ago. The actions taken today by those who are working to improve our communities and our world are therefore based on assumptions and expectations we have inherited from that past.

If we are to consciously create a future that looks different from the path we have already trod, we need to be conscious about which twists and turns in the old path have created our present situation. Only then will we have any chance of creating a path better suited to our intentions.

In considering the occurrences and conditions that have led to the way community organizations commonly do their work - especially in the developed world - some of the most meaningful explanations appear at first to have little to do with that work. Yet, they are at the root of why these organizations that were supposed to change the world have not yet accomplished that goal.

The World that Created the Present

The continuum of history provides thousands of years to look back upon - the years that created the path we are currently walking.

In the earliest of those years, our survival relied on the natural resources surrounding us. Over time, we learned to enhance those resources. We developed agriculture. We developed tools and weapons, giving us control over not only our own natural resources, but over the resources of others.

We continued to evolve. We developed commerce. We developed religion. We developed charity, to help those who could not help themselves, or who were not as fortunate. Those who had more than plenty also developed systems for ensuring they would be entertained - the arts in their various forms.

These institutions have been around, in some form or another, for thousands of years. The world's civilizations are experienced at working inside those systems. We almost instinctively know what to do there.

These days, however, a significant percentage of the world's population does not worry about meeting the basic needs of food and shelter. From that very new reality comes another new reality: items formerly considered a luxury are now seen as simply a part of life - owning a television or a car.

One of those luxuries is the ability and desire to invest in the greater good of our communities, helping those who are less fortunate, supporting arts, science, education.

This is indeed a new reality. It was not the reality 100 years ago, and was barely so even 60 years ago. As historian Arnold Toynbee observed, the world has, for the first time, evolved to the point where we have the ability "to think of the welfare of the whole human race as a practical objective."

The continuum of time we are on - the path we have been walking from the dawn of civilization to today - includes thousands of years of conditioning, thousands of years of habits. The centuries have taught us how, as a global people, to take care of our own in order to survive. The centuries have taught us to govern to protect our countries against those who would cause us harm.

The centuries taught us to run businesses that provide goods and services for profit. The centuries taught us to run institutions of worship for spiritual comfort, and taught us to provide one-on-one charity to help improve individual lives. And the centuries have taught us that only those of considerable means had the luxury to partake in the arts.

All this history has created our cultural norms. It is that history that informs what we think is possible. When we look back over those thousands of years, working to enhance the welfare of the whole human race simply has no precedent, no deeply ingrained cultural norms to fall back on.

The work being done by Community Benefit Organizations[1] is brand new.

---

1 We encourage using the term "Community Benefit Organization" over the more commonly used "nonprofit" or "nongovernmental organization, as it states precisely what organizations are expected to accomplish. For more detailed reasoning behind the term, see Chapter 11

Independence from Natural Forces

The path we are walking began when life was slow, when we relied upon the seasons for our survival, and we had to plan for that survival based on what the earth dictated.

For the past few centuries, however, our technologies have conquered the seasons. We no longer must rely on the earth's rhythms for our material needs to be met. Multiple generations have now grown up with the assumption that technology can provide whatever humankind might need or want.

That expectation has become another part of the history and culture that informs our view of the present and the future.

We can do anything, we can do it fast, and we have become impatient with any effort that fails to do so.

In 1961, when John F. Kennedy said he would put a man on the moon in ten years, the world was impressed with his audacity and his vision. The world was more impressed when it took not ten years, but eight.

These days, less than 50 years later, we think of eight or ten years as a ridiculously long time. We want a SHORT war, a FAST solution, a QUICK and SPEEDY economic recovery. In the words of Jim Morrison of The Doors, "We want the world, and we want it NOW!"

But we are still part of this planet. Our intentions and our technology cannot turn summer into winter, cannot make a human learn lessons any faster than he/she is going to learn them, or create immediate human understanding between long-term enemies.

Some changes, regardless of our intentions or our technology, simply take time. Because that goes directly counter to the accelerated expectations we have learned to see as "the norm," it is not unusual to hear the following when it comes to the work Community Benefit Organizations are trying to do:

"We can only fund what we can accomplish and measure quickly. We therefore have neither the luxury to consider, nor the dollars to implement programs for such long-term results. We must keep our focus on what we can accomplish and measure in the short term."

Our colleague Joel J. Orosz, Distinguished Professor of Philanthropic Studies at Grand Valley State University's Dorothy Johnson Center for Philanthropy and Nonprofit Leadership, speaks of the need for short-term immediate gratification.

"If we were to provide the typical one-year funding for a project to teach an infant to walk, after that year, we would measure our work, and we would declare the results marginal at best. The kid falls down. He can't walk a straight line. The project had some success, but overall, we would likely not fund such work again. Does it matter that by the time he is sixteen, he is running marathons? Not when all we measure is the immediate effects, so we can move on to the next short-term project."

The Culture of Can't

The path of our history is certainly filled with contradiction. We have thousands of years of training in what is not possible, and then hundreds of years of training that says, "We can have anything!"

Much of that contradiction relates to skepticism about anything we cannot see or feel. We know we can have material comforts because we can see them and use them.

But the intangible comforts - peace, compassion, joy - are another story entirely. If I do not already have the material comforts of a house or an ice cream cone, I still know they exist. But a global spirit of living together harmoniously? Our lack of experience with such a life tells us it is not likely to happen.

Our culture therefore believes that physical change is boundless - a Culture of Possibility. That same culture, however, reinforces that global spiritual / social change is impossible - a Culture of Can't.

The Culture of Can't is the culture that says, "get real!" It is the culture that gives the litany of seemingly reasonable reasons why something cannot be done. Coming as it does from the thousands of years of "reality" that have come before us, the Culture of Can't pervades our world view.

Logically, we know that much of what we assume to be impossible is merely unproven. Columbus proved the world was not flat. The Wright Brothers proved people could indeed fly. The Apollo missions proved we could not only go to the moon, but play golf there!

We know in our material world that what is unproven is not impossible. It is, in fact, where all our potential lies.

But we have not yet translated that to the world of the intangible.

We have direct experience with making payroll or feeding one person at a time.

We have no experience, however, with living joyfully in peace with everyone else on the planet. We have no experience with living in a community that is healthy in all ways - materially, intellectually, spiritually.

Because such a world is not part of our past or our present, we assume it will not be part of our future.

Visionaries and the Culture of Can't

Because we see a compassionate, healthy world as highly unlikely if not downright impossible, our culture and our history do not show much regard for those who assert the unwavering belief that such a condition is not only possible, but likely.

At best, we discount such individuals as unrealistic naive souls with their heads-in-the-clouds. Bleeding hearts. We mock them as Utopians who tilt at windmills. We call them Pollyannas.

At worst, we crucify them, assassinate them. (See Jesus. See Gandhi. See Martin Luther King.)

Mostly, though, we patronize and pacify them, and then get on with "dealing with reality" as defined by the path of our history. There has always been war, poverty, hatred, abuse. To imagine a world that is significantly different from that may be a nice dream, but it is not something we would waste time discussing as an attainable goal.

Knowing the best they can hope for is to be patronized or ridiculed, visionaries take one of two approaches. The strongest stand up for what they believe, fighting to build the world they envision.

Most of the rest, however, have learned that it is simply not culturally acceptable to talk about such things. This anti-visionary Culture of Can't affects the boards of Community Benefit Organizations every day.

> "Yes, it would be nice if we could eliminate poverty. But let's get real. There will always be poor people, and we could go broke as an organization if we try to help everyone. Our job is to do what we can for those people who walk through our doors, and to make sure we can pay the bills. To consider anything else is simply unrealistic. And we can't waste our donors' dollars on 'unrealistic.'"

While the visionary tries to get the group to see BEYOND what is right in front of them - beyond the payroll and the rent, to lead the group to what they can imagine - the Culture of Can't is the safe bet. The cause of creating an equitable society is considered the cause of the dreamer; the cause of providing a meal at a time to those of limited means is considered noble. The cause of creating true peace is considered childish; the cause of war, while admittedly painful, still far more "adult and realistic."

As a result, year after year, despite frustrations of visionary board members and visionary staff, leaders of Community Benefit Organizations create the future in the exact image of the past and present they so badly want to change.

Our Animal Nature

Consider the phrase "Human Nature." Do we invoke that phrase when we are talking glowingly about our brethren? Hardly. We use the phrase to focus on our greed, our fear, our selfishness - all the things we dislike about being members of this species.

In reality, though, virtually every one of the traits we "chalk up to human nature" is not what distinguishes us as humans at all. Those "human nature" traits are those we share with many, if not most or all, of our animal brethren.

Animals other than humans steal, kill, cheat, and deceive. Animals other than humans are greedy, fearful, thinking of their own survival above all else. Animals compete, they are violent.

When animals feel threatened, their immediate choices are either to run away or to fight back. As humans, our history suggests one of those approaches evidences valor and courage, while the other is evidence of cowardice. But in truth, either of those reactions is one my dog might also show. If threatened, she might run away, or she might bare her teeth. No valor, no cowardice; just being a dog.

That is not human nature. That is our animal nature.[1]

Neuroscientists have found physiological / chemical sources for many of the reactions we have come to call "human nature." The rush of adrenaline, the virtually immediate reactions that allow us to respond physically to danger without having to think about it first - those fight-or-flee response mechanisms are part of the physical composition of our species, the organs and chemicals that are our

---

1 In addition to the "human nature" traits we would just as soon blame on the animal world, we have also inherited some terrific animal traits. Many animals aside from humans use language, express love, loyalty, compassion, sharing, a sense of family. While those traits may not exist in all animals, at least some animals other than humans exhibit many of our positive traits. That begs this question: When we anthropomorphize animal behavior, noting how human-like a particular behavior seems (and often punctuating those observations with a long "Awwww, how cute!"), were these traits in those other animals before they were in us? Are they acting like us, or do we act like them?

physical being. We do not have to learn that; it is in us from before the time we were born.

Our species' long history of the survival reactions we call "human nature," therefore, are not just cultural. They are physiologically and chemically hard-wired into our being from a time before we were even human. That means overriding those physical reactions - aiming at something beyond our fears - requires something special; it requires that we make a concerted effort to use logic, and to exercise free will.

Our Human Nature is Our Potential

If our "negative" traits are not what set us apart as humans, what exactly *is* our human nature? What do we have that other animals do not?

Our "humanity" is a bundle of traits that combine to create our unique potential. While some other species may exhibit one or more of these behaviors, there is no other species that has all this and then some.

- A sense that we are part of something bigger than just our own selves and our own families / tribes
- The ability to comprehend that each of us is one life among a vast whole of billions of people we cannot see, but whom we acknowledge and understand are there
- The capacity to consciously de-program our instincts and re-program new instincts - free will
- An almost tangible sense of connectedness to something we cannot see or touch
- The ability to imagine things that do not currently exist - to invent, to create something from nothing but our imaginations
- The ability to express all these more ethereal capacities through language, through art, through music, through various means that allow us to transmit to other humans that which one cannot touch / taste / smell / see / hear
- The ability to envision the future, to envision what is possible
- The capacity for self-awareness, to strive for self-betterment. The ability to be conscious that we are conscious!
- The combined capacity for empathy, compassion, logic and reason, imagination - and joy at experiencing any or all of those

The human part of our nature provides a choice beyond fight-or-flee - a choice my dog cannot make. My dog is incapable of facing her attacker and choosing to neither run nor fight back, but to instead engage. Sweet as she is, she cannot appeal to her attacker's higher faculties, to learn why he is attacking, and to try to find a better way.

That is the *human* part of our nature. That is what defines our humanity. Our *human* nature is all about our potential. Through that uniquely human nature, we have the power to create the future of our world.

Chapter 3:
The Origins and Effects of "Nonprofit" Systems

Moving forward from the path of human history, we begin to see what has led to the path of the current systems in the "nonprofit" world. It has been a relatively short time - a matter of decades, not centuries - that the work once associated with churches and perhaps a few handfuls of private charities and community benefactors has become a multi-billion-dollar economic force with millions of employees and an even larger volunteer force. Just a few short decades ago, this massive force for community and global change did not exist.

Instead, as the quality of life in the developed world grew beyond survival needs, one by one, individuals and small groups who cared took action.

Had the "nonprofit sector" begun with intent, someone might have looked up and said, "Hey, we'll need some tools to do X or Y - let's craft those!" But, of course, what happened instead is that individuals used whatever tools were available.

Folks doing Community Benefit work did their best to adapt those systems to their own needs and goals. So what tools and systems has the path of our history led us to use? What were the origins of those systems and approaches? From those origins, what assumptions and expectations were built into those approaches, and what effect do those historic assumptions have on the work we are trying to do today?

A brief look at the two most common sources of the systems used within Community Benefit Organizations - Old-World Charity and the Business World - will help clarify the past that has led to our present. From there, it will help us see more clearly what the path ahead must be, as we look to create an extraordinary future.

The Old-World Charitable Model

Charity has been around since there have been people who care about each other. There is not a holy book of any faith that does not mention charity in some form. The habits formed from this part of our history have been long-held indeed.

The origins of the current charitable model lie in several places. First and most obviously, there is religious charity. In addition, the current model stems from private philanthropy, which grew dramatically during the Industrial Revolution, when certain individuals gained enormous wealth and wanted to provide some of that wealth for the greater good.

Both religious charity and private philanthropy helped the less fortunate, and both have also traditionally been significant patrons / supporters of artistic and educational endeavors.

The assumptions in the Old-World Charitable Model hold true whether the work originates from religious or private philanthropy. Those assumptions include the following:

Assumptions re: The Role of Assistance: The Old-World Charitable Model assumes the role of assistance is to help one individual or one family at a time. Even in circumstances where many thousands of people are helped, they are helped one person or one family or (usually in crisis circumstances) one village at a time.

Assumptions re: The Role of All-Knowing Benefactor: Private philanthropy generated by the successes of the Industrial Revolution expanded upon another assumption of the Charitable Model - that the benefactor knows what is best for the party receiving the gift, choosing what to give and how to give that gift. Whether the benefactor was granting his/her gift to a direct-service organization who then provided service to individuals, or the benefactor was delivering that service him/herself, it has been assumed that the party doing the giving (whether that party is giving money or direct services) has wisdom and knowledge the recipient does not have. After all, if the recipient were as wise as the grantor, the recipient would be in the same position as that grantor; he/she would have wealth and power (or in the case of religious philanthropy, divine wisdom)!

Assumptions re: Limited Resources: The Charitable Model assumes there are only a few individuals and institutions with the financial wherewithal to assist those in need. This not only leads to the assumption that their own philanthropy is a scarce resource, but also reinforces the assumption that resources overall are scarce. This reinforces the social distance between the grantor and the recipient, between service provider and client. From there, the scarcity assumption reinforces a sense of dependency, as the many who need such resources clamber around those "few" who will share what they have.

From these assumptions, tools and approaches rooted in the Charitable Model will measure results against questions such as:

How many people will it help?

How much will it help them?

Are some recipients more deserving than others?

Are we being accountable to our benefactors's wishes?

Is it better to help a lot of people with a little bit of help, or a few people more intensively?

How can we prove to our funders that our programs work?

Where can we find professional expertise to deliver our services?

How can we get our share of the scarce resources being offered?

What will we do when the money runs out?

The Business Model

Over the past decade or more, "nonprofits" have overwhelmingly been encouraged to "run more like a business."

As we look at the path of our human history, such emphasis is not surprising. While commerce has been part of that continuum since the early days of humanity, the industrial revolution brought to the fore a global emphasis on the making of money that has only strengthened with time.

Just as there are assumptions inherent in the approaches that come from the Old-World Charitable Model, there are assumptions and expectations inherent in the business approaches organizations are encouraged to use.

Assumptions re: The Bottom Line: The last line of a Profit & Loss statement shows whether a company has profits or losses - are they making or losing money? That literal "bottom line" is also the metaphorical bottom line in a business... profit.

Yes, there are businesses who care about the planet, about doing the right thing, about giving back. There are small, privately owned firms that make decisions based not only on profits, but on what is fair and just, sometimes to the detriment of profit. There are even the rare publicly held firms that make clear to their investors that they operate by a code of values that may place "doing the right thing" above profits.

But even for businesses with socially conscious investors, if the business is not making money, the investors will eventually find other places to invest. Profit is the bottom line.

Assumptions re: Organizational Strength: Planning for and ensuring that the business survives and thrives is imperative if there is to be an ongoing mechanism for generating profits.

Assumptions re: Market Demand: In a business that relies on revenues to create profits, market demand is opportunity. Without demand, there are no sales, no profits. Marketing, advertising, and other promotional activities therefore exist to create demand, to ensure ongoing sales and profits. And the more demand, the better.

> The purpose of a business is to create a customer.
> *Peter Drucker*

Assumptions re: Profit Centers: If the goal of a business is to make money, then to make the very most money, every aspect of the company will generate a profit. "Profit Center" thinking assumes each effort of a company will pay for itself and make money.

Assumptions re: Investors' Short-term Focus: Investors are a major source of capital for public corporations. The benchmark for investors used to be annual earnings. But just as the rest of life has sped up, the fast pace of the industrial age has become the "now" pace of the information age. Annual earnings have become quarterly earnings have become daily announcements on the Internet.

Investors may be patient for a little while as something is promised to develop. Some savvy investors actually seek out big-picture investments such as research and development or venture funds, that naturally take more time. But for the average investor, the most attractive project will be the one that consistently proves itself in the day-to-day of the short term.

Assumptions re: Scarcity of Revenues and Investment Resources: Revenues (and the customers who provide them) are not believed to be limitless, but finite. Therefore, the only way one company can gain as much revenue / customers as possible is if others in that same industry gain fewer customers, less revenue. Industry leaders work hard to be the #1 soft drink, the #1 selling car, or the #1 business automation system.

In addition to finite revenues and profits, it is also believed that investment resources are finite. If an investor invests heavily in one company, it is assumed she will have less to invest elsewhere.

Assumptions re: Competition: If revenues and profits are limited, and investment capital is limited, then logic tells us we must compete for those scarce resources, to ensure the business can survive and to ensure the profits will continue to roll in. Cola wars. Burger wars. Network TV wars. We are used to hearing such military terms when it comes to business, as we assume the aggressive, competitive stance of warfare is the only way to survive and thrive - to be #1.

From these assumptions, then, the systems rooted in the Business Model will measure results against questions such as these:

Will it bring in money?

Will it bring it in fast?

Will it generate more demand for our products?

Will it make our company strong, durable for the long haul?

Will it make investors move away from our competitors and instead invest with us?

Will it sell more product?

Will it leave our competition in the dust?

Will it result in profits both in the short term and the long run?

Chapter 4:
The Present Created by Our Past

The Results of Our Past

The past has created the present. What, then, has the path of our history meant for all these groups who have wanted to change their part of the world?

The Path of Human History

As a planet, we have thousands of years of "that's the way it's always been," with a long history of increasing ability to conquer our natural world. But because we have not seen such evolution on the social side, we believe the Culture of Can't to be fact - that humans will always be greedy, selfish, competitive, violent; that that is simply human nature. Visionaries who try to lead us toward our potential, while revered after their deaths, are often treated with the opposite of such respect and honor while they are alive.

The Result

As a result of the Culture of Can't, community organizations do not aim their efforts at the vision of a compassionate, vibrant, resilient planet. Instead, we react to what is troubling us, rather than aiming to create something extraordinary. We seek to end what we do not like about today, rather than seeking to attain what we do want for tomorrow and the next tomorrow.

> The greater danger for most of us lies not in setting our aim too high and falling short; but in setting our aim too low, and achieving our mark.
>
> *Michelangelo*

The Path of Old World Charity

Along the path of our history, Old-World Charity provided systems for helping one individual at a time. It assumed that scarce resources are provided by a relatively few benevolent parties of significant means, creating competitive systems for acquiring those scarce resources. Approaches developed under the Old-World Charity Model assume the people doing the helping are wiser than the person who needs the help - whether that recipient is an individual poor person, an artist in need of a stipend, or an organization asking for the dollars with which to serve others.

The Result

Programs (from the arts to human services and everything in between) focus on helping one individual life at a time. Evidence of this one-at-a-time approach is apparent in the recent surge in "Blueprints to End" this or that, whose provisions include ensuring all food banks have enough supplies to feed all individuals in need ("ending" hunger), or that every individual homeless person would have a roof over his/her head ("ending" homelessness).

Such programs are typically developed by the staff of social change organizations, with little to no participation from the individuals who will avail themselves of the services, rooted in the assumption that the organization's staff knows best. (In one case, a board member was incredulous at the suggestion that the staff ask community members about the issues that affect their community. "What if we ask them and they're wrong?")

Communities are seen as places of abundant need, with few who have the wherewithal to assist. That sense of need is confirmed by Needs Assessments that assume "need as reality" in their very line of questioning, and then, not surprisingly, find the need they are seeking.

From that sense of need, positive forces such as the arts are seen as a luxury for those of means. Arts groups work to refocus their message and their work on the power of the arts to build upon the strengths of people otherwise seen as needy. Yet even the language of the arts continues to reflect a history of elitism, where a supporter is called a "patron," with all the history that word implies.

Programs rooted in Old-World Charity are not funded upon a model of equal partnership between funder and grantee. They are funded by "benevolent benefactors," leading to a sense among grantees that funders create hoops through which organizations reluctantly jump, to be able to compete with others who also wish to qualify for those scarce resources.

The Path of Commerce

Business Model systems weigh decisions against a financial bottom line, with a strong focus on organizational strength. Systems built upon the Business Model see demand as opportunity. Such systems assume both resources and investors are scarce and that we must therefore compete for them.

The Result

Results of the Business Model are seen primarily in an organization's infrastructure, with a strong emphasis on organizational capacity and survival, and significant attention to a bottom line of financial viability. Decisions at such organizations often favor organizational and financial viability to the "bottom line" of community results.

Business-focused discussions often reflect "profit center" thinking, asking questions such as, "How long will that program take to pay for itself?" A program that does not pay for itself is often said to be "subsidized" (i.e. supported by general operating revenues). Regardless of its value to the community, a "subsidized" program in a business-focused organization is less likely to be supported than one that carries its own financial weight.

Under the Business Model, organizations lament the need to compete aggressively with others who want the same end results for their community, as they assume competition for scarce resources (funding, clients) is the only reality.

The Business Model has strong influence in organizational board rooms, where volunteer board members are often business people in their "real" lives. Boards spend considerable time addressing financial matters, as they are encouraged to hold themselves primarily accountable for the organization's fiscal well-being.

Business assumptions influence "strategic" planning, with short-term goals and a strong emphasis on organizational capacity as the end goal of many such plans. As organizations examine opportunities and threats in a situational analysis, demand is an "opportunity" (despite the fact that increased demand for child abuse services may not be a good thing), while increased numbers of organizations addressing that demand is a "threat" (despite the fact that more people addressing that need may indeed be a good thing).

Organizations who are most adept at using business tools are often exalted with awards for "excellence" and a local reputation for being "the best" - the best fundraisers, the highest profile, the "best" boards (defined by the participation of powerful community leaders, many of whom enjoy raising money).

The Present as the Gateway to the Future

The work of Community Benefit groups is about nothing less than our humanity - the elements that combine to create the uniquely human potential that sets our species apart from all other animals.

No animal but a human animal can envision a future different from the present and the past. And no animal but a human animal can create a path to that healthy, vibrant, compassionate future.

Community Benefit work is about what it means to be fully human. It is why so many of us, knowing the rolled eyes we will get when we make those Pollyanna-like statements, make those statements anyway.

Humans have huge stores of untapped potential. That human potential is what Community Benefit work is all about.

If we assume it is a pipe dream to think our communities could be amazing places to live, we will have no expectations that our work could achieve such monumentally significant results. Those low expectations will inform our actions and decisions. They will inform the systems and tools we use and the way resources are provided for those efforts. From there, our work will have no chance of achieving the visionary result of building resilient, vibrant, compassionate, healthy communities.

What if the systems most commonly used by Community Benefit Organizations helped us reach for and accomplish that uniquely human potential?

What if the most commonly used tools provided practical means for accomplishing visionary ends?

What if the tools we used were rooted *not* in the expectations and assumptions of what is not possible, but the expectation and assumption of what *is* possible?

Changing the Work that will Change the World

The definition of insanity, as the saying goes, is doing the same thing over and over, within the same conditions and in the same way, and expecting different results.

The path we have been walking has led us to the point where we are ready, as a species, to do what Arnold Toynbee suggests in the opening quote to this book: "To think of the welfare of the whole human race as a practical objective."

We humans can indeed change the world. Such change is possible, simply because it is not *impossible*. We can create whatever future we can imagine.

Creating such change is at the heart of what Community Benefit Organizations are all about.

To accomplish such change, the work of those groups must be defined not by those who believe such dreams are utopian fantasies, but by those who believe that aiming at creating a healthy, compassionate, vibrant, resilient future is the ***only realistic, practical and effective context for doing our work.***

To accomplish such change, Community Benefit Organizations will need to transform the way they do their own work, to ensure their means are not working at cross-purposes with the end goal. That will require more than a piecemeal change here or there. It will instead require true, systemic transformation. Clearly, no one party to this work can make this happen on its own.

In the words of a funder we met in Grand Rapids, Michigan, "If we are going to aim our work at creating extraordinary communities, we are all going to be uncomfortable for a while. We all need to decide whether those results are worth stepping outside the comfort zone."

That is what the rest of this book is about.

What's Next?

The path from here is ours to create.

In the first part of this book, we have disassembled the work Community Benefit Organizations are currently engaged in, to determine what has brought those groups to the way they do their work today.

From here, we will reassemble that work in the image of the future we want to create.

First, if our historic assumptions and expectations have not led to the sorts of change we want to create, we must identify sets of assumptions and expectations that would create such change - The Pollyanna Principles.

With those changed expectations guiding us, we must replace the tools, systems, and approaches that have not created the results we want, with tools, systems, and approaches that are aimed at those results.

And then, quite simply, we need to get to work.

Part 2

Creating the Path
to the
Future We Want

The Pollyanna Principles

Chapter 5:
Creating a Path to the Future

Moving beyond the path we have been walking, and consciously choosing to take a different road, can be compared to any major life change. In our personal lives, we can either lose weight by trying a fad diet, or we can instead focus on living a healthy life for the long term. For a true life change to occur, we need to change our thoughts. From those changed thoughts, we then need to change our habits.

But the thinking comes first.

When we change our actions without first changing our thoughts, we flit from fad diet to fad diet. When we change our assumptions and expectations, though, we not only lose weight; we become healthy overall.

To date, as Community Benefit Organizations have tried to accomplish more, they have leaned toward the fad diet end of the spectrum: the latest fundraising or governance fad, the latest planning fad. Not surprisingly, like dieting, our organizations have not grown more healthy, and neither have our communities.

Here is what we know about creating lasting behavioral change:

Assumptions About Reality **LEAD TO** Expectations of Results **LEAD TO** Actions **LEAD TO** Results

THOUGHTS **LEAD TO** **ACTIONS**

Where the Buddha Meets Aristotle

> We are what we think.
> All that we are arises with our thoughts.
> With our thoughts, we make the world.
>
> *Siddhartha Gautama*
> *The Buddha*

> We are what we repeatedly do.
> Excellence, then, is not an act, but a habit.
> *Aristotle*

The very first words in the most noted of Buddhist holy books, the Dhammapada, inform us that we are what we think, that everything we are arises from our thoughts.

That is what the first half of the formula is about - the assumptions and expectations that comprise our thoughts.

Our assumptions about reality are the beliefs we take for granted as simply "what is." Those assumptions are acculturated from the time we are born and stem entirely from what has come before us - thousands of years before us, and just yesterday. Our assumptions create the context for everything we think about, everything we expect to happen, and everything we do.

If I assume the world is flat, I will expect to fall off if I sail long enough, and my actions will be guided by that. My assumptions about reality will start that cascade of effects.

Rooted in those assumptions, then, our expectations will either stop us from taking action or encourage us to go for it. It is not our assumption that the world is flat that stops us; it is the expectation of what will happen when we encounter our "reality" - the expectation that we will fall off the planet. I am not afraid of a flat earth (my underlying assumption); I am afraid of my expectation that I will fall off it.

If, on the other hand, I assume the earth is round, then I establish a whole different set of expectations of what might happen. I might expect to just see a whole lot more water. Or I might expect to find strange new lands (or perhaps a new route to India?). Those expectations will then inform my actions.

The Culture of Can't is an expectation. If we expect things will never be different, that is the expectation we will act upon.

A Culture of CAN is also an expectation - the expectation that we can and will create considerable and significant improvement in our world.

We have all seen the quotes on inspirational posters, telling us, "Whether you think you can or you think you can't, you are right." Our results are ultimately rooted in those assumptions and expectations.

• •

That leads us to Aristotle.

Aristotle tells us, "We are what we repeatedly do." As our assumptions and expectations produce our actions, our actions produce our results, which then, in turn, reinforce our assumptions. And the cycle begins again.

As we consider the cause and effect between our thoughts, our actions, and our results, we see that aiming is an action. It is not a thought; it is not passive. Aiming is the first step in doing.

If we *assume* "the poor will always be among us," we will *expect* that we can neither eliminate poverty nor create an equitable world. From that expectation of "Can't," it would not even occur to us to aim at a different result. Instead, we will *aim* at what we expect is indeed possible - feeding hungry people, sheltering the homeless. Regardless of what target we aim at, it is that first action - aiming - that will determine all our other actions, and ultimately determine what *results* we can achieve.

As Aristotle points out, excellence is found in what we repeatedly do. To date, Community Benefit Organizations have become quite excellent at what they do. The issue, then, is to re-aim what they are doing, so they can then do ***that*** work with equal excellence.

· ·

In this part of the book, we will consider the Buddha's half of the formula: *We are what we think.* We will establish assumptions that logically aim our expectations at the end results we really want - incredible places to live.

From assumptions about end results, we will move to the assumptions about the work we do to get to those results - the means we use to achieve our desired ends. Unless we change the assumptions inherent in the tools we use to do our work, we may find ourselves using a hammer to try to open a bottle of wine.

As we re-consider the assumptions behind both our ends and our means, a set of principles emerges - The Pollyanna Principles. Those principles liberate us from the Culture of Can't of our past, laying the groundwork for creating our future.

From there, it will be Aristotle's turn to put the Pollyanna Principles into action.

Some Thoughts Before Diving In

No Shoulds
The Pollyanna Principles are not "shoulds." They are instead simple assumptions and expectations about reality. Once our work is rooted in these undeniable truths, the "shoulds" simply become what we naturally do, without having to be told to do them.

The difference between prescriptive measures - telling people what they should or should not do - and approaches that encourage and inspire, is all about the difference between aiming at something positive vs. trying to fix something negative. The Pollyanna Principles are not about fixing what we do not like. They are about inspiring and encouraging our human potential to achieve what we do want. When we inspire people to what is possible, prescriptive "shoulds" are no longer necessary.

Linking Arms Means Everyone
The Pollyanna Principles do not apply only to groups providing direct community service. As observations and assumptions about reality, if they are true, they are true about everyone and everything.

These principles apply to everyone who participates in Community Benefit work - direct service providers, funders, board members, nonprofit resource centers, academics, consultants, associations, coalitions, government departments, and any others connected to the work that improves our communities.

The principles also apply to all facets of Community Benefit work, from human services to the arts, from environmental work to animal welfare, from historic preservation to the preservation of human rights, and everything in between.

If this is reality, it is reality for everyone, at all levels, for all disciplines. If, as you will read in Chapter 9, everyone and everything is interconnected and interdependent, it is important that we all see ourselves as part of the same team.

As such, we have added some thought-starters for those whose work is not considered "nonprofit" but who certainly are doing Community Benefit work, with equal potential to change our world - elected officials and government leaders. If your work is about creating a better world, regardless of what that work is, we encourage you to re-examine the assumptions and expectations behind that work as well.

Our overwhelming human potential is what the work of Community Benefit Organizations is all about. What will it will take to unleash that potential, to create the path to the future we want?

The Pollyanna Principles

The Ends:

#1. We accomplish what we hold ourselves accountable for.

#2. Each and every one of us is creating the future, every day, whether we do so consciously or not.

The Means:

#3. Everyone and everything is interconnected and interdependent, whether we acknowledge that or not.

#4. "Being the change we want to see" means walking the talk of our values.

#5. Strength builds upon our strengths, not our weaknesses.

#6. Individuals will go where systems lead them.

Chapter 6:
Holding Ourselves Accountable

Pollyanna Principle #1:

We accomplish what we hold ourselves accountable for.

It is hard to imagine how limitless our potential is simply as a result of what we choose to hold ourselves accountable for!

If we hold ourselves accountable for fiscal prudence, we will be fiscally strong. If we hold ourselves accountable for staying the course and maintaining our current programs, that is what we will accomplish.

Imagine the potential, then, if we held ourselves accountable for making our communities healthy, vibrant, resilient, humane places to live? If we accomplish what we hold ourselves accountable for, our potential is limited only by us!

What might it look like in practice when we choose to hold ourselves accountable, first and foremost, for creating a better future for our communities? What actions might come from the expectation that we will reach for exceptional community results?

> For provider organizations, it might first mean holding themselves accountable for creating extraordinary end results for the individuals and families they serve (their clients, patrons, participants), doing whatever it takes to make sure that is possible.

> From there, those organizations might extend that accountability to the people whose lives are touched by those program participants - their families, their friends, their schoolmates.

Finally, if provider organizations choose to reach for their very highest potential, they could hold themselves additionally accountable for creating a better future for their whole community, in the short term and the long term.

Regardless of where the organization chooses to focus its accountability, those expectations will be where they aim their efforts.

Similarly, funders could choose to hold themselves accountable for using their dollars to create extraordinary results for the individuals served by the programs they fund. Or they could choose to hold themselves additionally accountable for creating a better future for the whole community. Either way, those expectations will be where they aim.

Nonprofit Resource Centers could choose to hold themselves accountable for creating extraordinary results for all the organizations in their community. Or they could hold themselves additionally accountable for creating a better future for the whole community, period, through their work with those organizations. Either way, those expectations will be where they aim.

Membership associations. Coalitions. Neighborhood groups. Government offices. Depending on what we choose to hold ourselves accountable for, that choice will create our expectations, and those expectations will create our actions and our results.

The choice is ours. Either way, we will accomplish what we hold ourselves accountable for. That accountability will guide our expectations, which will determine where we aim, which will determine how we measure our success.

What the Pollyanna Principle of Accountability Looks Like In Practice

What would it look like if an organization's decisions were all rooted in accountability for making their community a healthy, vibrant, compassionate place to live?

First, organizations would take only those actions, and make only those decisions, that would further their ability to create a better future. Their decisions and actions would consistently aim at achieving great results for both the individuals whose lives they affect, and for the community overall.

Second, they would diligently work to avoid actions and decisions that either do not further those ends, or might actually preclude them.

Boards would continue to monitor the activities for which they are legally accountable. But they would consider their decisions regarding means within the context of their larger accountability both to their community today and to future generations.

Lastly, organizations would work closely with those to whom they hold themselves accountable, to ensure they are, in fact, meeting both the community's expectations and their own.

To put this assumption into practice requires more than just having lofty goals; it requires ensuring that an organization's means align behind those ends.

We Already Do That!

Many organizational leaders feel they are already putting at least some of this into practice. They feel they are already basing their decisions on what is best for their clients, and that they absolutely avoid actions that go counter to those interests.

But these are often the same boards who will vote to eliminate a program that is highly effective but not paying for itself. These are often boards who cut program effectiveness when funding for that program is cut. They are often the boards who spend considerable board time discussing how to thank donors, or where to shop for the new fax machine, but virtually no time at all discussing how they will measure the impact of their programs in the community.

They are also the boards who may even feel that creating visionary end results is simply not their job.

> The Executive Director of a food bank was nationally renowned for her visionary approaches to hunger and poverty issues. But at home, her board wanted to put a short leash on all that "visionary hogwash."
>
> In our work with this group, one by one board members told us the same story: "Yeah, she's the visionary alright - she thinks we can end hunger and poverty. But where does she think the money will come from for this utopian 'ending hunger' dream? She never thinks of that, does she?" (In fact, the organization was always in the black, with a huge donor base - a fabulous track record in all ways.)
>
> Not surprisingly, the board put the kibosh on virtually every effort the Executive Director attempted towards making more visionary community-wide change.
>
> When the Executive Director finally announced her retirement, a committee of board and staff assembled to write the new job description. When it was read to the board, one of the qualifica-

tions was, "A passion for social justice." As the director of a food bank, that is certainly not a surprising part of the job!

One of the board members vocally rebelled. "What is this social justice garbage?" And the committee members told him, as if quietly confessing, "We included it to make the staff happy."

The intent of these organizations and their leaders is not at fault. They are just doing what they have been taught - that boards are primarily accountable for fiscal, legal and operational oversight. In some quarters, this "accountability education" has even been codified into Standards of Excellence. Unfortunately, such teaching is not merely incomplete (means without ends). It is actually the root cause of the day-to-day board actions that preclude creating a better future.

On the other hand, when organizations hold themselves accountable for the higher expectation of making a huge difference for their clients and their communities, their actions change. Accountability for the means without first considering the end results is seen as illogical and thus irrelevant.[1]

Our favorite example of what this looks like in action comes from a story told to us by Steve Zabilski, Executive Director for the Society of St. Vincent de Paul in Phoenix. Steve had been an accountant in his prior life, and so it is no surprise that during his first year on the job, he brought the board's attention to a program that was not paying for itself, and likely never would. The board was intent on keeping the program, as it was doing tremendous good for many people.

Here is what the board advised:

Our mission has been our mission for almost 200 years. It has done tremendous good for those 200 years. That is what we are about. And that will define what we will do.

Because the board held itself accountable for creating a better future for the clients and for the community, the critical issue was a mat-

---

1 Again, no shoulds. Just a change of expectation that makes a different course of action the only logical choice.

ter of impact rather than a matter of money. From there, the board trusted that Steve would find a way to pay for continuing the program, whether through program-specific funding or general organizational fundraising (which he did). They knew that being accountable for the end results meant they must absolutely be accountable for the means as well.

But their primary expectation was that they would make life better for the people they served. There was no question what they held themselves primarily accountable for, nor to whom.

The same approach, when taken by Nonprofit Resource Centers and by funders, would encourage those groups to ask similar questions, both about the providers they work with, and about their own work.

A Nonprofit Resource Center, holding itself accountable for creating a better future for the community, might look more critically at the content taught at the center, to ensure they were not teaching approaches that go counter to creating significant community impact.

A funder, holding himself accountable for creating the future of his community, might reconsider the requirements for receiving a grant, to ensure his funding systems are aligned with the impact he is holding himself accountable for creating.

Accountable to Whom?

In addition to having different expectations about an organization's results, if provider organizations held themselves accountable first and foremost to the communities they served, they would also have a different expectation about their relationship and level of engagement with that community.

Most community organizations will admit they do not currently "work with" as much as they "work for" their communities and their program participants. The relationship between program participants and those organizations is most often the one-way relationship of the top-down, provider-knows-best Charitable Model, rather than a real give and take. But if the party to whom a provider organization holds itself accountable is the person whose individual life that organization is affecting, that relationship will logically be quite different.

The same often holds true for an organization's interactions with the community. "Going out to the community" is more often a euphemism for "asking for support" (and most often financial support) than it is a real dialogue about determining how to create a better future together.

However, when groups hold themselves accountable to those they serve, both individually and collectively, that dynamic often changes.

Providers stop seeing the people they serve as units needed to maintain funding. (The most egregious example of this is public school districts in the U.S., whose leaders often admit that their motivation for having kids at least show up for half the day is that their funding increases along with those attendance figures.) Providers will instead expect to work with their program participants, engaging those participants to work together as one with the organization, towards their mutual goal.

> At KIPP charter schools all across the U.S., everyone involved signs a contract, obligating themselves to each other. Students agree to certain conditions that will impact their ability to excel. Parents agree to hold themselves accountable for creating the conditions at home for their child to succeed. And the teach-

ers agree to make themselves available to the students, 24 hours a day, seven days a week. When that student graduates from school, everyone has succeeded together.

When the "Us vs. Them" dynamic changes for funders, they stop making rules. They begin asking instead of telling, inviting instead of requiring. They begin working together, side by side.

In Lincoln, Nebraska, the Community Health Endowment funded and worked alongside area hospitals for three years. The end result was the virtual elimination of the use of hospital emergency rooms as primary care for low-income patients, ensuring instead that all those individuals have a primary care physician - a "Medical Home." [1]

In Phoenix, Arizona, St. Luke's Health Initiatives has funded and convened learning communities to explore what it will take to create a healthy, resilient community. After two years, they are still meeting and learning alongside their grant recipients. [1]

As a result of their deep sense of accountability, first and foremost, to the communities they serve, such efforts build real two-way relationships, so the parties can all work together to create a better future for their communities. That is a far cry from the "We know what's best for you" of the Top-Down Charitable Model.

One of the best examples of this change in focus of accountability is found in the disability community, where the rallying cry worldwide has been, "Nothing about us, without us!" Do not make decisions about what is best for us ("nothing about us") if we are not part of those decisions ("without us").

In other words, "Act with accountability to us. We are the reason your organization exists."

What if your community held your organization accountable for the results you provided - the impact you were having on their quality of

---

1 Read more about the efforts of these two organizations in Chapters 44 and 46.

life? What if there were consequences if your organization survived and was fiscally sound, but the community was no better off? What might those results be? How might the community define *success*? Those are just some of the questions that can guide a board to put Pollyanna Principle #1 into practice - holding itself accountable for creating significant community results.

Our expectation that "boards are about oversight" has led to actions that keep organizations accountable for the means. However, when our expectation is that we will hold ourselves accountable for creating a healthy, vibrant, compassionate place to live, our actions will reflect that higher level of accountability. We will then conduct our oversight along the way to building that extraordinary community.

In our work with a rural health clinic, we encouraged them to consider what they held themselves accountable for. We asked them to fill in this blank:

> When we have tough decisions to make, the right decision will always be the one that _____.

The group immediately responded, "The best decision will always be the one that is in the best interests of our patients."

Then a voice came from the back of the room. "As long as we have the money to pay for that!"

The group argued back and forth for a long time. Finally, they took a break, during which time we wrote up the following statement, and asked them how they would feel if this were hanging in the lobby of the clinic:

> "Our decisions will always reflect what is in the best interests of our patients, as long as we have the money to pay for it."

Suddenly they saw that this was precisely how they had been making decisions. This was indeed what they had been holding themselves accountable for - the money first, and the patients second.

Their decision became a simple one. "If we don't have the money to do what is best for the patients, we had better find it!"

Holding Ourselves Accountable to our Donors / Funders

If you still feel organizations should hold themselves primarily accountable to their donors, consider these questions:

1) Consider that rare entity - the fully funded, fully endowed organization. With no donors to be accountable to, does that mean the organization is not accountable to anyone?

2) If organizations are primarily accountable to donors, are they more accountable to the person who writes a $1 million check than to the person who gives $10? What if the $1 million check came from Bill Gates (representing a fraction of his total wealth), and the $10 came from a homeless person who had little more than that $10 to his name? Would that change the extent to which the organization is accountable to either of them?

3) If organizations are accountable primarily to donors, are they only accountable to those donors who give cash? What if someone provides $1 million in free rent every year, or someone volunteers full time (40-hour weeks) for free? Are organizations equally accountable to those in-kind donors as to their cash donors?

4) If an organization is receiving government funds, is the organization accountable only to the government officer who approved the grant? Or to the whole government, or to just that division of the government? And what exactly does "government" mean - is it the individual employees who work there, or the elected officials? Or is the organization accountable to every single taxpayer?

The list goes on. It is easy to fall into the trap of believing we are accountable only for the money. But if, as would be legally true, we are equally accountable for being honest and fair with anyone with whom we have the same type of contractual relationship we have with our donors, then it may be time to consider holding ourselves to a higher standard.

Joyfully, that higher standard is where our potential lies.

A Note for Public Officials (Elected or Appointed)

Who are you holding yourself accountable to? Where are you aiming the results of your efforts?

Are you considering that you are accountable to the voters who elected you? To your campaign donors? To the region you represent?

Or are you holding yourself accountable to anyone and everyone who will be impacted by the decisions you make?

Your potential to create a better future will come down to the question of whom you hold yourself accountable to, and what you hold yourself accountable for.

That accountability will create your expectations, your actions, and the results you are able to achieve. It is ultimately what will separate the politician from the statesman.

Pollyanna Principle #1:

We Accomplish What We Hold Ourselves Accountable For.

If we accomplish what we hold ourselves accountable for, our actions will flow from those expectations.

Therefore, to aim our actions at our highest potential to create an extraordinary future for our communities, we will hold ourselves accountable to the community we serve, and we will hold ourselves accountable for creating that extraordinary future.

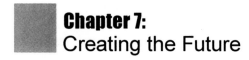

Chapter 7:
Creating the Future

Pollyanna Principle #2:
Each and every one of us is creating the future every day, whether we do so consciously or not.

If we accomplish what we hold ourselves accountable for, and we are creating the future every day, logic holds that we can hold ourselves accountable for consciously working to create an extraordinary future for our communities.

Talk about unleashing our potential! And talk about a huge responsibility! Imagine the power each of us has to create an extraordinary future! Imagine the collective potential our organizations all have to create the communities our children will live in and our grandchildren will inherit!

Having a visionary focus does not mean abandoning our current work. It does not mean we would stop addressing the very real issues of the present. It simply means we could do both. We could simultaneously aim at creating a better future tomorrow for the individuals we serve, **and** a better future in the long term, for the whole community.

> We could provide a safe haven for animals today, and simultaneously aim at creating a future where communities were more compassionate places overall, towards all beings.

> We could save sensitive lands from harm today, and simultaneously aim at creating a future where all the actions of our communities were aligned behind a deep respect for the natural environment.

We could provide theater performances today, and simultaneously aim at creating a future where our communities understood the arts to be the way humans express all aspects of their spirit.

As the Buddha and Aristotle remind us, the power to create that extraordinary future lies in changing our assumptions and expectations - the context of our work - and from there changing the way that work is done.

Changing Expectations from Problem-Solving to Vision-Based Results

As we reinvent the work of Community Benefit Organizations to aim at creating more significant improvement to the quality of life in our communities and our world, the most critical step we can take is to change the context of our work from problem-solving to vision-based expectations.

By definition, problem-solving is about ending something we do not like - poverty, drug use, terrorism. By definition, vision-based expectations are about creating the future we DO want.

This is not semantic. That seemingly simple change of assumptions and expectations can change every single thing about the way an organization does its work. From there, that changed work cannot help but produce more visionary results.

When we expect to work towards a powerful vision, we imagine the positive future we intend to create, and we head for that future, solving current problems along the way. We embrace and work with all the complexity it will take to achieve that positive goal, immersing ourselves in the whole picture. We are able to more clearly see what might otherwise become "unintended consequences." We expect to work closely with everyone whose future we are creating (which is, in reality, everyone!). We expect to consider both the forest and the trees.

Problem-solving, however, encourages us to focus on the trees to the exclusion of the forest, and often to focus on only one or two of those trees at a time. If a community has a drug problem, a substance abuse prevention effort might aim at the drug dealers and the drug users. It is less likely to simultaneously aim at building strong families in all ways, strong schools, strong spiritual support systems - at building strong individuals who may not be as inclined to use drugs, or who have support systems to help if they do. Such community programs are far more likely to aim instead at intervention, where they know they can make a difference quickly.

If we expect to create a healthy, vibrant, humane community, we know such intervention is critical to our ultimate success. But we also know there is much to be done beyond that intervention.

Taking all this into consideration, vision-based expectations allow us to see why, for all the work and dollars poured into solving both global and community problems (e.g. poverty, drug use, terrorism, immigration issues, etc.), those problems still persist. Further, it allows us to see that the next problem-solving effort in the war on poverty, the war on drugs, the war on terror, the war on illegal immigration cannot succeed, regardless of what such efforts include, who creates them, how well they are funded, and how much support they have. By narrowly focusing on the symptoms, staring at each tree individually with little attention to the "unintended consequences" that may result from our actions, and aiming at the elimination of something negative rather than attaining something grand, problem-solving efforts prove repeatedly that they are not very effective at solving complex social problems.

The only road to visionary end results is to have visionary expectations. If we are to create the future of our communities, our image of that future must guide all our decisions and actions. Along the way, we will solve our problems. Then we will keep going, intent on attaining the future we do want, instead of simply eliminating the current circumstances we do not want.

Creating the Future

> You never change things by fighting the existing reality. To change something, build a new model that makes the existing model obsolete.
>
> *R. Buckminster Fuller*

The American Civil Rights movement did not have problem-solving as its expectation. The goal was not simply to end something bad - segregation - but to create something extraordinary - the lasting and all-encompassing goal of equality and possibility. The Reverend Dr. Martin Luther King made that abundantly clear:

> "I have a dream that my four children will one day live in a nation where they will not be judged by the color of their skin but by the content of their character."

This is not a reactive, problem-solving statement.

It is a statement that describes a promised land. It envisions a time when a man of African descent could be president of a country that was built, in large part, by the blood of African slaves. Nelson Mandela. Barack Obama. Both are images not of a problem that was solved, but of an extraordinary future envisioned and created, with strong intent and great sacrifice.

Such visionary achievement is possible only when we aim beyond our problems - when we stop asking, *"What are we going to do about what we do not like about today?"* and we begin asking, *"How can we build the future we **do** want to live in?"*

To reinvent the work of Community Benefit Organizations to create the future of our communities and our world, we will need vision-based expectations to be at the heart of our work. It is that vision that will create a path to the promised land.

The Power of Positive, Visionary Expectations:

When former Arkansas Governor Mike Huckabee lost over 100 pounds and kept it off, he wrote a book and hit the PR circuit. On television and in the newspapers he repeated the same words (quoted here from an interview in USA Today): "I don't have a weight goal. I have a health and fitness goal. If you get healthy and fit, **the weight will take care of itself."** (Emphasis added)

Determining whether we will aim at the problem or aim at the future we want to create is not semantics. It is not consultant mumbo-jumbo. Deciding where to aim is, instead, everything.

When we aim at the problem, the discussion begins with all our baggage. We begin at the place where we all disagree, and that sense of disagreement sets the context for all our discussions.

However, when we aim at the future we want to create for our communities, for our world, for our grandkids and their grandkids, we begin that same discussion at the point where virtually all of us agree, simply because our current livelihood is not threatened by that future. Our baggage all resides here in the present.

Aiming at the future inspires us to be the very best we can be, for ourselves, for each other, for our heirs and their heirs. It inspires us to consider our legacies as individuals and as communities. It inspires us to consider our boundless potential to keep getting better - potential that builds more potential, the more we tap on it.

Aiming our work at the future we want to create makes us realize every day that unless something is scientifically impossible, it is possible. That realization can inspire us to act with responsibility to all beings on our planet, now and in the future, because each of us is creating that future.

Such inspiration is a far more effective long-term motivator than our animal fears. We can accustom ourselves to living in fear, and eventually stop reacting and just get on with life.

But living with ongoing inspiration is like a constant caffeine rush. It pulls us out of bed invigorated in the morning, and inspires us to do even more the next day.

And that is power we could all use.

Inspiration, Human Potential, and Creating the Future: Education and the Arts

Education and the arts are all about our human potential. They are entirely about what is possible, what is inspiring, what is glorious about humanity.

One result of our culture's intellectual and emotional pull towards problem-solving is that we have relegated arts organizations to second-class status. Because the primary goal of the arts is not to attempt to solve society's many woes, they are considered superfluous, fluff. In talk after talk, and in workshop after workshop, I am asked about how this "creating the future stuff" applies to the arts, when funders repeatedly tell arts groups there is just too much need in the world for them to begin funding something that is, yes, wonderful, but is also "unnecessary."

Further, when it comes to education (at least in the U.S.), we have actually turned one of the most inspired and inspiring human acts - learning and expanding our minds - into a problem-solving venture. From the failure of public schools to the needs of our local economies to have a trained and educated workforce, the "education issue" has become a series of problem-solving arguments about curriculum, drop out rates, gangs, plummeting test scores, and all the other issues related to a failing education system.

Again, the bigger picture context of vision-based expectations can make all the difference.

How would our expectations and our actions change if we assumed art was the key to building a healthy, vibrant, humane, resilient community - not because of its economic impact, but because the arts encourage us to express ourselves and help us interpret the world around us in the healthiest and most human of ways?

How would our expectations and actions change if we assumed education was the key to building strong communities, not simply as "workforce development," but as a force for creating more engaged citizens in all ways?

A colleague who works for a human services organization shared her thoughts one day, telling us, "The worst thing about poverty isn't the poverty of our bodies - hunger or homelessness. The worst thing is that it breeds poverty of the spirit, and once poverty invades the spirit, it is almost impossible to rise above it."

We build spirit through the unleashing of our human potential, our curiosity, our ability to synthesize a variety of thoughts and emotions to create something new. We build spirit through our ability to explore, to dream. That is what education and the arts are at their core.

We see repeatedly that education and the arts have the ability to inspire, often when everything else fails. We all know the stories about Harlem kids who learned the violin; about kids in East Los Angeles who learned to excel at calculus; about Compton, California kids who not only produced Thornton Wilder's "Our Town," but modified it to fit THEIR town. These stories (and the movies that have been made about them) leave us feeling engaged and inspired by the potential that exists inside us all - potential that is reached through education and the arts.

Among its many programs, Reno, Nevada's Sierra Arts provides unrestricted grants to local artists, to encourage and further their work. Through the *Razor Wire* poetry workshop at the Northern Nevada Correctional Center, a literary arts fellowship was awarded to Ismael García Santillanes, who expressed his boundless gratitude:

Today, Shaun brought news - great news, he said - that I won a literary arts fellowship. He had to repeat it a few times. I was, at that very moment, the happiest man on Earth - I laughed and curled my legs beneath the chair to keep from flying off. Prison suddenly lost its gravity. The rest of the workshop session was a dream sequence. Segments of ideas. Morsels of hearts. Rituals. As I read my poems to the workshop, I felt a sense of prayer.

I thank you and everyone involved with the Sierra Arts Foundation. From now on, when I think of the word "fellowship," I will

think of you, Sierra Arts, and a workshop where men struggle to
write their way back home.

That is the inspirational power of education and the arts. It is the power of what it means to be human. It is no less than the power to change the world.

Putting the Pollyanna Principle of 'Creating the Future' Into Practice

As we consider the powerful difference between aiming at problem-solving (or problem-preventing) and the vision-based approach of aiming at the future we want to create, we see once again the effects of changing the assumptions and expectations at the core of the systems we use.

If we consciously aimed day-to-day systems such as governance, planning, program development, and evaluation at creating a better future, the results would ripple in ways we can only imagine.

We could aim at creating an extraordinary future for our clients, for our employees, for our board members. We could aim at creating an extraordinary future for our whole community, and beyond our community.

Such a change will require that our actions and decisions be rooted in two questions:
1. Will the future created by this decision be the best possible future for those affected?
2. If not, what will we do?

The result of those two questions can be astounding:

When the funding context of a healthcare foundation moved from "care that treats the sick" to "building a healthy, resilient community," everything discussed in this chapter came to pass. Their funding priorities changed, and their board discussions changed. After two years, a larger group than they ever dreamed possible remains at the table, inspired and motivated to see what comes next. [1]

When the academic context of a masters level degree program changed from the standard "leadership education" to "a change-the-world, leave-a-legacy, make a difference" program,

---

1 See Chapter 44 for more about this work.

everything discussed in this chapter also came to pass. Their curriculum and their faculty changed. After only a few short months, new questions arose about "the way we do things," as the program's leaders began questioning how they might better walk their own talk in light of the changes they had embarked upon for their students.[2]

In the end, our power to create the future is about more than potential. It is about responsibility. What future do you want to be responsible for creating?

---

2 See Chapter 20-22 for more about this effort.

A Note for Public Officials (Elected or Appointed)
As a public official, are you problem-solving or aiming
at creating the future? Are you aiming the power be-
stowed upon you at ending something you do not want,
or at beginning something you do want?

Is your end-the-war strategy focused on simply ending a
war, or is it instead focused on creating a spirit of peace
in that region and around the world?

Is your strategy on immigration aimed at closing down
the borders now, or creating a circumstance where
perhaps, 20 years from now, the country from which
you are experiencing that influx will have such a strong
economy, or such a focus on human rights, that individuals will neither need nor want to leave?

Is your strategy on the economy focused on ending a
crisis, or is it aimed instead at creating equal opportunity for prosperity for everyone, at every level of the
economic spectrum, for the long term?

It is the rare elected official that aims at anything that
cannot be proven to work before the next election
cycle. Aim at the future you want to create, and the
unintended consequences of your actions may just be
greater short-term *and* long-term success than you had
imagined possible.

Pollyanna Principle #2:

Each and every one of us is creating the future every day, whether we do so consciously or not.

If we are creating the future every day, then every day we can expect to aim our work at the cause-and-effect that will create a healthy, vibrant, humane future for our children, our grandchildren, and their grandchildren. Our actions will then flow from those expectations.

Chapter 8:
From Ends to Means

As we change our expectations about the extent to which vision-ary community results are possible, we see that the means we use to achieve those results must be aligned behind those visionary expec-tations. When we fail to align our means behind creating visionary community results, we encounter obstacle after obstacle. When we embrace means that align behind those community results, things fall logically into place.

When we hold ourselves accountable for creating the future of our communities, we will expect to do our work in a way that embraces anyone who is doing similar work, and we will expect our whole community to work alongside us. We will expect to build our work upon the higher values we all share. We will expect our work to be built upon our individual and collective strengths. And we will ex-pect that work to be self-inspired, relying upon logical, self-sustain-ing systems, aimed at our end goals and aimed at the positive means we will choose to achieve those goals.

When the tools and systems we use to do our day-to-day work are aligned behind the visionary results we intend to achieve, the means become not just a path towards those end results, but in many cases, become inspiring end results unto themselves.

The following chapters address the assumptions and expectations embodied in the means Community Benefit Organizations use to do their work.

Chapter 9:
Interconnected & Interdependent

Pollyanna Principle #3:
Everyone and everything is interconnected and interdependent, whether we acknowledge that or not.

There is something powerful about sitting atop a mountain, realizing we are part of something bigger than just ourselves. We feel connected, whole, as if time is not something that happens to us, but instead runs through us.

That is what it feels like when we focus on what connects us, rather than what divides us. It is one of the many things that separates us humans from the rest of the animal world. As such, it is a big part of our potential.

None of us is completely independent. I am not simply "me," but the genetic combination of my parents, their parents, and generations of grandparents that go back for thousands of years. Each of us is connected to our genetics in that way.

We are also the sum of the experiences of family who came before us. All my grandparents were sent away from their homes at the tender ages of 11 and 15, put on boats to America, never to see their families again. That impacted how they raised my parents, how my parents raised me, and how I raised my daughter. Each of us is similarly connected to our family's experiences.

Just as I am the sum of everyone who has gone before me, I am also the sum of my own life's experiences. None of us is who we were ten years ago or fifty years ago. The interwoven stories of our own lives have created who each of us is today.

We are all little bits of everyone else and everything else.

We are also each part of something yet to come. Bits of me are in my daughter, and in her children yet unconceived, and their children still further unconceived. Just as we are all part of what was 500 and 5,000 years ago, we are also part of the future you and I are creating right now.

The interconnectedness that is true for us as individuals is true for our communities.

What happens in one neighborhood affects other neighborhoods. What happens in the Federal Government affects our tiny town. Our communities are all affected by economic, environmental and social issues that are sparked halfway around the world and just across the tracks.

Each of us - as individuals, as organizations, as communities and as nations - exists because something else was and something else is. We are all the effect of many causes, and we are the cause of effects we can barely imagine.

That connectedness is a great source of power as we seek to create the future of our world.

The Impact on Our Work

The impact of this one assumption on the way we do our work can be staggering. We have seen it be exhilarating. We have seen it be the one aspect of the work that makes everything else function well, and makes everyone seem to come alive with a sense of possibility.

In part, it comes down to another change in assumptions - the one we will discuss in Chapter 11 - the assumption that resources are not, in fact, scarce, and that competitive approaches may therefore be wholly irrelevant as we consider gathering those resources.

But let's focus on the issue at hand. The impact of our interconnectedness on our work begins when we realize that yes, in some ways, each of us is an individual. But in more ways, we are part of other, more collective wholes. We are part of families, schools, organizations, regions. Our organizations, while legally individual entities, are also parts of a collective whole - many collective wholes.

Because none of us can change the world on our own, we will be more likely to create such change if we learn to focus through the lens of our collective interdependence and interconnectedness. Through that lens, we acknowledge that what is often felt to be missing from the lives of people who have reached the pinnacle of individual success is the sense of being part of a bigger whole. We cannot be highly realized individuals if we are not part of a highly realized collective whole.

Western culture has spent centuries teaching the art of being an individual, taking our animal instinct for individual survival and raising it to heights unimagined. The next step, the step towards creating an amazing future for all of us, is to begin integrating that individual potential into the collective potential we have when we realize we are individuals within a collective, and not merely individuals living on our own, fighting to survive.

That is the opportunity Community Benefit Organizations have before them. The reward goes beyond attaining the end goal. The reward is also that when we work collectively, the work itself is more rewarding.

As you begin working more closely with anyone and everyone who also wants what you want for your community, you will begin to see changes in the way you do your organization's own work, as everyone involved feels more energized, more inspired, more connected. Yes, there may be more opinions and personalities to take into account, but there will also be more hands and hearts and minds dedicated to the cause. Slowly, you are likely to realize that for the whole effort to be strong, the individuals within that group need to be strong. You will start to care about the survival of all those other organizations with whom you used to compete. You will want them to succeed, because you will all be succeeding together.

Putting the Pollyanna Principle of Interconnectedness / Interdependence into Practice

Improving our communities is a large, complex, interdisciplinary task. No one individual, organization or jurisdiction can accomplish it alone. We can only create an amazing future for our communities if we link arms and work together.

> If all the groups in our community were working together,
> we could ___ fill in with your vision for what is possible ___.

What possibilities exist in that simple statement! It is so much easier to link arms when we are focused on what connects us, rather than what separates us.

Building tools and systems that are rooted in our interconnectedness and interdependence will include our internal systems of governance and program development and planning. But tools must also be developed on a larger scale, focusing on the more overarching systems at play throughout virtually all Community Benefit Organizations.

We cannot build trust if the only time organizations are brought together is when we are either facing a crisis or learning to compete with each other. We cannot build common ground if building relationships and collaborating are seen as tools and mechanisms, rather than a way of being.

The seeds of cooperation cannot simply be planted and then left to grow on their own. Cooperation must be nurtured and tended to.

Cooperation also cannot be forced - not if it is to have any lasting effect. Systems that bring groups together with the expectation of building a better community are systems that focus on the things we all share, the spirit that has brought us all to our work in the first place.

Systems that acknowledge that, at the core, our communities' organizations all share the vision of a humane, vibrant, resilient community

- those are systems that will build a better future, with expectations deeply rooted in our connections.

In practice, when we have convened such groups in our own work, the common theme among all those groups is that they cannot wait to meet again, and again and again.

> After a first meeting with a group of funders and capacity building leaders in Danville, Virginia in 2005, the energy in the room prompted one foundation president to ask, "When can we set another play date?" The resulting group has been meeting and working together ever since.

We all want that connection. We want to be encouraged to see the good in each other, to sense that we are all, together, part of something bigger.

In practice, here is what we have found repeatedly: It works.

Tearing Down Walls

Putting our interconnectedness into practice will mean consciously tearing down the myriad walls that have been constructed throughout the Community Benefit Sector.

- The walls that divide organizations who do similar work, with similar missions
- The walls that divide organizations whose missions seem unrelated, but who might be pursuing dollars from the same funding sources
- The walls that divide funders from the organizations they fund (and the organizations they do not fund)
- The walls that divide funders from other funders
- The walls created by nonprofit resource centers, dividing "members" from "nonmembers"
- The walls that divide academics and practitioners
- The walls that segregate "donors" from "volunteers" and treat them differently
- The walls that divide provider organizations and their communities

We will also have to be more conscious of the extent to which each of us bemoans competition with our words, yet perpetuates competition with our actions.

- Funders who bemoan competition, yet maintain competitive grant processes
- Funders and nonprofit resource centers who teach (via workshops and consulting support) competitive funding techniques
- Nonprofit resource centers who compete with other nonprofit resource centers (yes, such situations do exist!)

When we destroy the us-and-them spirit of competition created by these walls, we can accomplish anything. That is what happens when we are accomplishing our goals together.

Our Highest Potential

When we assume everyone and everything is interconnected and interdependent, we expect to work together towards our highest potential.

As such interconnected work takes hold, though, groups begin to see that all the other assumptions we have discussed thus far (as well as those to come) become interwoven as we consider our deep connection with and dependence upon each other.

When we hold ourselves accountable for creating a better future for our communities, we are holding ourselves accountable to each other. When we realize we are creating the future, we realize that we are creating that future together and for each other.

We realize that in the big picture of what we want for our communities, we all want the same thing. Our narrowly defined mission statements are, in fact, all interconnected, as they collectively aim at building a better future for our communities.

> Because we want to build a better future for our community, we provide shelter for the homeless.

> Because we want to build a better future for our community, we teach young people about dance and movement.

> Because we want to build a better future for our community, we work to keep our community's rivers clean.

When we focus on that which unites us, focusing on our true interconnectedness and interdependence, it is easy to inspire ourselves and those around us to reach for our highest potential.

A Note for Public Officials (Elected or Appointed)

This is one planet, with many people, many animals, and many other living things all sharing this space together.

What divides us hurts us. Whatever decision you are about to make, if that decision is based on the assumption that we are all one planet-full of people, it is more likely to take us in the right direction than a decision intended to benefit only one group - whether that group is a single organization, a single community, or a single country.

There is no "us and them." There is only us all, together.

Pollyanna Principle #3:

Everyone and Everything is Interconnected and Interdependent, whether we acknowledge that or not.

If everyone and everything is interconnected and interdependent, then if we expect to create a better future for our communities, we will develop and use tools, approaches and systems that encourage and nurture those connections.

Chapter 10:
Being the Change We Want to See

Pollyanna Principle #4:
"Being the change we want to see" means walking the talk of our values.

Imagine what our organizations could accomplish in our communities if the behaviors of the staff, board and volunteers were a model of the values we wanted to see reflected throughout our communities.

If we wish people were more compassionate and humane; if we wish human dignity were respected more; if we wish decisions were made by first considering the least powerful among us - imagine the impact we could have if we took to heart Gandhi's suggestion that we put those values to work by being the change we want to see in the world.

When we consider the practical meaning Gandhi's quote suggests, the word that comes to mind is "integrity" - the word whose Latin core is all about that wholeness, that soundness of being and doing. While we often see the word "integrity" paired with the word "honesty," integrity moves beyond mere truthfulness. Integrity speaks to an honesty that aligns "being" with "thinking" and "doing."

That alignment is what Gandhi was addressing. It is the alignment that comes when we are putting our core values into action.

Values are the signposts that guide our decisions. Because decisions are often about tradeoffs, values are the measuring stick against which we answer the question, "What is more important, this or that?"

When our work is not aligned behind the values we would want to see reflected in the community, we often find we are fostering the very conditions we wish to eliminate. That contradiction of purpose and action cannot lead to the change we want to create in our communities. It can only lead to frustration, blame and rationalizing.

Rooting decisions in the values we want to model to the community often requires practice, as it asks us to use what is unique about our humanity to override our animal survival fears. Consider the reasons typically given for making choices that cause us to rationalize: money, time, expediency, short-term benefit, political concerns. These survival-driven concerns can make the simplest and most seemingly obvious choices more complicated.

> When a substance abuse recovery organization has the choice of allowing a beer distributor to sponsor an event, what values might guide that decision?

> When an organization has the opportunity to participate in a three-year project to make significant strides regarding a community issue related to the organization's mission, and that effort will require that the ED be out of the office one half day per week for that whole three years, what values might guide that decision?

> When a donor offers to provide substantial funding for an initiative that only marginally fits with your mission but would meet your short-term revenue needs, what values might guide the decision of whether or not to accept that gift?

At their core, these day-to-day decisions come down to the simplest values question of all: "What is most important?"

Stories

When the subject of "values" arises, many people (especially board members) see the topic as touchy-feely "fluff." But there are no questions more practical than values questions.

"When we have tough decisions to make, how do we know which is the right one?"

"How do we know what lines we will never cross?"

When a choice requires that we reconcile our day-to-day concerns with the change we want to create in our communities, there is nothing more practical to discuss than the question, "Which is more important, this or that?"

The following stories evidence the practical nature of such questions. From these stories, we see that virtually every major organizational decision is, at its root, a values decision.

Story: The Disability Care Group

The Disability Care Group provides residential assistance to homebound disabled adults. They called our office asking for assistance with employee morale. When we met with their board and key management staff, we learned the organization had 125% annual turnover in care staff. Yes, 125% every year! That is more than a morale issue; that is a catastrophe!

We asked about the people who provide the care. We learned they are responsible for daily visits to help bathe, groom, and otherwise attend to the needs of the disabled adults in their care, many of whom are elderly. They do light housework. They change diapers. The work requires compassion and wisdom; it requires physical strength; it requires the patience of Job.

Realizing the combination of skills and qualifications this work required, we asked about the pay scale. Their answer: $7 per hour.

We were stunned. We shared our observation that this was not a morale issue, but an issue directly related to those less-than-livable wages. We noted that their care workers were taking care of the basic bodily needs of clients for the same money they could be making at a telemarketing center, where their whole job would be to make calls and sit in an air conditioned office.

We asked if they had considered paying a better wage, so they could find caregivers who were more devoted to this line of work. That is when they told us, "That's impossible. This is a State contract, and that is all the State allows us to pay. We are stuck with those wages."

We pointed out that this was not, in fact, the case - that they could choose to raise money to increase those wages to a more professional scale. The group thanked us for our time. We later learned they hired a different consultant to do the morale work with their employees.

The Disability Care Group was faced with a choice: "Shall we work to raise money to address our core purpose, maintaining the highest possible standard of care for the people we serve? Or shall we instead continue to pay low wages and treat the symptom - morale?"

At its core, this discussion, seemingly about money and morale, is a question of values and integrity. The extent to which the Disability Care Group can create significant change in its community is directly linked to the extent to which the group consciously decides to be the change they want to see.

Story: American Red Cross

Between the September 11th attacks on the World Trade Towers and the devastation to New Orleans caused by Hurricane Katrina, the American Red Cross can't seem to catch a break. Every few months, it seems we are reading yet another story about the Red Cross jamming its toes in the door.

In each case, the Red Cross has an explanation - a rationalizing argument for why they did (or did not do) whatever the press and the general public have accused them of at the time.

Of all the issues laid at the feet of the Red Cross, however, there is none as blatant as the situation for which they have been ordered to pay almost $10 million dollars in fines by the U.S. Food and Drug Administration (FDA).

According to the FDA, the Red Cross failed to ensure the safety of the nation's blood supply. In a 2001 article about the Red Cross, New York Times reporter Deborah Sontag noted, "Food and Drug Administration inspectors found that some Red Cross blood centers would keep testing blood until the tests delivered the desired results; for instance, blood that tested borderline-positive for a given virus would be retested five or six times until the numbers came out negative."

Because blood equals revenues for the Red Cross, if it looked like one more pass through the machine might make that blood usable, they would run it through until it passed.

While these stories make it easy to spot the discrepancies between *walk* and *talk*, they are not at all unusual. The same stories could be told of a Nonprofit Resource Center that teaches measurement but fails to measure its own results, or a consultant who teaches about the importance of planning but does not have a business plan for his own business. They could be told of a yoga center that is neither compassionate nor encouraging in its approach to its students. They could be stories of a neighborhood center in a low-income area, whose annual fundraiser is a neighborhood street party, where they raise money by selling beer to the very people they serve.

While any of these actions might have strong rationalizations about why it was the best action to take, in the end, none of these groups will be able to effect significant change in their communities if their work is not aligned behind the values they say are important.

To create an extraordinary future for our communities, therefore, does not require that we choose between "practical reality" and "values." It requires that we find the decision that aligns that practical work behind the values we envision as part of that extraordinary community. It requires that our practical work walk the talk of the change we want to see.

Putting the Pollyanna Principle of Values-Based Work into Practice

> Integrity requires courage and intelligence, because every significant ethical choice entails risk.
>
> *Stephen Batchelor, Buddhism Without Beliefs*

When an organization's walk and talk are aligned, the leaders of that organization, as well as its staff and volunteers, work diligently and consciously to incorporate their values into their decisions and actions. The community knows what the organization stands for. Community members are attracted to incorporate that organization's work into their lives.

In the end, the practical truth is that organizations who walk their talk are able to accomplish more, simply because their integrity is doing part of their work for them. The very act of "being the change they want to see" is, in and of itself, working to create that change.

> When the board of directors of the Society of St. Vincent de Paul (See Chapter 6) told their new Executive Director that their first concern was not that a program pay for itself, but that the lives of their clients be better, they modeled the kinds of behaviors they expected to see in their staff, their volunteers, and their clients.

Modeling the behaviors we want to see in our communities is not beyond our abilities. Yes, we all enjoy telling the seemingly hypo-critical stories of groups and individuals who have defaulted to their survival instincts rather than reason out the cause and effect of a different approach.

But we also know stories of those who have done just the opposite, like the board of St. Vincent de Paul. We all know of instances where individuals have reached beyond their own comfort and survival, to find the decision that is powerful, clear, elegant in what it accomplishes.

We feel good about those stories. We tell them with pride, from both our organizations and our personal lives. We place such high value on the ability to live with such integrity, that we are especially proud when those stories are about our own children.

> As my best friend and business partner, Dimitri has always been like a second dad to my daughter. When his mom was dying of cancer, Lizzie was only 14. She had never seen someone who was dying. We knew Mamou had very little time left - perhaps just a few weeks. The cancer had moved from her breasts to her liver, causing the yellowed skin of jaundice. She was a shadow of the amazing woman who, although not Lizzie's natural grandmother, had cared for her as if she were her own.

> I was heading out to visit Mamou, and I asked Lizzie if she wanted to come along. She hesitated. "I'm scared," she told me. I told her it was ok, that she didn't have to go, that the decision was hers. She grabbed her coat and said, "I'm going. This isn't about me being scared. This is about making Mamou happy. I want to do that."

In practice, doing our work with integrity requires two steps. First, organizations must take the time to deliberate and determine what values they want to see reflected in their own actions.

> What could we accomplish if our own internal behaviors were a model of the behaviors we wanted to see in our community?

> What could we accomplish if we walked our talk?

> What values do we want to cultivate in our community, and how can we use our own decisions and actions to show what that looks like in practice?

> What would it mean to actually be the change we want to see in our community and our world?

The second step in working with integrity requires that we use those values as a touchstone to guide our decisions and our actions. Once actions are taken, it means then measuring and evaluating those actions against our values, asking not only, "Did we do what we said we would do?" but, "Were we true to our values as we did that work?"

We humans have the ability to work through the various factors weighing on a decision, to take action based on something more than our fears, our worries, our discomforts. We have the ability to consider the potential consequences of actions not yet taken, and to base our decisions on what we value most.

That ability is much of what sets us apart from the rest of the animal world. Because of that, it is also a big part of our potential.

When Your Mission is to Change Community Values

> I am not going to allow anybody to pull me so low as to use the very methods that perpetuated evil throughout our civilization.
>
> *Martin Luther King, Jr.*

The expectation that an organization will walk its talk is especially important to advocacy groups, who are dedicated to changing their community's values.

Consider two extreme cases, two movements that were indeed about changing the community's values: The Inquisition in Europe, and the Civil Rights Movement in the United States.

In Europe in the Middle Ages, the desired values change was a religious one: making Europe wholly Christian. The actions taken to effect that change went so heinously counter not only to the religion they were intended to establish, but to values the world has shared since the dawn of time, that that entire period is ranked among the darkest times, both for Europe and for Christianity. Five hundred years after the end of the Inquisition in Spain, it remains an example of how horribly we humans can treat each other.

The desired values change for the Civil Rights Movement in the U.S. was related to equity and justice. Having been moved by watching the nonviolent means by which Mahatma Gandhi led the people of India to independence over the British, American Civil Rights leaders vowed to use means that aligned with the heart of their purpose. After almost 500 years on this continent, and 100 years after slavery had been legally abolished in the U.S., nonviolence was adopted as the primary means for creating a future of opportunity and potential for African Americans.

Year after year, during the 1950's and 60's, average Americans turned on their televisions to see peaceful Civil Rights demonstrators - many of them young children - being set upon by dogs, beaten with night sticks, knocked down by fire hoses. While many Americans may have shared the bigotry of local officials who used these violent means, those same Americans could not sanction siccing dogs upon a young child or beating a woman who is simply sitting on a sidewalk, doing no harm to anyone. The triumph of the Civil Rights movement was a triumph of means that walked the talk of values we all hold dear, over means that were clearly abhorrent to any thinking, feeling person.

As for results, both movements could claim short-term victory. Given the choice of conversion, banishment or death, the Inquisition did indeed convert many people to Christianity. And not ten years after the first bus boycott in Montgomery, Alabama, the U.S. adopted sweeping Civil Rights legislation in 1964, deepening that commitment with further legislation in 1965 and 1968. Both parties could easily claim their efforts attained the desired end results.

But in the end, which of those movements created lasting values changes - the goal they sought in the first place? Which is looked upon with disgust, and which with admiration? While the Catholic Church, after 500 years, still cannot find a way to rationalize what the Church did in the name of Jesus, the leaders of the Civil Rights Movement are venerated, a source of pride not just for African Americans, but for *all* Americans.

When it comes to changing values, it is not just the mission that matters; it is the degree to which every part of our work can act as an example of what those values would look like in practice.

A Note for Public Officials (Elected or Appointed)

Public service is one of the highest callings in our world. As a public servant, are your actions and decisions modeling the reasons you chose public service as your life's work? Are your actions fostering the conditions you hope to see become the norm throughout your community?

Integrity is not simply about following the letter of the law. It is about putting your values into action in everything you do. And there is no end to what you can accomplish when you spend every day being the change you want to see.

Pollyanna Principle #4:

"Being the change we want to see" means walking the talk of our values.

If being the change we want to see means walking the talk of our values, then if we want to create an extraordinary future for our communities, we will be conscious of which values we intend to model to the community, and we will be conscious to put those values into action in the way our work is done.

Chapter11:
Strength Builds Upon Strength

Pollyanna Principle #5:
Strength builds upon our strengths, not our weaknesses.

Imagine what it would be like if Community Benefit Organizations had everything they needed to get the job done. Imagine if we had all the human resources, all the physical resources, all the mission resources it would take to reach for our highest potential.

Now imagine that we already have all that, because, in fact, we do.

As community organizations, as communities, and as individuals within those communities, we have more strength to build upon than the Culture of Can't suggests.

Year after year, organizations think it is "a miracle that we are still here!" Year after year, they tell of the miracles that allow them to provide more and more service to their communities.

It is not a miracle. It is the myriad strengths inherent in our communities, our organizations, and the individual people who comprise both.

What could the future hold for a poor black girl, born to unmarried teenage parents in Mississippi in the 1950's, perhaps the most racist state in the United States at that time?

Raised by a single mother who so neglected her that she was sexually abused by several male relatives, the girl ran away often. At age 14, she gave birth to a premature baby, who died shortly after birth. As this child grew into an adult, she battled a weight problem that made her the target of relentless jokes.

Oprah Winfrey.

Is Oprah a pile of needs or a pile of strengths? Did she get where she is today by building on her needs, or by building on her strengths, often turning those very weaknesses into strengths?

Is Oprah the abused overweight black girl, or is Oprah gorgeous, vivacious, powerful, compassionate and incredible?

Oprah has plenty of "not good enough." So do we all. Oprah also has far more "wow" than she has weaknesses. And so do we all.

Roger Hughes, Executive Director of St. Luke's Health Initiatives in Phoenix, Arizona, suggests that we start, "Counting the strengths and assets, and look for ways to extend them vs. counting the holes and looking for ways to fill them up."

Just like Oprah.

Community Benefit Organizations - We Are Oprah!

As individuals, as organizations and as communities, we can either see ourselves through the lens of what we have, or through the lens of what we do not have.

Often, we choose the latter.

Organizations plead. We ask. We need.

We need volunteers. We need board members. We need money - God knows we need money.

And the work we do? We help the needy. Vulnerable people. Those who cannot help themselves. We help at-risk kids.

We work in poverty-stricken areas, ghettos, "third world" nations. We give people a chance who might not otherwise have one. Just one dollar a day can help this child.

And if our organization is an arts group? Oh my goodness! We are tiny, neglected, seen as unimportant. People want to donate to flood victims. People want to give to disasters. 9/11. We can never compete with that.

Burnout. Low pay. Widespread fear of Executive Directors retiring with no one to replace them.

Seen all on one page (and no doubt we could fill several more pages), such negativity becomes almost laughable. How overwhelmingly horrible life must be in our organizations and our communities!

Changing Our Assumptions and Expectations: Strength Builds Upon Strength

It is inspiring to listen to Jody Kretzmann talk about the asset-based work he and his compadre, John McKnight, have done over the years. It is empowering to hear the stories he tells of small groups of citizens accomplishing what years of government and other efforts could not.

Jody often shares the story of a soup kitchen, whose leaders realized there was far more power in giving than receiving, and began asking each food recipient what gifts they might share with others. Visiting that soup kitchen these days, one cannot tell the volunteers from the recipients. Everyone is working, sharing what they have.

We all have so much that is strong and powerful. Those strengths are the roots from which our potential grows.

> The feeling of wealth is enhanced when you give, not when you take, since, subliminally, giving means you have enough to share, while taking means you may not be getting enough. Giving is a relief. Taking is a burden.
>
> *Robert Thurman - Infinite Life*

A charter middle school in the United States has as its mission to provide exemplary education for low-income children whom the public school systems have written off as either unable or unwilling to succeed. When one mother saw how the program built upon the strengths of her son, she was encouraged to share her own strengths and volunteer. Soon she went back to school for her own education. Eventually, she graduated from college, becoming a teacher herself. She found her potential when she was encouraged to see the gifts and assets everyone, including her, assumed she did not have.

The same holds true for foundations. In one particular effort, the foundation staff participates alongside grantees and nongrantee organizations, as well as average community members, to learn a new way of doing their work, to help build a healthy community. Attending those meetings, like the soup kitchen Jody Kretzmann speaks about, one would never know who is the funder, who is the mental health advocate who herself has schizophrenia, or who is the professor at the local university. Meeting after meeting, the participants share their aspirations and their wisdom, building upon the experience and skills shared by all the others in the room.

When individual organizations believe they are weak and that resources are scarce, they sense they must compete for their survival. They live day to day. They focus more on internal needs than external community building. They weigh every potential contact against the degree to which that person might help them out of the hole.

But organizations are not weak. They have storehouses of strengths upon which to build. When they are encouraged to see those strengths, they repeatedly say the same thing. "We had no idea we had so much to work with!"

Putting the Pollyanna Principle of Strength into Practice

Eliminating the assumption that "scarcity is reality", and replacing it with the assumption that we have incredible strengths to build upon, changes our expectations. That change of expectations then ripples throughout all the systems we use to do our daily work.

In program development, rather than beginning with the question, *"What do we need?"*, we begin by asking, *"What do we already have to build upon?"*

In resource development, the work begins with the joyful exercise of identifying assets that are hiding in plain sight - the people we already know, our buildings and other physical assets, our mission, and especially the assets that exist throughout our communities.

In governance and planning, building on strengths means building upon the most powerful asset of all - the passion and commitment of people who care.

The very act of building upon our assets strengthens the assets themselves. When we tap into our wisdom, that wisdom grows. When we build upon our existing relationships, those relationships flourish and multiply.

When organizations begin seeing the abundance that surrounds them, another fact becomes clear: the simple assumption that they are strong becomes one more strength to build upon.

The Culture of Can't begins to vanish. In its place we find the Culture of Possibility.

Nonprofit / Nongovernmental Organizations

Words matter. They build the images from which we create our assumptions.

The words most commonly used to define the extraordinary work done by Community Benefit Organizations, however, do not focus on what is extraordinary. Those words focus on what is lacking.

If we are going to put the principle of "strength" into practice, therefore, we must address the names that are commonly used for the work our organizations do.

Nonprofit. Nongovernmental.

We are not a business. We are not a government. We have no money. We have no authority.

We have built a sense of scarcity, need and weakness into the very names we use to describe our work.

Imagine this:

> From now on, all persons of European descent will be called NonAfricans.
> From this day forward, all Christians will be called NonJews.

Preposterous, right? One can quickly see that a group defined by what it is NOT will spend much of its time defensively comparing itself to the group it was defined against.

Not African. Not Jewish. Well then, what are you?

Nonprofit Organization. Nongovernmental Organization.

Well then, what are we?

Like Oprah, are we strong, powerful, capable? Or are we simply what we lack?

What if our name reflected assumptions of strength and abundance? What if our name proudly proclaimed what we do, and the very reason we exist - to make our communities extraordinary places to live? What if we called ourselves by what we *are*?

We are Community Benefit Organizations!

We are *not* "not" anything. We **are** something amazing, powerful, and filled with every bit of our human potential.

To build an amazing future, we cannot build upon a base of scarcity, weakness and need. We must build that future upon what is strong in our communities and what is strong in ourselves.

Strength builds upon strength. And we Community Benefit Organizations are a lot stronger than our assumptions (and our names) have led us to believe.

A Note for Public Officials (Elected or Appointed)

Our communities are places filled with visionary possibility and abundant wisdom. They have much to build upon.

As you seek to create legislation that will directly affect your constituents, can you do so in a way that taps on the collective strengths of the people living in those communities? Can you bring them together to share their wisdom, to find approaches that are born of their own life experience?

Building on what is strong will build strength. Identifying and building upon that community strength cannot help but be an asset as you seek re-election the next time around.

Pollyanna Principle #5:

Strength Builds Upon Our Strengths, Not Our Weaknesses.

If strength builds upon our strengths, then if we expect to create a better future for our communities, we will develop and use tools, approaches and systems that build upon our strengths - the abundance of gifts, assets and resources each of us has to share.

Chapter 12:
Systems

Imagine that all the systems used by Community Benefit Organizations were aligned behind creating visionary community change.

Imagine that governance, planning, program development, resources development and all the other systems used by organizations were aimed at the expectation that organizations would create an amazing future for our communities.

Those systems would not only be powerful themselves, we would feel powerful whenever we used them. Building strength upon strength, the systems themselves would tap into our potential and help that potential grow.

Now that's being the change we want to see!

Systems that Aim at Our Potential

What might systems look like if they were to point us towards our highest potential to create more visionary results?

Governance systems
- would make it easy for boards to hold themselves accountable, first and foremost, for creating the future of their communities. Within that community context, those systems would then make it easy for boards to hold themselves accountable for the means they use to accomplish those results.
- would focus on an organization's interconnectedness with individuals and organizations who care about the same thing that organization cares about, rather than focusing on competitive advantage.

- would make it easy to develop and use a code of values as the litmus test for all decisions and actions.
- would assume boards are strong, needing only encouragement and inspiration, rather than assuming that boards are weak and must be addressed prescriptively.

Planning systems
- would provide a practical, step-by-step way for organizations to hold themselves accountable for creating the future of their communities, and for simultaneously holding themselves accountable for ensuring they had the means to make that difference.
- would assume the organization will do its work by linking arms with others who care about the same cause.
- would be tethered to the organization's core values, providing a concrete way for the organization to walk its talk.
- would not only build upon the strengths of the organization and the community, but eschew approaches that focus solely on the problems or weaknesses of either the community or the organization.

Program Development and Sustainability systems
- would align behind the organization's primary accountability for creating the future of the community, rather than a primary accountability for donors and dollars.
- would be rooted in the assumption that the key to sustainability lies in our interconnectedness with others who want the same results we want.
- would be guided by the organization's core values, allowing organizations to point to those systems as their proudest example of consistency between "walk" and "talk."
- would embody a spirit of abundance rather than assuming resources are scarce. And as happens when resources are not scarce, competition would become a non-issue.

If our systems were all rooted in the assumptions and expectations at the heart of The Pollyanna Principles, that is what we would expect from our systems. It is what our work would be aimed at and what we would achieve, because individuals and groups will go where the systems lead them.

Warning Signals

When a system is failing - whether that system is under the hood of a car, is in the internal workings of our own human bodies, or is a system in our communities (our schools, the environment) - we often receive a warning before those systems fall apart entirely.

This is as true for the systems used in Community Benefit Organizations as it is with our cars, our cars or our schools. The key, then, is not only to be able to identify the warning signs, but to know what to do once we receive the warning.

"What to do" will be addressed in Parts 3 and 4. For the remainder of this chapter, however, we will identify some of the most common indicators that warn about potential misalignment between the work a group is doing and the end results they are seeking to achieve.

It is likely you will recognize these signals - perhaps in your own organization, perhaps among Community Benefit Organizations overall. However, until we realize that the circumstances we encounter every day may, in fact, be warning signs, the corrective action we take is likely to be aimed at the symptoms rather than the more critical need for systems change.

Warning Signal: Frustration, Blame, and the If Only's

One of the boldest warnings that a system is failing is the degree of blame one encounters within that system. When it comes to the work of the participants in the Community Benefit Sector, blame is not targeted at one clear villain. It is so widespread that the targets instead depend upon who is doing the blaming: Founders, boards, funders, the government, and a whole cast of others.

Clearly, when everyone is certain someone else is at fault, the odds alone say it cannot be the fault of every one of those groups individually.

That level of blame is instead a clear indication of an overall failure of systems.

To quickly identify warning signs for blame, one can listen for more than just the actual finger-pointing. Blame is also expressed in the wishful-thinking phrase, "If Only."

> *If Only* we had more money.

> *If Only* we had stronger boards.

> *If Only* we had a change in government leaders.

"If Only" is the language of blame. The more we hear those words and other blame-ridden phrases, the stronger the warning of system failure.

Warning Signal: A Tendency Towards Prescription (vs. Inspiration)

Another signal that a system is failing is the degree to which authorities promote prescriptive systems as the "solution."

The work of Community Benefit Organizations is the most inspiring work one could do. The potential inherent in that work is the epitome of the human side of our nature.

Prescriptive systems, on the other hand, are not intended to inspire or encourage people to reach for that high potential. Prescriptive systems are intended to force individuals to toe the line.

In Community Benefit Organizations, such systems are most commonly found in board development work. Type the phrase "board roles" into Google, and you will find website after website with a list of *shoulds* - the eight or twelve things every board "should" do. That word - *should* - is the primary indicator of a prescriptive system.

When we create systems based on high expectations for extraordinary end results, we inspire ourselves and others to action, reaching for what is possible. People no longer need to be told how they should be doing their work. They just do it.

When we notice long lists of prescriptive *shoulds*, however, we are witnessing another warning of a system failure.

> If you want to build a ship, don't drum up people to collect wood and don't assign them tasks and work, but rather teach them to long for the endless immensity of the sea.
>
> *Antoine de Saint-Exupery*

Warning Signal: Complexity to the Point of Confusion

> Everything should be as simple as possible, but not simpler.
>
> *Albert Einstein*

Systems that require the ongoing intervention of experts are another warning sign of system failure. Such systems simply cannot self-perpetuate, and the result is often blame, frustration, and then prescription of often more complicated systems!

Does it seem every board in the world is a candidate for board development work? This might be an indication that governance systems have become immensely complicated.

Do the majority of organizations feel they need resource development counsel? This might be an indication that current resource development approaches are either too difficult to do, too complex, or too far outside-the-comfort-zone for organizational leaders to grasp and run with. Or it might be an indication that the funding system itself is not working well.

If we expect Community Benefit Organizations to become a force for creating significant community improvement, their success will be more likely if the standard operational systems they rely upon are simple enough for anyone to learn, maintain, and replicate.

When that is not the case, and we find systems becoming more and more complex to the point of creating an ongoing need for consultant intervention, that is another signal of system failure.

Putting the Pollyanna Principle of "Systems" Into Practice

Following the Community Benefit Sector's first several decades of growth and development, the next stage of development has the potential to create an extraordinary future for our communities and our world. To accomplish that, however, we will need systems that are consciously built for that purpose.

We will need systems that are aligned behind high expectations, inspiring us to our highest potential as human beings. These systems will need to be consciously created, because the world-changing results our organizations have the potential to achieve has not been attempted on this scale before.

We will also need systems that make it easy to not only do that work well, but to continue doing it well - systems that are both practical for this world full of practitioners to use now, and replicable after this crop of practitioners has given way to the next group, and those after that.

Having developed and used such systems, and having seen the inspired success those systems create, I will turn the reigns over to Aristotle for the rest of the book, as we consider that "we are what we repeatedly do." It is in that "doing" that we will see these assumptions and expectations transform into action and results on behalf of our communities and our world.

A Note for Public Officials (Elected or Appointed)

The next time you suggest legislation to regulate individual behavior, search to determine if there is instead an underlying system that is maintaining the very behavior you are seeking to eliminate.

Whether the legislation will imprison drug users or penalize employers of illegal immigrants, before finding ways to punish individual behavior, search to find if that behavior is rooted in a system that is actually encouraging it. Without considering, for example, that there are multiple economic systems that encourage the cheap labor provided by illegal immigrants, punishing those employers is simply putting a finger in one hole in the dam.

Seeking comprehensive systemic change may be far more complex than the ease with which one can blame and punish individual behavior. But the results might finally solve the problem. Better still, those results might begin to aim us at creating better circumstances for all of us together.

Pollyanna Principle #6:

Individuals will go where systems lead them.

If individuals will go where systems lead them, then if we expect to create a better future for our communities, we will develop systems that align behind our vision for a better world, and we will shun systems that preclude reaching that destination.

Chapter 13:
Using the Pollyanna Principles to Create a New Path

We will have done our best to create an extraordinary future for our world when we have aimed all aspects of our work at the highest possible expectations for our potential. From there, it is time to move from the Buddha to Aristotle - from "We are what we think" to "We are what we do."

Whatever systems we build to do our work, it will be critical that those systems set expectations and aim first, and develop means second. Aiming at visionary end results will mean tethering those systems to the future we want to create for our communities, to ensure we do not continue to default our focus to the day-to-day.

It will then be critical that we rely on *all* the Pollyanna Principles to achieve results, rather than choosing to focus on one expectation or another. Building on our connectedness alone will not change the world, nor will only building on our strengths or building solely upon our values. None of those means-related principles will accomplish the end goal on its own, as the assumptions behind those principles are as interconnected and interdependent as everything else in the vast universe in which we live.

In addition, as Community Benefit Organizations consider the adoption of new systems, we must be mindful of the degree to which our assumptions to date have been limited by our animal nature. By re-focusing the end result of our work on our potential to live compassionately and joyfully together in a world that is healthy, vibrant and alive, we will be celebrating the evolution of our species beyond those traits we share with the rest of the animal world. We will be moving towards our potential to be this uniquely human animal.

Doing our work in this way will take conscious effort. The reflexive responses of our history and our evolution will continue to tug on our hearts and minds, screaming like a game-show contestant, "Pick me!

Pick me!" But that is again where our human potential can assist us, as we have the ability to override our reptile brains, to see what cannot be seen with the eye.

It will take diligence. It will take creating support systems to reinforce what we learn along the way.

But the first step is creating the expectation that we can and will make it happen. If that is the world we want; if we know there is a path to create that world; and if there are simple, practical systems that support and encourage our efforts, we will have already made huge strides along the road to a better future. Like flying to the moon, which also took diligence, support, and effort, it is possible, simply because it is not impossible.

Whether we are soaring to the moon or creating an amazing future here at home, it will all come down to what we expect of ourselves, what we hold ourselves accountable for accomplishing, and how that translates into the nuts and bolts of how we do the work we do.

Part 3

Creating the Path to the Future We Want

The Pollyanna Principles
in Action for
Individual Organizations

Chapter 14:
From Thought to Action

The Buddha was correct - we certainly are what we think, and with those thoughts, we create the world. But Aristotle reminds us: we are also what we repeatedly do. If excellence is "not an act, but a habit," then creating a force for change will require transforming our "changed thoughts" into "changed habits."

In the following chapters, I will share some practical day-to-day approaches my business partner at the Community-Driven Institute - Dimitri Petropolis - and I have developed and used. These systems embody the Pollyanna Principles. They are rooted in high expectations for the visionary community and global success we know this sector can achieve.

By raising our expectations for governance, that leadership role is aimed at creating the future of our communities.

By raising our expectations for planning, we have aimed at providing practical means for creating the future of our communities.

By raising our expectations for the way programs are developed and sustained, those activities at creating the future of our communities.

If our goal is to create a better future for our communities and our world, maintaining high expectations - our thoughts - will be a powerful tool, all on its own. But when those expectations become the basis for all the practical day-to-day work a group does to accomplish its dreams - well, stand back!

It is those practical systems that finally provide us Pollyannas and do-gooders with a response to the frustrating (and inaccurate) observation that "Vision and hope are all well and good, but they just do not translate beyond feel-good platitudes.".

Before diving in to celebrate what is possible when day-to-day systems and tools embody the Pollyanna Principles, there are a few considerations to keep in mind.

It's Not Just One Thing; It's Everything

If we could just fix governance. If we would all just use the X method for planning. If we only engaged the community more. Everyone seems to have his/her own panacea.

We know that none of the assumptions about organizational means will create significant change if we do not first change our assumptions about our desired ends. We also know that none of the individual Pollyanna Principles can, on its own, be as effective as they all can be collectively.

The same holds true for the practical parts of the work Community Benefit Organizations do. It cannot be one thing or another thing. It is, instead, one thing AND another thing.

To see significant change in the results Community Benefit Organizations achieve, *all* parts of their day-to-day work need the wake-up call of increased expectations. From there, *all* that work must align behind achieving those visionary, community-focused results. The change that is required is systemic, as piecemeal change has repeatedly proven not to work.

To achieve significant, visionary community and global improvement, it will require different approaches to governance, planning, program development and program sustainability.

But any one of these efforts will miss the mark of building healthy, vibrant, humane communities if the whole system is not addressed.

Further, to be effective in creating real change, that systemic change cannot come from the standpoint of solving organizational problems (the problem of governance, the problem of sustainability, etc.) but must derive from the potential of those internal systems - the potential of this whole sector. Without that comprehensive and aspirational change to all the systems organizations use to do their day-to-day work, each narrowly targeted effort will continue to come and go as the latest quick-fix, problem-solving fad, dooming each individual piece to the eventual graveyard of "We tried that, but after a while, nothing changed..."

In this section, we therefore address the sector's major operational systems.

- Governance systems aimed at creating the future of our communities.
- Planning systems aimed at those outcomes.
- Program development and sustainability systems, again aimed towards the end goal of creating significant, visionary, comprehensive outcomes.

As we move to Part 4, the interconnectedness of these systems will expand to include funding for community outcomes, teaching for those outcomes, convening for those outcomes.

It is critical to consider all these pieces, because, like any complex living organism, nothing that happens within an organization or a community occurs in a vacuum. Everything builds upon and affects everything else.

High Expectations

In this review of practical, day-to-day systems that aim organizations at their highest potential, you will note the absence of prescriptions about what organizations or individuals "should" do. There are many reasons for excluding the *shoulds* wherever possible, but the overarching reason is purely practical: The *shoulds* do not work.

We all know we should lose weight, we should work out, we should quit smoking, we should do this or that. Some people do what they know they should do, and some people do not.

Our organizations are the same.

Boards are told they should fundraise. They should plan. Boards should engage the community. They should create succession plans.

In reality, some boards do, and some do not. The classic list of "10 Things Every Board Member Must Do" might easily be re-labeled "10 Things Most Board Members Avoid."

But when high expectations guide the work of an organization's leaders, those leaders self-actuate and self-motivate. They come up with exactly what the prescribers have wanted them to do, only now it is inspired from within. Suddenly, individuals are doing the very things they could not have been dragged to do before!

As you read through this section, therefore, if you are tempted to say, "But they have to do X first!" consider what is possible when the group itself determines what needs to be done, rather than performing a task simply because "our consultant says we have to do this."

When systems avoid prescribing to our animal side and instead inspire our human side, those systems are more practical, as they are far more likely to be maintained once the consultant is gone.

However, the results of such an approach go beyond being merely practical. The most critical result of having a board that is inspired is just that - having an inspired and energized board.

Just Examples

The goal of this section is to celebrate that creating visionary community change is not only possible; it is practical and doable. Cynics may suggest that visionaries "Get Real!", but as this section shows, changing an organization's internal functions to aim at creating visionary community change is as real as it gets.

Therefore, the approaches and examples on the following pages are not intended to show "the way," nor are they intended to show all the how-to steps in implementing these approaches.

Instead, they are just examples to show how practical it is to base an organization's internal functions on the Pollyanna Principles, and to further show the immediate and dramatic nature of the results.

In addition, while the case studies themselves tell the stories of organizations, the lessons learned from those stories will be applicable for anyone doing Community Benefit work, from elected officials and other government officers, to individual citizens who care.

Governance
& Planning

How the Pollyanna Principles
Create Boards
that
Create the Future

Chapter 15:
Governing for What Matters Most

We accomplish what we hold ourselves accountable for. And we are creating the future with everything we do.

In a Community Benefit organization, accountability resides with the board. In part, that accountability includes Legal and Operational Oversight. However, if a board wants to hold itself accountable for more than oversight of organizational means, the board can choose to hold itself accountable for creating an extraordinary future for the community.

Imagine what might be possible, then, if boards had governance systems that would aim their accountability at what matters most - dramatic community end results!

Accountability and the White-Hot Core of Governance

Over the years, boards have been taught to hold themselves account-able for the internal means by which the organization does its work.

- Legal Oversight

- Operational Oversight

- Board Mechanics (the day-to-day work of the board, including recruitment, orientation, etc.)

When governance is considered by its simplest definition, however, governance is about leading and making decisions on behalf of others. Leadership is what focuses the board beyond the organization's internal means, all because of that simple phrase - "on behalf of others."

In a for-profit corporation, the "others" to whom the organization is primarily accountable are the shareholders - those individuals who will receive the benefit the corporation was created to provide (profits).

An organization whose purpose is Community Benefit is also making its decisions on behalf of others, and those "others" are also those individuals who receive the benefit the organization provides. For Community Benefit Organizations, it is obviously the community that will receive that benefit. Therefore, stripped down to its core definition, *Governance* in a Community Benefit Organization is the act of *leading, guiding, and making decisions on behalf of the Community*.

There are two parts to that statement - the "leading/guiding/decision-making" part, and the "on behalf of the community" part. If we are to ensure that governance is aimed at creating the future of our communities, it is worth examining both parts of that statement.

Leading, Guiding, Making Decisions

Who is making the decisions that lead and guide the efforts at most community organizations?

Leadership is far more than simply reacting well to current circumstances. True organizational leadership is instead about aiming at a goal, and aligning resources to achieve that goal. Leadership is about making decisions and then following through on those decisions.

To be true leaders, then, boards must be conscious of the impact of their decisions as they create the future of their organization, the future of every life the organization touches, and the future of the community overall.

That level of conscious decision-making is at the heart of a board's leadership role.

On Behalf of the Community

Governing to build an amazing future for the community is only possible if the community is considered in every discussion and every decision (focusing back to the question raised in Chapter 6 - "To whom is the board holding itself accountable?").

Boards who are holding themselves fully accountable to the community - acting as the community's conscience as they guide the organization's work - are actively engaging the community in a dialogue about the community's vision for its future, and the shared values that will bring that vision to reality. Those boards are spending their meetings talking about what success would look like in their community, and/or the way the mission is carried out in the day-to-day, on behalf of its clients / patrons. The effect of their work on the community is at the heart of every decision.

When a board is holding itself accountable to the community, the board undertakes proactive planning to ensure the community is healthy and vibrant. Such boards understand that ongoing monitoring is then the only way to ensure the community that those plans are on track to be accomplished, and that the organization is doing its best to ensure nothing will stand in the way of their ability to achieve those goals.

The community wants a better place to live. The staff is in charge of doing the on-the-ground work it will take to make that happen, as it relates to the mission. *The board's leadership role is therefore to provide the linkage between what the community aspires to have happen (vision), the work that is being done to achieve those aspirations (mission) and the way that work is done (values).*

Governance that Creates the Community's Future

Governing to create the future takes the basic definition of governance to the next level. Instead of merely "making decisions on behalf of the community," governing to create the future is *leading, guiding, and making decisions on behalf of the **community's highest aspirations.***

Boiled down to its essence, the community's highest aspirations can be found in three simple words: Vision, Mission and Values.

When a board's accountability is focused on vision, mission and values, that board is Governing for What Matters Most. Such a board places those three words at the core of every action they take and every decision they make, aligning organizational means behind Community-Driven end results.

Because the Pollyanna Principles implore us to create systems that are practical and replicable, Governing for What Matters is not complicated. In fact, aligning means behind Community-Driven ends is far simpler than the complicated layers boards have been encouraged to use to date.

Ironically, the simplicity of Governing for What Matters allows it to accomplish what other systems have not been able to do - keep boards proactively accountable for Legal Oversight, Operational Oversight and Board Mechanics while aiming their work at making a real difference in their communities. As you will see in the examples, it is no wonder boards who are Governing for What Matters are energized!

The following chapters describe the two simple steps at the heart of this Community-Driven approach to governance.

Step 1: Defining what matters.

Step 2: Putting what matters into action

Chapter 16:
Defining What Matters

When a board is Governing for What Matters Most, the definition of what matters most to them is found in their *3 Statements*: Their Vision Statement, Mission Statement and Values Statement.

When a board is using its *3 Statements* as a touchstone for every single decision it makes and every action it takes, the board is rooting the community's highest aspirations into the heart of its leadership. Further, the board begins to realize that the most powerful of those three statements is not their Mission Statement - the one they have been the most accustomed to using. The most powerful are the statements of their Vision and their Values.

So what, then, are the differences between all those statements? What falls under the heading of *mission vs. vision?* What should be included in a Values Statement? Do we really need all three statements?

Because governance has not, to date, emphasized *The 3 Statements* as the touchstone for every single thing an organization does, these elementary questions are often followed by more practical questions. *Aren't these statements really just consultant-speak? How can the touchy-feely mumbo-jumbo of vision and values possibly be practical?*

As you will see on the following pages, when a board is using *The 3 Statements* as the guideposts for all their decisions and actions, and as the key evaluation criteria for those decisions and actions, those statements are neither irrelevant nor impractical. They are, in fact, everything.

Vision vs. Mission Defined

Every consultant has his/her own ideas about how to define vision and mission. The most direct way to determine the difference between those two words is to defer to standard English usage. A simple trick for accomplishing that is to add the letters "ary" to the end of each word.

VisionARY
MissionARY

It is easy to understand what those two words mean. A visionary is someone who sees what is possible, who sees the potential. A missionary is someone who carries out that work.

Jesus of Nazareth was a *visionary*. He saw the potential, the possibilities for making life better. Jesus's *missionaries* carry his work and his words to the world, putting his vision into practice.

An organization's vision is all about what is possible, all about its potential. The mission is what it takes to make that vision come true.

The Vision Statement

When an organization is holding itself accountable for creating the future of its community, its vision will be defined as follows:

> Vision is the picture of the future your organization will aim at creating for the community it intends to impact.

This is different from the Business Model, where a vision statement is, "the picture of the future you want for the *organization*." In a business, self-perpetuation is indeed the vision, to keep the company generating profits, long into the future, for those who own the company.

But when an organization is Governing for What Matters Most, its vision will be for the community, not for itself. If the organization were to disappear tomorrow, that vision would still remain.

Therefore, an effective Vision Statement will tell the world what community improvement the group intends to create.

> Our vision is a community where _____.

> Our vision is a community that _____.

When an organization is Governing for What Matters Most, its vision is for the community's highest aspirations, its highest expectations. Through that thought-process, we see that using a traditional business Vision Statement for a Community Benefit Organization is actually a statement of *low* expectations. Claiming that the best future an organization can envision is for itself, the organization will have no expectations for creating any visionary change outside its own four walls.

If a board is governing with its vision for community success always in mind, it is always coming back to the big question: "Why are we doing what we are doing?"

We are doing that work so we can create an amazing place to live.

We are doing it so that individuals' lives will be better, and so that all the lives of everyone in the community will be healthy, strong and joyful, long into the future.

That vision for building an extraordinary future for the community becomes the board's context for all its decision-making.

Example: Vision for a Recovery Organization

The Recovery Organization was 30 years old when we began working with them on governance issues. We began the discussion with this question:

**What will the community look like
if you are 100% successful in accomplishing your mission?
When we aim at "success" for our community,
what will we be aiming at?**

As the group discussed this question, the conversations quickly jumped beyond the immediate issues of treating and preventing substance abuse.

The group talked about the emerging science of substance abuse. If there is evidence that other animals besides humans seek euphoria / escape, the group wondered if it was realistic to envision a community where that somehow did not occur.

They therefore turned their vision to a community-wide attitude of acceptance, to replace attitudes of condemnation, fear, judgement, and self-loathing. They discussed the elimination of stigmas, where individuals dealing with substance abuse were treated much as a doctor treats the flu - without being judged.

They described a sense of spiritual "wholeness" in the community - a place with rich opportunity for spiritual interaction, communication, awareness, and education. They talked about acceptance and celebration of religious diversity.

The group also envisioned more realistic understanding about the cycles that contribute to substance abuse, as well as the cycles for which substance abuse itself is a contributing factor - a community that understood cause and effect, rather than considering individuals in a vacuum. They saw a place with equality of opportunity for education, for artistic expression.

The discussion eventually led to a picture of compassion, not just regarding those dealing with substance abuse, but an overall compassionate community regarding how we all deal with each other, period.

These are the sorts of conversations in which few boards have the opportunity to regularly partake, and which some boards feel are too "esoteric" - not at all practical.

But what could be more practical than clarifying precisely what success a group is aiming to achieve? Without such conversations, how will a group know what it is aiming all its work at accomplishing? How can it measure whether or not it is making progress?

How, then, could it be at all practical to NOT have these conversations?

The Recovery Organization's Vision Statement

Our vision is for a safe, nurturing, compassionate community that respects individuals and their families, and encourages their spiritual, intellectual, emotional, and physical development.

The Mission Statement

Like the Missionary does for the Visionary, the Mission Statement turns a group's vision into practice. The Vision Statement will define where the group wants the community to end up; the Mission Statement is the one that will actually do the work to get there.

Again, it is easy to see what the Mission Statement needs to do if we go back to plain English usage. Consider the phrase "mission accomplished" - the work is done. Or "mission impossible" - the job cannot be done. The mission is the doing part - it is what a group will do to bring its vision to reality.

While it is powerful to talk about the work an organization does (the mission), it is more powerful to talk about that work in the context of why you are doing it - the context of creating an amazing place to live.

> Our vision is a community where _____. To
> bring that vision into reality, we do _____
> _____.

This is powerful for a number of reasons. First, it states right up front, "Our intent is to create significant community change."

Equally as important, though, that vision is the point at which all members of your community agree. While each organization in a community may be *doing* something different, we all want the same end result for our communities - healthy, vibrant, resilient, joyful places to live.

Lastly, making the Mission Statement a condition of the Vision Statement reminds the board and staff to align the organization's means (what we do) behind its desired end results (why we are doing it).

Example: Mission Statement for the Recovery Organization

Our vision is for a safe, nurturing, compassionate community that respects individuals and their families, and encourages their spiritual, intellectual, emotional, and physical development.

The Recovery Organization advances this vision by providing treatment for people recovering from substance abuse, to help them build lives of wholeness and health.

The Values Statement

Mission Statements and Vision Statements are relatively common in organizations. It is the rare board, though, that takes the time to then define HOW it will do that work - the talk they intend to walk.

When the purpose behind an organization's work is to reach for the community's highest aspirations, the organization will be able to accomplish significantly more impact if it is conscious to "be the change it wants to see" in the way it does that work. In practice, that means behaving and acting in ways that become a case study model to the community, showing them how such work can be done.

The Values Statement is therefore the cornerstone upon which the organization will rely for that guidance.

> If we are to be the change we want to see in our community, what will be the most critical values to uphold as we do our work? How can we show our community what those values look like in practice? How will we model to the community the values we wish to see embraced?

Example: Values at the Recovery Organization

The discussion of core values was another energizing discussion for the Recovery Organization. How do we know which is the right decision in any given situation? What is the talk we want to walk, the behaviors we want the community to emulate? For a group where many of the participants were either in recovery themselves, or had dealt for years with the substance abuse of family members, these were not arms-length issues; they were what mattered most about the work they were doing.

While the group acknowledged that Western Society's (and particularly the United States's) current emphasis on "pulling oneself up by one's bootstraps" was detrimental to building a compassionate and sober community (the dictate that any individual not only can, but should merely pull him/herself into sobriety), they were equally resolute that responsibility be both collective and individual.

Understanding that responsibility and compassion, diligence and humanity, did not go counter to each other but instead must go hand in hand, made these discussions especially rich.

Some of the words the group used during this discussion included:

- Compassion
- Respect
- Sensitivity
- Confidentiality
- Responsibility
- Attention to the health and safety of our clients
- Modeling of the behaviors we want to see - from dress and speech, to positiveness and all our values
- High ethical and moral standards
    - Sobriety
    - Honesty
    - Open communications

The Recovery Organization's Values Statement:

The Recovery Organization will be able to provide our mission and reach for our vision only if our work is true to the following core values:

1. We will do our work in a way that treats the health and well-being of the individuals in our care as the highest priority. What is in the best interest of the greatest number of clients at the Recovery Organization will be in the best interests of the Recovery Organization.
2. We will do our work in a way that complies with all Federal, State, Local and industry regulations.
3. Our behaviors will evidence the highest ethical standards, including compassion, respect, sensitivity, confidentiality, honesty and sobriety.
4. We will do our work in a way that models those behaviors to the staff, to the clients and to the community.

Chapter 17:
Putting What Matters Into Action

> The truth of the matter is that you always know the right thing to do. The hard part is doing it.
>
> *General H. Norman Schwarzkopf*

When a board is Governing for What Matters, it uses its Vision, Mission and Values Statements as the core for its work. Those *3 Statements* provide the context for every decision and every action taken. By governing through *The 3 Statements*, the organization's work is always aligned behind its vision for success in the community, and the organization is always doing its best to walk its talk.

To accomplish this, the board uses *The 3 Statements* to guide its work wherever the board does that work. Primarily that work happens in two places[1] :

    1) In annual planning sessions and other retreat settings

    2) At the board table

To show how a board can ensure *The 3 Statements* are guiding its actions in both those settings, Chapters 18-23 will focus on putting *The 3 Statements* into action via a board's annual plan. From there, Chapter 24 will focus on how boards put *The 3 Statements* into action through their day-to-day work at the board table.

---

1 Individual board members may do their work in many other places, from committees to individual advocacy and other arenas. The focus of a Governance System is, however, on the actions of the board as a whole. As such thinking becomes the culture of the board, individual board members would be encouraged to align their individual actions behind that way of thinking and being.

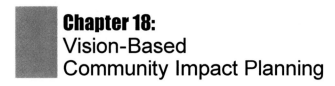

Chapter 18:
Vision-Based
Community Impact Planning

The most crucial act of a board's leadership role is planning - the process by which a board actually leads and guides the organization's work. When a board is Governing for What Matters Most, its planning is aimed at creating significant community improvement. From there, the plan also assists the board to proactively address its Legal Oversight, Operational Oversight, and Board Mechanics roles.

To accomplish all that, an organization's planning would need to be guided by two critical questions:

1. How will the community be a better place because of our work? (Leadership)

2. How can we ensure we have the capacity to make that happen? (Legal and Operational Oversight, Board Mechanics)

Such questions are not typically at the heart of organizational strategic planning. Traditional planning approaches do not reach proactively for creating an extraordinary community. Instead, such planning reacts incrementally to community circumstances and needs (*We have seen an increase in the need for behavioral health services. We cannot meet that full demand, but we can respond by increasing staffing in our behavioral health department by 10%...*).

Classic strategic planning also does not aim at overall organizational health, but instead reacts to narrow organizational circumstances and needs (*We need a fundraising plan; we need board development work; we need to brand ourselves, etc.*).

A plan that is rooted in reactive problem-solving cannot aim an organization's work at making the community a better place to live. However, when a plan is instead tethered to the positive future it intends to create, that plan can indeed aim a group at accomplishing visionary community impact. With such a proactive plan, problems are solved along the way to creating an extraordinary community.

Organizational infrastructure is developed along the way as well, to be sure those efforts remain strong. The key aspect of the plan is that it proactively aims at what is positive, what is possible.

That is what Vision-Based Community Impact Planning is all about.

Before showing how the planning process works, it is important to clarify what this relatively straightforward term means.

- What exactly is *Vision-based*, and how is that different from what organizations currently do?

- In this context, what is the definition of *Community*?

- What exactly is *Impact*?

- And how can *Planning* accomplish that impact?

Vision-Based

Traditional "nonprofit strategic planning" begins at today and moves forward to establish goals for what the group will accomplish over the next several years.

To ensure the plan is tethered to today's reality, such planning typically begins with some form of situational analysis, such as a SWOT Analysis (Strengths / Weaknesses / Opportunities / Threats), an Environmental Scan or a Needs Assessment. These systems create the plan's context, which creates the context of the organization's focus.

In truth, though, the focus is not simply on "today's reality," but on what we do not like about that reality. Whether it is focused on the needs of the community or the organization, traditional "nonprofit strategic planning" is about problem-solving - reacting to what is wrong.

If an organization's annual planning session is when the organization dreams its biggest dreams, the results will be severely limited if those dreams are tethered to what we do not like about the current reality. We can accomplish considerably more if our plans are instead tethered to the reality we do want to create - our community's highest aspirations.

That is what is meant by Vision-Based.

Vision-Based planning aims at the extraordinary future we all want for our communities, establishing that visionary future as the foundation of the planning process.

Along the way, Vision-Based planning enumerates and addresses today's problems. It also addresses adjustments to today's programs, as well as internal organizational issues.

What this approach does not do, however, is to allow those negative and ever-changing factors to become the context of the plan. Vision-Based planning instead addresses all those issues within the context of the one thing that remains constant - our desire to create an amazing future for the communities we care about.

Community

With all this talk about community improvement, how can one effectively define *Community*? Is it a geographic location? Is it a community of interest?

If the goal is to effect more visionary change in communities, the definition of *Community* will be *the geographic area your group intends to impact.*

This could be a neighborhood, a town or city, a region, a nation, or perhaps the whole world. Whatever geographic area is the focus of your organization's aspirations, concerns and mission, that is your community.

Where do you intend to make a difference? Where do you intend to aim your vision for the future? Whose future? Where?

By directly linking your definition of "community" to the difference your group is aiming to make - for whom and where - the definition will have specific and logical meaning to your group. From there, group members will be more motivated to hold themselves accountable to that community.

Impact

If ever a word were bandied about communities to the point of non-meaning, it has been the word *impact*. These days, words such as "impact" and "outcomes" and "results" have become little more than overused buzzwords.

Program leaders tend to think of such words in conjunction with funder / government mandates to "measure outcomes" and "measure impact." Programs are encouraged to determine the extent to which that impact is directly attributable to one source of funding or one project.

Mike Morris, a professor of Psychology at the University of New Haven, has assessed this trend with his own tongue-in-cheek distinction between all the terms that relate to *impact*. He tells us, "Impact is what a ripe peach looks like after you've hit it with a baseball bat. The outcome is what comes out of the peach after you've hit it with the baseball bat."

To get past the never-ending semantics issue (and to escape the peach juice!), we encourage groups to define impact as ***the future you wish to create, for whomever you wish to create it.***

What do you want life to be like? For whom? That is the impact you will aim your Vision-Based Community Impact Plan at creating.

Planning

Planning is the path to conscious governance. It is the most practical and effective tool boards have for consciously leading, guiding, and making decisions about the future of the organization and the future of the community.

Planning makes the board's leadership role practical and doable. A board that annually plans for what the organization will accomplish is less likely to spend its time reacting to circumstances that are seemingly outside the organization's control. During budget discussions, such a board has a barometer by which to determine whether or not the budget should be approved, simply by asking whether or not the budget reflects their planning priorities.

On the flip side, a board that does not make time to thoughtfully and proactively plan for what the organization will accomplish that year is destined to be whipsawed by circumstances. That board is likely to spend its time reacting rather than proactively leading and guiding. Budget decisions will typically be a reaction to staff's recommendations, often based on incremental adjustments to the prior year, or based on outside circumstances such as funding cuts. Board members on such boards often report that they do not have time to focus on improving their community, because they are always focused on some immediate circumstance or another.

A board that plans annually is therefore executing the most important role of the board - its leadership role. Without planning (and then monitoring the progress of that plan), the board's oversight activities are of little consequence. But with planning as the centerpiece of the board's activities, the board is consciously leading and guiding the organization - consciously governing.

Chapter 19:
Planning: Nuts & Bolts

To accomplish everything boards need from a planning process, Vision-Based Community Impact Planning breaks into three phases:

Phase 1: Focus 100% on the community. Phase 1 focuses the board on the future it will aim to create for the community, providing concrete steps to create that future. Phase 1 is therefore all about the "Leadership" part of governing.

Phase 2: Focus on connecting the future of the community with the present-day work of the group doing the planning. In Phase 2, the group will determine what work it will do in the short-term, to begin creating the long-term change they want to see in their community. They will determine how they will engage the community in that work, and will determine what they need to know that they do not know now. In addition, the group will determine how the organization and the community might chart how community conditions are changing and improving.

Phase 3: Focus 100% on the organization. Phase 3 aims the group at ensuring it has everything it needs internally to accomplish what it will do for the community. As part of that work, Phase 3 also aims the group at preventing undue risk and liability that can harm its ability to accomplish those goals. Phase 3 is where "Legal and Operational Oversight" proactively come into play, as well as "Board Mechanics."

The process starts in the community with its focus on the future. The process then narrows to connect the organization's current work with the future of the community. It then narrows again, focusing solely on the organization's internal capacity to take on the tasks it has in store.

Through the simultaneous focus on creating community impact and developing the organizational wherewithal to create that impact, a board is able to hold itself accountable for both the end results the organization provides, and the organizational means with which it provides those results.

That is why Vision-Based Community Impact Planning is the cornerstone for Governing for What Matters Most.

Reverse Engineering the Future of Our Communities

Vision-Based Community Impact Planning is Reverse Engineering for the future of our communities. That means the plan begins by considering the grandest ends we wish to achieve, and then works backwards to determine both the community conditions and the organizational conditions that will cause those results to become reality.

This is not as unusual an approach as it may seem. As a matter of fact, reverse engineering is how most of us plan to accomplish the normal events of our day-to-day lives.

Example:
You need to be at the airport for a 9am flight tomorrow. What time should you set your alarm clock to wake you?

We all know instinctively how we would determine what time to get up. We would start with that 9am flight, and we would work backwards:

- If the plane leaves at 9am, I'll need to be at the airport at 7am.

- To be at the airport by 7am, I need to leave the house by 6:30.

- I still have about an hour of packing to do, so I must begin packing no later than 5:30.

- I have to shower and feed the dog - that's about ½ hour - so I will have to get up at 5am.

That is reverse engineering. It is the same process one might use to determine how to ensure a complicated dinner is timed to coincide with the arrival of our guests. It is the thought-process we use to determine what time to leave the office to get home in time for our kids' soccer game. It is, for the most part, how we humans plan to accomplish the day-to-day of our lives.

Because reverse engineering is how most effective planning is done, it is how Vision-Based Community Impact Planning works. It starts with the powerful positive image of the extraordinary future we will aim at creating. Then, tethered to that vision for the future of the community, the planning process walks backwards along the chain of cause-and-effect, until the process arrives at what steps the organization will take today, to begin moving towards that visionary end goal.

Using reverse engineering, a group can transform the seemingly overwhelming goal of "creating an extraordinary future for our community" into a series of simple and doable steps. The group will accomplish that simply by considering the question, "If this is where we want to end up, what has to happen before that can happen? What causes will create that effect?"

CHAPTER 20:
Planning: Vision for the Community
Phase 1: Focusing on the Community

The Community Impact planning process begins by asking participants to envision the future they will aim at creating for their community - the same discussions that are at the root of creating the organization's Vision Statement.

- If we were to wave a magic wand and create the community we want for the grandkids of our grandkids, what would that community look like?

- As we consider the mission of our organization, what would 100% success look like in our community?

- What would "amazing" or "extraordinary" or "Wow!" look like for our community? What would success look like?

From there, the reverse engineering begins.

If it is true that all our actions today are creating the future, then we can certainly envision what kinds of community conditions might create the future we intend to build. We can then consider the interrelated causes-and-effects that might create those conditions, and the sets of pre-conditions prior to those, and so on going backwards, just as if we were setting the alarm clock to head to the airport.

Eventually, we work our way backwards through interwoven causes and effects, to the conditions an organization's clients / patrons / participants and community at large are facing today.

The group is encouraged to discuss the precursor conditions that go beyond just their narrow mission. What will it take for our community to be what we want it to be? What conditions must be present for our vision to become reality? We all know the answer is not found solely in the mission of one organization. By focusing on the big picture first, and then working backwards to consider how smaller conditions fit into that big picture, the process encourages listing as many of those causal conditions as possible, whether they are directly related to the organization's current mission, tangentially related, or seemingly unrelated.

The examples on the following pages show how Phase 1 worked for three organizations with whom we have done this work. The first is the Recovery Organization, to show how the themes in their *3 Statements* translated into their planning.

The other two examples include a Public Broadcast Group, and a University Masters Degree Program in Community Leadership.

The Recovery Organization
Community Impact Plan Phase 1

Stats:

Age: ± 30 years old
Budget: $1.5 Million
Staff Size: 35 Full Time
Status: Effective but dated residential substance abuse treatment program. Many loyal, high profile board members, the result of the organization helping a family member. Poor relationship between board and long-term ED had persisted for many years, with board frustrated / unable to focus beyond day-to-day problems. Program was stagnant, with community reputation (and funding) in decline.

Motivation for Plan:
Part of overall governance improvement strategy.

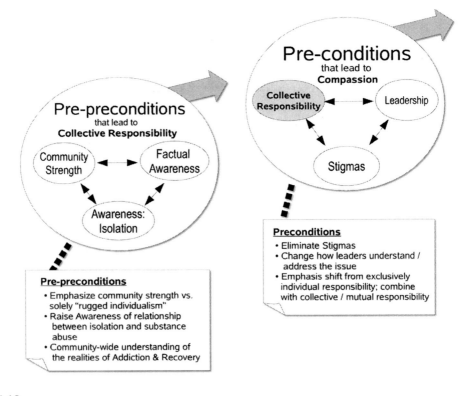

Pre-preconditions that lead to **Collective Responsibility**

Community Strength ↔ Factual Awareness

Awareness: Isolation

Pre-conditions that lead to **Compassion**

Collective Responsibility ↔ Leadership

Stigmas

Pre-preconditions
- Emphasize community strength vs. solely "rugged individualism"
- Raise Awareness of relationship between isolation and substance abuse
- Community-wide understanding of the realities of Addiction & Recovery

Preconditions
- Eliminate Stigmas
- Change how leaders understand / address the issue
- Emphasis shift from exclusively individual responsibility; combine with collective / mutual responsibility

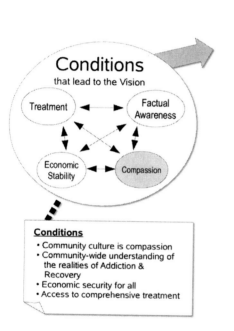

Conditions
that lead to the Vision

Treatment ⟷ Factual Awareness

Economic Stability ⟷ Compassion

VISION
A safe, nurturing, compassionate community that respects individuals and encourages spiritual, intellectual, emotional and physical development.

Conditions
- Community culture is compassion
- Community-wide understanding of the realities of Addiction & Recovery
- Economic security for all
- Access to comprehensive treatment

For purposes of simplicity, space and clarity, this page shows reverse engineered discussions for just one condition (Compassion) and one pre-condition (Collective Responsibility) at a time. In the planning session, there were discussions of pre-conditions, pre-preconditions, and so on, for each condition leading to the organization's vision.

The Public Broadcast Group
Community Impact Plan Phase 1

Stats:
Age: ± 40 years old
Budget: $8 million
Staff Size: ± 100 Full Time and Part Time plus ± 400 volunteers
Status: Mid-market public radio and television stations. Highly stable group, with only three General Managers in almost 40 years.

Motivation for Plan:
We provided planning assistance to the station twice, the first time six years prior to the second. Motivation for Prior Plan: Eliminate fiefdoms between and within radio and television divisions. Motivation for Current Plan: How to remain relevant / How to survive given rapidly changing technologies and other competition for viewers / listeners.

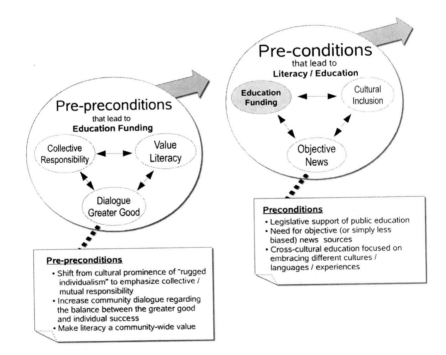

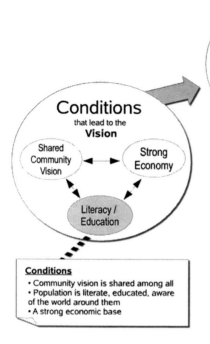

VISION

A community where community members have an engaged and participative sense of ownership of their community, within a spirit of celebration for each other's differences.

Conditions that lead to the **Vision**

Shared Community Vision ◄──► Strong Economy

Literacy / Education

Conditions
• Community vision is shared among all
• Population is literate, educated, aware of the world around them
• A strong economic base

As with the Recovery Organization, discussion during the planning session included pre-conditions, pre-preconditions, and so on, for each condition leading to the organization's vision. This page narrows the focus on one condition (Literacy / Education) and one pre-condition (Education Funding) for the sake of simplicity, clarity and space.

The University Leadership Program
Community Impact Plan Phase 1

Stats:
Age: ± 40 years old
University Stats: 10,000 students in major metropolitan area. University is over 100 years old.

Status and Motivation:
Relatively new masters program with standard leadership curriculum. Acceptable enrollment and levels of satisfaction among students. New Dean was dissatisfied with "acceptable," seeking to transform the program into a "Change-the-World, Make-a-Difference, Leave-a-Legacy" program.

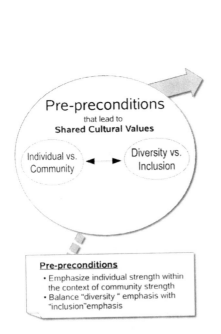

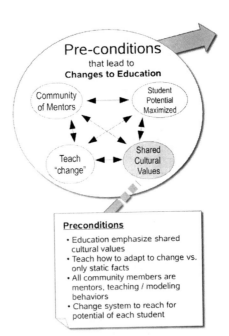

Pre-preconditions
that lead to
Shared Cultural Values

Individual vs. Community ◄─► Diversity vs. Inclusion

Pre-conditions
that lead to
Changes to Education

Community of Mentors ◄─► Student Potential Maximized

Teach "change" ◄─► Shared Cultural Values

Pre-preconditions
• Emphasize individual strength within the context of community strength
• Balance "diversity " emphasis with "inclusion"emphasis

Preconditions
• Education emphasize shared cultural values
• Teach how to adapt to change vs. only static facts
• All community members are mentors, teaching / modeling behaviors
• Change system to reach for potential of each student

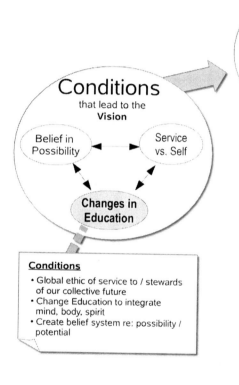

VISION

A world where all systems are aligned behind bringing out our highest potential to live joyfully together.

Conditions
that lead to the
Vision

Belief in Possibility

Service vs. Self

Changes in Education

Conditions

- Global ethic of service to / stewards of our collective future
- Change Education to integrate mind, body, spirit
- Create belief system re: possibility / potential

Again, the planning session discussion included all pre-conditions, pre-preconditions, and so on, for each condition leading to the program's vision. This page narrows the focus on one condition (Changes in Education) and one pre-condition (Shared Cultural Values) for the sake of simplicity, clarity and space.

Phase 1 - The Pollyanna Principles in Action

Pollyanna Principle #6 notes that people will go where systems lead them. Where does Phase 1 of Vision-Based Community Impact Planning aim those who are participating in that process?

Pollyanna Principle #1:
We accomplish what we hold ourselves accountable for.

Pollyanna Principle #2:
Each and every one of us is creating the future, every day, whether we do so consciously or not.

As we saw in Chapter 6, accountability is all about aiming. Whose expectations are we aiming to fulfill? Where are we aiming our efforts?

The answers to those questions are clearly defined in Phase 1 of the Community Impact Plan. All three groups defined the future they would be holding themselves accountable for creating in their communities, by influencing the chain of cause-and-effect that would create that future.

Phase 1 thus immediately begins to negate the Culture of Can't, showing through cause-and-effect how individual actions will become the "reality" of the future. Participants create their own path of causality from today to the future they want to create, seeing that they can take realistic and practical steps that align with their accountability for those ultimate results.

Pollyanna Principle #3:
Everyone and everything is interconnected and interdependent, whether we acknowledge that or not.

As we see in the diagrams for each of the plans, the cause-and-effect conditions move forward along a trajectory between today and the future. But because long-term community change occurs not along a single, direct path, but along a more circuitous route, the forward motion of the plan is not the narrowly defined straight-line image we would see in short-term "strategic" plans.

That is because focusing on the causes and effects of what it will take to build the kind of literate, compassionate, engaged community these groups sought to build, requires that a planning process embrace the interconnectedness and interdependence of all those causes and effects. Further, the process must acknowledge the many missions that might fall outside a group's own mission but are, nonetheless, critical to success.

Therefore, rather than feeling overwhelming by that sense of interconnectedness and interdependence, the discussions in Phase 1 feel natural and not at all intimidating.

> **Pollyanna Principle #4:**
> "Being the change we want to see" means walking the talk of our values.

A cursory glance at the examples shows that discussion of the cause-and-effect community conditions that will lead to the vision quickly becomes a discussion of values.

While there are material conditions that must be present, all three examples focus heavily on the need to realign community values, to aim those values at what is possible and desirable. Again, rather than being seen as "impossible" or "too tough for one group to accomplish," the cause-and-effect of reverse engineering simply encourages the group to look back another step, to ask, "What needs to be present to change those values?" The Culture of Can't is thus dealt another blow!

> **Pollyanna Principle #5:**
> Strength builds upon our strengths, not our weaknesses.

There are two interwoven observations about the issue of strength. The first is that Vision-Based planning starts the conversation at the point where we all agree - the desire for a safe, healthy, humane place to live. The process then continues to be rooted in that sense of agreement as it focuses on the conditions that would need to be present for that vision to become reality.

The second observation is that this process is rooted not in the perceived weaknesses of our communities, but in their potential for strength. The process is not about problem-solving (eliminating a negative condition); it is about attaining something proactive and positive.

From the combination of those two observations, we see that a plan focused on ending a negative condition is not only rooted in weakness; it also causes dissension from the beginning, as participants disagree about which aspects of the problem should be addressed first, etc. That dissension itself creates a further base of weakness.

However, when the discussions begin with agreement, and slowly walk through additional sources of agreement, by the time the process arrives at the point where participants do disagree, they encounter that disagreement within the context of having already agreed about a great many issues. The spirit of agreement has become a strength upon which to build.

By beginning with the powerful vision of the future they want to build, and slowly walking backwards, step by step, to create the causes and effects that will build that future, the process itself adds strength to every step by generating agreement and inspiration about what is possible.

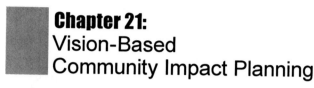

Chapter 21:
Vision-Based
Community Impact Planning

Phase 2: Connecting the Community's Future with the Organization's Present-Day Work

Phase 2 is where a group will see that creating visionary community change is not only possible, but practical and doable.

Having started by focusing exclusively on the community in Phase 1, Phase 2 determines the various ways the organization will work to change the community conditions that will lead to their ultimate picture of success.

Vision-Based Short-Term Goals / Objectives

The end result of the reverse engineering process is the question, "Which of the cause-and-effect conditions that will lead to our vision could we begin to address now?"

Those first steps will become the plan's goals and objectives.

Sometimes those first steps are grand and mighty. More often, first-time goals are small steps, a bite at a time. As long as those goals reflect the vision and values of the organization, then regardless of the size of that first effort, even the smallest steps will be aimed in a direction that will create a better future.

Aligning Existing Programs

The discussion then examines the organization's current programs, to determine whether those programs are aligned with the group's vision, and its stated values. It is not unusual for a group to look up in dismay, realizing its current programs go counter to the vision they have defined, or that they have allowed funding limitations to prevent a program from accomplishing all it can accomplish, or that in some other way, their programs go counter to one or more portions of the values they have determined are important, per their *3 Statements*.

Gaining Knowledge

To ensure their first steps are well-informed, groups also consider what they need to know that they do not already know - research, inquiry, learning. It is not unusual for a first-time plan to include a significant research component.

Engaging Others

Groups also consider the critical question of Community Engagement. How can engaging the community enhance each of our efforts? Whose lives will be affected by what we are considering? Whose wisdom can make our efforts stronger? And how will we engage those individuals as partners in this work?

Measurement

What indicators might the group employ, to measure the extent to which their work is indeed changing the conditions they have discussed?

Through reverse engineering, these first steps become obvious as the logical next step on the cause-and-effect path that led backwards from the group's vision for the future.

Using this approach, organizations are less likely to come up with ideas in a vacuum. Instead they will have considered a whole host of potential consequences (as well as a whole host of potential partners) they might otherwise have ignored.

All this occurs as the organization looks first at its dreams for the community, and only then at how the organization will interact with and fit into that community, becoming one part of the chain of cause-and-effect that will create the community's future.

The following pages provide examples of Phase 2 for each of the case studies.

The Recovery Organization
Phase 2: Goal-Setting

Goal #1: Make Sure Our Current Program is Effective

Condition to Impact: Broader Access to Comprehensive Treatment
- Research and define treatment program effectiveness
- Institute changes to make the treatment program as effective as possible

Implementation Steps:
1. Board and staff meet to determine what questions they want their research to answer
2. Staff to work with professors at the local college to develop research methodology
3. Research state of the art: Literature scan, interview leaders of innovative programs
4. Report research to the board, to inform next-step decisions about the program

---

Goal #2: Develop Program for Working People

Condition to Impact: Broader Access to Comprehensive Treatment
- Establish program to meet needs of non-indigent / non-wealthy clients, who must work for a living and therefore have few options for long-term, residential treatment. Program up and running within 2 years.

Implementation Steps:

PART 1:
1. Promote availability of existing program to working individuals (current clients primarily low-income)
2. Document response of working individuals (Were objections raised? What were they?)
3. Document experience of those who go through the program

PART 2:
1. Form committee of board / staff / outside experts / community members
2. Committee: Research and develop program for working population

---

Goal #3: Increase Awareness of Addiction / Sobriety Issues

Condition to Impact: The Community's Culture will be More Compassionate than Judgmental
- Develop / implement plan to raise awareness of issues of sobriety and addiction, and the effect of those issues on the community, with measurable goals. Host an awareness event within 18 months.

Implementation Steps:
1. Immediately include larger issues in all the organization's outreach and marketing
2. Immediately include "issues awareness" in board orientation
3. Form committee of board / staff / outside experts (including board members / staff from other substance abuse groups) / community members, to draft a Community-Wide Issues Awareness Plan

Recovery Organization - Phase 2

In the goals for the Recovery Organization's Community Impact Plan, we see how all aspects of Phase 2 are logically incorporated in their goals and objectives.

Vision-based:	Each goal takes steps to impact the community conditions noted in Phase 1
Aligned:	Ensuring programs align with the vision is a goal unto itself
Research:	Each goal includes research and knowledge-building
Engaged:	Each goal includes community engagement
Measurement:	Each goal includes an element of outcomes measurement

The Public Broadcast Group
Phase 2: Goal-Setting

Goal #1: Mission / Vision / Values Statements

Condition to Impact: Shared Community Vision

- Re-work mission, vision and values statements to provide the public with a firm understanding not only of what the organization does, but why.

- Use the airwaves to provide ongoing message: "This is the talk we will be walking. These are the values we will uphold. This is the future we want to create for our community."

Implementation Steps:

1. Form internal committee to re-work *The 3 Statements*

2. Cross-division committee to develop plan for getting that message on the air

Goal #2: Strengthen Emphasis on Literacy / Ability to Communicate

Condition to Impact: Literacy / education

- Maximize and expand the group's existing in-school literacy efforts.

Implementation Steps:

1. Work with other literacy groups to collectively enhance current literacy work in the community

2. Research to determine how to maximize the impact of the group's current program

3. Determine most effective ways to expand existing program, as well as indicators of success

Goal #3: Convening the Community to Enhance Civic Dialogue of Issues

Condition to Impact: Shared Community Vision

- Broaden the reach and impact of current "we-broadcast-out" mission work, by creating true dialogue, engaging and convening the community face-to-face.

Implementation Steps:

1. Engage community in discussion around what such an effort might accomplish and how it might work

2. Develop a plan to put results of those discussions into action

Goal #4: Embracing Cultural Diversity

Condition to Impact: Shared Community Vision AND Increased Literacy

- Move beyond smattering of cross-cultural programming, to more deeply integrate diversity into programming (cultural, socio-economic, age, etc.).

Implementation Steps:

1. Engage community in discussion around what an effort to truly "embrace" diversity might accomplish.

2. Develop / implement plan to accomplish those goals

Public Broadcast Group - Phase 2

The Public Broadcast Group wove the various aspects of Phase 2 throughout their Community Impact Goals. In these goals, we see that:

Vision-based:	Each goal takes steps to impact the community conditions noted in Phase 1
Aligned:	Each goal aligns programs with the vision, with one focused entirely on *The 3 Statements*
Research:	Where appropriate, goals include research and knowledge-building
Engaged:	Each goal engages others in the community
Measurement:	Each goal includes an element of outcomes measurement

In addition, it is clear from these goals that the "fiefdom" issues and issues related to relevance (page 150) are addressed in the course of aiming through and beyond those issues, rather than aiming at the problems themselves. The goals simply assume all divisions will work on all issues. Those issues will not lose relevance, even in the fast-paced world of broadcasting, simply because they relate to the broader community vision.

The University Program
Phase 2: Goal-Setting

> Goal #1: A "Change-The-World, Leave-a-Legacy, Make-a-Difference" Masters Program

Condition to Impact: All the conditions they noted!

- Engage individuals who are already working to impact any of the conditions we noted, to determine potential courses to reach for those conditions. Build on their strengths to build the program.

- Each semester, replace one existing course with a new course aimed at those changed conditions.

- Within two years, eliminate vestiges of the old program; in its place will be the fully revamped program.

Implementation Steps:

1. Engagement of faculty

2. Ongoing adjustment to curriculum and to individual courses

SUB-GOAL #1: RESEARCH SIMILAR EFFORTS

- Identify and engage similar visionary masters degree programs around the world

- Learn from each program: Successes / failures; pitfalls; measurement rubrics; use of technology; "What do you wish you had known when you started?"; long-term results; etc.

- Mandate: Do NOT research this to death! Ensure research is practical, ongoing, and evolutionary - not a drawn-out precursor to taking first steps.

SUB-GOAL #2: MEASURING STUDENT LEARNING

Condition to Impact: Walking the talk re: collective responsibility vs. competition

- Engage students, alumni, faculty and others in discussion re: grades as a measure of student learning. How can students be empowered to measure their own learning? What would we want to measure? If a student gets a D or an F, does that do anything to create the future we want for the world?

The University Masters Degree Leadership Program

The University program made goal-setting simple by articulating one overarching goal, with sub-goals within that goal: "We need to find faculty who agree with our vision, who can immediately start teaching these topics, to begin building a curriculum that will address these conditions."

The visionary roots of this planning session had clear intent: Overhaul the program. That overarching goal was therefore to address ALL the cause-and-effect pre-conditions to their vision, by creating an educational atmosphere centered around those values and those conditions.

The University's overarching and sub-goals address all the aspects of Phase 2:

Vision-based:	Goals are rooted entirely in the vision and conditions noted in Phase 1
Aligned:	The entire purpose of the plan was to ensure the courses aligned with the vision. The first courses to be eliminated were those that were the most misaligned.
Research:	An entire sub-goal is dedicated to learning what others have done
Engaged:	Each step includes engagement of faculty, students and other programs
Measurement:	An entire sub-goal is dedicated to measurement of meaningful outcomes, from the perspective of core values articulated in the plan

Phase 2 - The Pollyanna Principles in Action

Pollyanna Principle #6 notes that people will go where systems lead them. Where does Phase 2 of Vision-Based Community Impact Planning aim those participating in that process?

Pollyanna Principle #1:
We accomplish what we hold ourselves accountable for.

Pollyanna Principle #2:
Each and every one of us is creating the future, every day, whether we do so consciously or not.

It is one thing to inspire the potential in a room full of community leaders; it is quite another to give them practical, doable steps for turning that potential into action. That practicality is the only path to replacing the Culture of Can't with a Culture of Can. As each of the goals of the case study organizations shows, this is as real as it gets. It is those practical steps that allow a board to hold itself accountable for creating the future of the community.

> "Our cultural instincts may say it is impossible to create a healthy, vibrant, compassionate community. But look - we just created a step-by-step plan to accomplish just that!"

Pollyanna Principle #3:
Everyone and everything is interconnected and interdependent, whether we acknowledge that or not.

For years, organizations have been told to collaborate. Funders have tried to encourage / force them to do so as a condition of funding. Corporate funders have urged mergers. As I write this, a U.S. foundation is even offering a $250,000 prize to some lucky collaborative effort, to provide an incentive and to allow that amazing collaboration to serve as an example to others.

Through the Community Impact Planning process, though, organizational leaders do not need that outside push. They realize on their own, "We cannot do this alone. We must see who else is doing this work, and get to know them." That spirit of cooperation is not prescribed. It is self-inspired.

The three plans in the case studies are not unique in their desire to engage others doing similar work. In the many years of doing planning in this way, there is not a plan I have facilitated where this has not been the result. In every single case, organizational leaders who had entered the planning session seeking competitive advantage left the session seeking others from whom they could learn, and with whom they could work together to get the job done.

Pollyanna Principle #4:
"Being the change we want to see" means walking the talk of our values.

The question of whether current programs are aligned with the Vision and Values of Phase 1 is revealing. In all three case studies, aligning their organizational means behind their intended end results was a critical goal, not only because to do otherwise would be illogical and counterproductive, but because of their desire to be consistent in walking their talk.

In all three case studies, the desire to "be the change they wanted to see" was consciously and deliberately incorporated into each of their goals and their plans.

Again, this is not an anomaly - it is what we have seen happen in every single Community Impact Plan we have done, both because the process encourages such discussion, and because groups realize it would be counterproductive to do otherwise.

Pollyanna Principle #5:
Strength builds upon our strengths, not our weaknesses.

The directive that "Our community will be healthy" is far different from "Our community will stop being sick." From such vision-based thinking, the goals of the plan are also forward-thinking, strength-based goals, aimed at taking positive steps towards a positive, visionary, community-focused end result.

No matter how small those first steps, they are powerful steps, focused not on fixing a weakness, but on building upon strengths that already exist, both in the organization and in the community.

The sense of organizational strength that comes from that simple change of perception is instantaneous, occurring in the course of an afternoon's planning session.

One can see strength in each of the goals of each of the organizations in the case studies. That strength is especially poignant to find in an organization that was experiencing the sorts of internal strife the Recovery Organization had been facing for years.

Pollyanna Principle #6:
Individuals will go where systems lead them.

While all the systems noted in Phase 2 point in the direction of visionary community results, one system in particular stands out - analyzing the current situation via data collection.

Unlike planning processes that collect "situational analysis" data first, and then root the plan in that present-day data, the Vision-Based nature of this planning system roots data collection in the organization's dreams for the future it is aiming to create. That vision then determines what data is needed, what questions need to be asked and answered, what information must be sought.

If the systems point towards today, that is where our plans will focus. If the systems point towards the future we are creating, our plans will aim us in that direction at every step.

Chapter 22:
Vision-Based
Community Impact Planning

Phase 3: Focusing Internally on the Organization

In the last phase of the planning, the reverse engineering continues, taking one last step backwards to examine what the group needs to have in place internally to ensure the organization can accomplish its goals.

How can the group ensure, to the best of its ability, that every functional aspect of the organization is strong enough to proactively pursue the community's future, vs. always reacting to circumstances? How can they proactively guard the organization against risks that could harm their ability to do so?

Vision-Based Community Impact Planning therefore ends with the question, "What do we need to have in place, to ensure every function of the organization is healthy enough for us to create the kind of community we dream of?"

That means addressing everything - every organizational function, including personnel, facilities, equipment, regulatory compliance, resource development, board development, community engagement, internal communications, cultural competence, internal financial controls, etc.

The organization plans to ensure each and every functional aspect is strong enough to take on the challenge of creating the future of the community. And they simultaneously plan to ensure that liability and risk do not eat away at that strength.

The process then ends the way any planning process should - by calendaring that plan and assigning it. Who will do what, and when? How will we monitor, to ensure we are on track? What do we want to measure, to know whether we are accomplishing what we intended to accomplish?

The Recovery Organization
Phase 3: Organizational Wellness

The Recovery Organization was in a tenuous position when it did
its plan, as the relationship between the Executive Director and the
Board had been as dysfunctional as any we have seen. Past efforts at
"fixing the problem" had failed.

In the Organizational Wellness portion of the Community Impact
Planning, all functional areas were discussed within the context
of the organization's vision for the community. This allowed for
dispassionate discussion of what it would take for them to reach for
their goals. It also allowed both parties - the Executive Director and
the Board - to be present for all discussions, as there was no blame
involved, just moving forward towards a future they all agreed they
wanted. The results, months and years later, have been staggering in
their sustained success.

For each functional area, the group addressed its aspirations and concerns. For every issue raised, the group prioritized and determined
steps to ensure the organization had the capacity to create the future
it envisioned.

The following prioritized Organizational Wellness goals came from that discussion.

Organizational Wellness Plan

Personnel
- Create a succession plan, in the event anything were to happen to the ED
- Have an outside Human Resources specialist perform annual review of HR manual. Calendar board review of the specialist's report.

Finance
- Create internal financial control policies
- Have auditor review financial controls and include in management letter
- Develop resource development plan to diversify beyond government reliance

Regulatory Issues
- Create annual calendar of regulatory issues, for board to monitor compliance

Facilities / Equipment
- Develop technology plan for adding computer capability

Community Engagement
- Develop Community Engagement plan

Board Mechanics
- Create monitoring systems for board directives, plans, operational and legal oversight issues
- Develop board recruitment process; implement recruitment efforts
- Develop plan for ongoing board education

The Public Broadcast Group
Phase 3: Organizational Wellness

The Public Broadcast Group was in a far better place during their second plan than they had been when we first assisted their planning efforts six years prior. The walls between the fiefdoms were so decidedly diminished that this Organizational Wellness plan was able to focus on enhancing the work they were already doing across disciplines and across divisions.

Unlike the Recovery Organization, the Public Broadcast Group was in a stable place in their growth cycle. As the group addressed its aspirations and concerns over each functional area of the organization, they found that many of those issues had already been addressed during their setting of Community Impact goals - issues such as Community Engagement and Cultural Inclusion / Diversity.

The following prioritized Organizational Wellness goals came from the group's discussion.

Organizational Wellness Plan

Programming
- Increase emphasis on local programming to maintain relevance and aim towards vision
- Enhance cultural competence in programming (per Community Impact Goal #4)

Finance
- Develop funding plans for new initiatives (requires more engaged approach than traditional on-air pledge drives)

Facilities / Equipment
- Create plan for dealing with lack of redundancy re: critical pieces of older equipment
- Create plan for facilities improvements to enhance informal communications (e.g. currently no lunchroom where staff can gather)

The Public Broadcast Group: Planning Epilogue

After the Public Broadcast Group completed their discussion of Organizational Wellness, I noticed a number of individuals passing notes as if they were in middle school. Finally it became comical, as I asked (in my best school-teacher voice), "Is this something you want to share with everyone?"

Indeed it was. These individuals had been working on a sweeping statement to address not only the conditions they intended to create for implementing the plan, but the conditions they intended to inject into their ongoing day-to-day efforts.

The following approaches and parameters will be incorporated into all actions taken at the Public Broadcast Group - for the goals of this plan, as well as ongoing day-do-day efforts:

1. *All divisions of the Public Broadcast Group will be consciously involved in planning and implementing all activities undertaken towards these goals and all our day-to-day activities, for a more integrated effort at creating impact.*

2. *The work we do inside the Public Broadcast Group will model the values we want to reflect outward to the community.*

3. *We will bring into our efforts as many collaborative partners from throughout the community as possible.*

4. *We will bring as many non-management staff and as many board members into these efforts as possible, to be inclusive inside our own house first.*

We smiled to recall that during our initial planning session with this group six years prior, the General Manager's personal goal had been the elimination of organizational fiefdoms. Now the group had, on its own, done just that, creating its own roadmap to a coordinated, integrated effort to build an incredible future for its community.

By aiming beyond the problem, and out towards what was possible, they had self-inspired to find the solution, as one step along the road to extraordinary.

The University Leadership Program
Phase 3: Organizational Wellness

Because the Masters Degree Program in Leadership was a single program in a large university system, the issue of Organizational Wellness was different from the other two groups, since the University took care of most of the needs that a smaller organization might have to handle on its own - issues such as regulatory compliance and financial controls.

In addition, like the Public Broadcast Group, many internal issues (such as the issue of Community Engagement) had been addressed in their Community Impact goals.

The issues that arose in this phase were therefore highly targeted.

In addition, because the group was embarking on creating something almost entirely new, they were mindful that they could not currently plan for all the internal issues that might arise. Rather than immediately incorporate issues into actual implementation goals at this early stage, therefore, they identified the following and noted them as issues to be mindful of during this formative stage.

The following prioritized Organizational Wellness goals came from that discussion.

Organizational Wellness Plan

Personnel
- Determine staffing levels to get beyond current limited staffing / low wage scales that will limit expansion of the program.
- Include in staffing discussions the need for interns or other volunteers to assist with both the research goals and engagement activities.

Finance
- Develop plans for funding additional personnel needs

Facilities / Equipment
- Research state-of-the-art technology for distance learning

- Determine how to encourage / teach faculty to use existing technology to its greatest effect, to address student complaints re: the distance learning experience

Communications
- Rewrite all communications to reflect new vision and purpose of the program - brochures, website, course catalog

---

The group chose to address its personnel, finance and technology needs as part of the budget process, which would give them time to see how the effort was evolving. Knowing that they did not yet know what they didn't know, the group wanted to see what additional issues would arise during their initial exploration of the changes they were about to embark upon.

Phase 3 - The Pollyanna Principles in Action

Pollyanna Principle #6 notes that people will go where systems lead them. Where does Phase 3 of Vision-Based Community Impact Planning aim those participating in that process?

Pollyanna Principle #1:
We accomplish what we hold ourselves accountable for.

Pollyanna Principle #2:
Each and every one of us is creating the future, every day, whether we do so consciously or not.

Traditional planning typically focuses its internal rays only on those operational issues that are "on fire." Like plans that focus on solving community problems vs. building "amazing communities," when these traditional plans aim inward, they aim to fix board problems, or fix funding issues, or add staff where it has been sorely needed.

To create the future of our communities, however, the groups doing that work cannot always be reacting to the circumstances that affect their operations. That is why Phase 3 of the planning process proactively aims at Organizational Wellness in all operational areas.

From the plans created in the examples, one can see that this is the only way a group can truly hold itself accountable for Legal and Operational Oversight. If a group is not proactively planning for overall wellness, its "accountability" in those areas is little more than reacting to organizational illness.

By planning for true Organizational Wellness, the board holds itself accountable for aligning the organization's means behind its ends, ensuring organizational strength to back up its strong, visionary end goals.

Pollyanna Principle #3:
Everyone and everything is interconnected and interdependent, whether we acknowledge that or not.

Ask any consultant who is asked to address one problem area of an organization, and that consultant will tell you - addressing one area in a vacuum always leads to uncovering issues in other areas that are affecting and affected by the one narrow issue they have been asked to address.

Rather than shy away from that complexity of interrelated internal issues, Phase 3 provides a simple system for observing, analyzing and taking proactive action to address *all* the interconnected internal issues faced by groups doing community work.

Pollyanna Principle #4:
"Being the change we want to see" means walking the talk of our values.

Feelings of organizational weakness and fear are often at the heart of the kinds of decisions that lead organizations to trade their values for a chance at financial security. When organizations proactively plan to be healthy, they find themselves in a far stronger position from which to model the kinds of decisions and actions they can be proud of.

Pollyanna Principle #5:
Strength builds upon our strengths, not our weaknesses.

Finally, planning for Organizational Wellness is planning proactively for strength in all functional areas. It assumes and expects strength, it aims at strength, and takes action to ensure that strength becomes *and remains* the reality.

Chapter 23:
Planning - Results and Observations

Vision-Based Community Impact Planning is the single most powerful tool a board can use for leading an organization to create the future of its community. By inspiring what is possible in a board, the process balances the need for proactive leadership with the need for proactive internal accountability, all in a single annual effort (followed up by ongoing monitoring).

The power of this system to effect both community change and internal change cannot be understated. Frequently, those effects happen faster than anyone could have imagined. Further, boards that could barely get a quorum become empowered and energized, all because they are aiming beyond problem-solving; they are aiming at creating something inspirational and exciting.

The following examples provide insights into these and other effects of using a vision-based approach to planning.

The Advocacy Group

The Community Benefit arena is filled with individuals who indeed believe it is possible to create a better future. Often, however, our cultural conditioning tells us that such change will take a l-o-o-o-n-g time to become reality.

In truth, though, it is consistently overwhelming how quickly things change when a group combines a change of expectations with practical systems for putting those expectations into action.

> A small issues advocacy group in a midwestern U.S. state requested planning assistance. For years their work had involved the kinds of actions that are all too common among advocacy groups: "If we can just wait until the legislative mood changes..." While recent elections had changed a few faces in their state's legislature, the group still had an overwhelmingly uphill climb.

The group's primary goal was clear cut - a simple, yet emotion-laden change of the law. They had been advocating for that change for over 20 years. For each of those 20+ years, they had failed to even have enough votes for the issue to be debated on the floor of the legislature, never mind having it actually come up for a vote. Each and every year, they could not even get the legislators to discuss it.

As a result, they did what many advocacy groups do when they are stuck in the Culture of Can't. As they waited for the magical day when the legislature would be filled with people who agree with their views, they held rallies and vigils. They wrote scathing editorials. And they waited.

As the 2006 legislative session opened, even with the changing faces of the legislature, the group could count only six supporters among forty-nine legislators.

But in that same year, the group created a Vision-Based Community Impact Plan. The question the process encouraged them to ask was, "What would success look like for the community?" The group responded easily, "The law would be changed." And before they could offer the 5,000 reasons that was unlikely to happen, the facilitator suggested, "Let's focus all our efforts on that."

From their Community Impact Plan, the group radically changed its course, including hiring a new lobbyist. Within a few months, for the first time ever, the legislature held a floor debate on their issue. From there, the group got its first-ever floor vote.

I wish I could tell you the law was changed in that first attempt; that would have truly been the fairy tale ending. But here is the next best thing to that happy ending. On an issue that had started the legislative session with only six supporters, the issue failed on a vote of 25 to 24. Within just a handful of months, the group went from feeling defeated before they even started, to getting their first floor debate, their first floor vote, and coming within 1 vote of accomplishing their 20-year dream.

This near-success empowered the group to step up their actions in other areas as well. Within a year of that first planning session, they were successful in having the courts strike down as unconstitutional the law they had been fighting so long to change.

The group not only proved such change was possible; they proved it could happen quickly once they realized that creating visionary change is not only possible; it is practical and doable.

The Arts Organization

Board members often feel inadequate and uncomfortable in their position at the top of the organizational chart. Frequently, this level of discomfort leads to poor decision-making, as they revert to the comfort level of the things they do understand.

Consultants often bemoan the Paper Clip Syndrome - where a board is so focused on budget line items for the things they understand (like paper clips) that they ignore the lion's share of what could easily be a $1 million or more annual budget. This is completely understandable. When we humans are held accountable for something we do not feel we understand well, we defer to the comfort zone.

The systems created by Vision-Based Community Impact Planning allow any board member, regardless of his/her level of expertise, to participate knowledgeably. The system acts as a catalyst for igniting what those board members DO bring to the table - their inspired passion for the mission, as well as their concerns for what could go wrong.

Here is just one example of that phenomenon.

> The Arts Organization is a tiny group in a midwestern U.S. community. Our first encounter was a full-day multi-organization educational session on Governing for What Matters, where the Arts Organization had almost all their board members present.
>
> At that time, the organization had just survived a number of years so close to disaster that community members had been placing bets on whether the group would survive. The Executive Director had been hired when the board was in tatters. Having little experience in Community Benefit work, she had set out to learn all she could. Through those efforts, the board had begun to shift from self-destruct mode to the position of, "We have nothing to lose, so let's take the time to learn to do this right!"
>
> During that time, a group of foundations had created a series of educational programs, bringing governance ex-

perts to town to share different approaches. We were the last in that series. When we left town, we had no idea what the ripple effects would be.

Then we received this letter from the Executive Director of the Arts Organization.

Dear Hildy:

Your break-through work on nonprofit governance is the really big news here. The ideas presented in your sessions were the most accessible and most actionable of any our Board considered.

Over the last two years, our board of directors had several opportunities to learn about different governance models. All the advice we received was germane to our situation, however, when it came time to adopt the advice, the path was unclear. Our board had been through some rough times while the organization changed its focus and reinvented itself. The last thing we wanted was to commit to a model that wouldn't work any better than before.

Frustration with our inability to cut through the limitations of our traditional board model and adopt any other board model was wearing on us all. Luckily, you were the final presenter in our series of visiting experts. Everyone from our board came away with the sense that we could adopt this model without a lot of study, that it was simple and direct, and that it would produce results.

First, each board member received and read the workbook from your workshop. Then, the board held a special meeting to draft our first plan.

It was a revelation to all. In the whole scheme of things, discussing what we want our community to be because of our organization's efforts was enlightening. From there,

*individual directors felt empowered to address their
aspirations and concerns about the internal workings of
the organization in this structured manner.*

*The discussion was meaningful, it was important, and it
covered all the areas salient to responsible oversight of a
nonprofit organization. No red tape, no lengthy agenda,
no agonizing process! We took two separate meetings to
get through the list of topics and completed a document
by the next day.*

*While the rest of the work provided much-needed con-
text for our board, in my opinion, the most important
result of creating the plan was that the board finally has
a handle on the scope of the organization's activities. I
don't think they were aware of the various pieces of the
organization and how they all fit together. Now they had
a good snapshot of the organization, and the board then
became aware of their accountability for these things.
This resulted in everything from the mundane - an update to the employee handbook and equipment purchases
- to the bigger picture - creation of a community engagement plan.*

*The monitoring matrix was simple to create, and easy to
update. It works for our board, which, like many others is composed of good people with busy lives. It helps
each director manage the abundance of information and
responsibility of oversight with relative ease.*

The Arts Organization had experienced so many critical infrastructure problems, that the act of governing had become completely
overwhelming to its board. By using the framework of Vision-Based
Community Impact Planning, the board's role in living up to the organization's vision, mission and values became manageable, doable.
Putting all that in the context of their vision for the community was
the key to having their governance finally make sense.

Planning: A Final Observation

In ten years of using this planning approach, it has been encouraging and inspiring that in every plan we have done - regardless of the size, age, or mission of the institution - groups consistently appreciate the power of this approach, creating meaningful plans that change both the way they *think about* and the way they *do* their work. Choosing a handful of examples to share on these pages was therefore a difficult task.

It is important to note, though, that in all that time, with the singular exception of the University Leadership Program in the examples on the prior pages, none of the myriad organizations with whom we have done this planning saw themselves as candidates for changing the world.

None of those organizations contacted our office asking for anything but traditional "strategic planning." In fact, none of those programs was any more visionary than any other average provider of community services. If we were to crystalize the highest goals of all those organizations into a few words, those words might be, "To get beyond struggling."

There was one difference, and one difference only, between these organizations and the millions of other organizations around the world: These folks happened to call us. We happened to suggest a different approach. And they happened to say, "Yes."

I share this because it is important to note that with one rare and revolutionary exception, every one of the organizations with whom we have done this planning has been just like the vast majority of organizations we all know and work with every day.

The key, then, is not finding exceptional organizations who want to create visionary community change. The key lies is finding the exceptional potential that lies waiting to be tapped in all organizations.

Chapter 24:
Putting What Matters Into Action at the Board Table

When a board has a proactive plan to aim a group's work towards making a difference in the community; when that plan ensures the group has everything it needs to make that difference, and guards against risks that could harm their ability to do so; when the board implements and monitors that plan, and uses the plan to guide all the group's work - that board is modeling the very best of governance practices. The four board functions of Leadership, Legal Oversight, Operational Oversight and Board Mechanics are all addressed in the development, implementation and monitoring of that plan.

From that starting point, however, for an organization to truly "be the change they want to see," the board will also incorporate the group's *3 Statements* into all the rest of its day-to-day board work. The board table is where the board will determine whether the organization's plans will become reality, or whether the board will have spent time creating yet another plan that changes nothing.

When a board is Governing for What Matters, *The 3 Statements* become the organization's version of the Ten Commandments. Those *3 Statements* are present at every board meeting and every committee meeting, and board members are encouraged to remind themselves to weigh all their decisions against what matters most. *The 3 Statements* are present as almost a living being in every discussion the board has and every decision they make.

Those who have done work in cultures foreign to their own quickly learn that "culture" is not about traditional songs or dances or art. "Culture" is the eyes through which we see the world. It is the perspective through which we filter everything we encounter.

An ongoing focus on *The 3 Statements* creates the culture of the board - the lens through which the board filters all its thinking, and from that thinking, its work. Discussions that might have previously caused schisms are brought back to the context of what matters most

- creating visionary community impact and walking a consistent talk in doing so. From there, new board members are recruited to fit into that culture.

Such focus takes diligence at first, becoming second-nature as time moves along. As Zen Master Thich Nhat Hanh notes about having such consciousness rule our everyday lives, "It is not a matter of faith; it is a matter of practice."

How does a board put that culture of conscious governance into practice? The following pages provide some examples.

Dollars Determining "What Matters" - or - "What Matters" Determining Dollars?

The story of Steve Zabilski and the Society of St. Vincent de Paul in Phoenix, as told on page 46, is a great example of what happens when Vision, Mission and Values guide a board's decisions. When Steve was concerned that a particular program was not paying for itself, the board told him, "Our mission is to provide service to those who need our help. We will find the money to pay for this program, because that is what this organization is about."

At the other end of the spectrum, however, a substance abuse organization had a highly effective six-month treatment program. When state budget cuts forced the state to only cover three months of treatment, the organization reduced its program to three months. When asked if the three month program was effective, both board and staff immediately said "no" - their recidivism rate had almost immediately increased. Yet finding funding to supplement the reduced state funds, to return to providing more effective treatment was never considered as an option.

The 3 Statements were clearly guiding the actions of the first group. The second group's mission, however, had de facto become, "Providing what service we can afford to provide, regardless of whether or not it is effective."

Dollars Determining Who We Serve - or - "What Matters" Determining Who We Serve?

Nonprofit Resource Centers all have pretty much the same mission - to develop and maintain a strong and thriving sector in their communities, filled with strong and thriving organizations. Their approaches to accomplishing that mission, however, differ dramatically, when seen through the eyes of "what matters most."

The Nonprofit Resource Center in one major metropolitan area funds its training and consulting by as many creative approaches as it can find. All activities at the Center are open to anyone who wishes to attend, as the Center spreads its arms wide to encourage learning and strength throughout all organizations in the community.

In another major metropolitan area, however, funding for that community's Nonprofit Resource Center comes primarily from memberships. While some activities at the center are open to everyone, many "special" activities are available only for members, as a way to show value / benefit to those members, so they will continue to pay their membership fees. Those who cannot afford that membership, however - who may need assistance the most - do not receive the same level of assistance as those who pay their dues. In one instance, we even heard those non-members who try to attend such special activities referred to as "freeloaders."

The first group's *3 Statements* are clearly guiding their work. The second group's mission, however - to strengthen the work of all the community's organizations - has de facto become "to strengthen the work of its paying members."

Inclusion as Part of "What Matters"

It is not necessary to provide examples of those who narrowly define their mission (and hence the results that mission can accomplish). We all see such work every day. A food bank board member who told us, "Our mission is not about poverty; our mission is about hunger," is a case in point.

Instead, consider how the vision for a more inclusive community can strengthen both the results and the day-to-day work of an organization.

In the past several years, the Human Services Federation in Lincoln, Nebraska, decided to include arts groups as full members. If art therapy is a human service, and art as gang prevention is a human service, the question that eventually became a policy change was, "How are the arts NOT a human service?" From that blurring of divisions, "human service" and "arts" organizations are discouraged from acting as competitors for public attention, and instead have significantly more opportunity to work together towards a shared vision of a vibrant, healthy community.

In Fresno, California, the Fresno Coalition for Arts, Science and History convenes and advocates for these seemingly disparate disciplines, because all three disciplines are about creativity and innovation, about education, about our higher selves. In walking its talk, the board and staff have begun aiming their work at the following question: "If these higher disciplines are about creativity and innovation, shouldn't we be the ones leading the way towards creating innovative change in our community?"

Financial Reporting and Budgeting for "What Matters"

Financial reporting and budgeting processes are pretty standard organizational functions. Some organizations, however, focus their financial lens on community results.

At a multi-million dollar human services coalition, in a major metropolitan area, the financials are reviewed by the finance committee quarterly, and salient points are reported to the board. At their monthly meetings, however, the board reviews a different version of the financials - a report that measures the finances against their strategic goals for the year, and against their values. "How are we doing against budget re: our goals? How are revenues doing re: a particular strategic initiative? Are we leveraging our resources into the areas we have said are important?" That is what the board reviews monthly.

At the other end of the size spectrum, the board of a $100,000 human services organization determines whether or not to approve its budget by focusing on how the budget reflects the goals it has set forth in its annual plan. "Are we budgeting to accomplish what we intended to accomplish?"

Fundraising for "What Matters" - or - Fundraising AGAINST "What Matters"?

The Recovery Organization, whose values statement is shown as the example on page 134, is the beneficiary of an annual dinner event produced by a third party. At that event, alcohol is served. After years of feeling uncomfortable about this circumstance, the board brought this issue into the open, debating the appropriateness of even that third party serving alcohol at an event benefitting an organization dedicated to sobriety.

After considerable debate, the board deferred to its Values Statement, noting their desire to model the 12 Steps in their work with staff, clients, and the community. That led them to the source - the Alcoholics Anonymous "Big Book" - where they found the advice that individuals in recovery not be adamant that everyone stop drinking, as such behavior is likely to backfire. From that wisdom, the group not only created a policy to reflect that sentiment; they created a written statement to be shared at the event, to help others understand how that decision actually furthered their mission.

At the other end of the spectrum, however, is another recovery organization, who produces its own annual fundraising event. On the flyers for the event, the first item listed to entice people to attend the event is this: **Beer, Wine and Local Libations**!

Yes, the main annual event for a substance abuse recovery organization is promoted as a drinking event. Those are the behaviors they are modeling to the community.

Board Meeting Agenda Focused on Circumstances - or - Meeting Agenda Focused on "What Matters"?

At every governance workshop I have ever presented, without exception, the concern is raised that boards do not have time to discuss "What Matters" because they are too busy with discussions of the day-to-day. Because the agenda is the list of what the board needs to accomplish each time it meets, the sentiment that boards are too busy to discuss their impact on the community is clear evidence that *boards* are not leading and guiding their organizations; instead, *current circumstances* are leading and guiding the organization.

That does not have to be the case. Prior to each board meeting of a mid-sized ($1.5 million) human services organization, the agenda committee evaluates prospective agenda items against a checklist headed by these questions:

- Does the item relate to *The 3 Statements* - to our Vision, Mission or Values?
- Does it relate to furthering our Community Impact Plan?

If the answer is "no" to either of those questions, the group then deliberates:

- Is this just a reporting item? (*If so, does it really need to be discussed? Or can it go on the consent agenda or be handled as pre-meeting reading?*)
- Is this a staff item? (*If so, the item is sent back to be handled by the staff.*)
- Is the item about the organization's means - Legal or Operational Oversight? (*If so, let's work right now at this Agenda Meeting to ensure this item is positioned within the context of our Vision, Mission and Values, and not discussed in a vacuum.*)

By eliminating from the agenda those items that focus narrowly on the day-to-day, the board has time to discuss its Community Impact Plan. It has time to deliberate questions such as, "How can we measure long-term community impact?" Further, board members have time to discuss the extent to which they are engaging the community in that work, moving forward not just *on behalf of* the community, but *with* the community.

Executive Transition for Day-to-Day Business - or - Executive Transition for "What Matters"

The Community Impact Planning work at the Recovery Organization re-inspired the board to make a dramatic difference in the community. Unfortunately, however, the organization's potential had outgrown the Executive Director's capabilities. This disconnect of vision had been the cause of considerable organizational stress for a long while.

The group's Community Impact Plan brought up the issue of succession planning, and their vision and values guided that process. Through that succession planning, it became clear that the organization was heading into an executive transition.

During their executive transition process, every aspect of the job description was rewritten to focus on the group's Vision and Values, including the prescription that the ED would be responsible for ensuring that the staff adhered to the organization's Values Statement. During interviews, the board's questions sought to uncover candidates' abilities to implement the vision at the heart of their Community Impact Plan, not just in the short term, but long into the future. In its final decision, the board chose the person they felt would best lead them towards the future they wanted to create for the community and for the organization.

Almost immediately one could sense the change simply by stepping onto their campus. The result of the joyful (yes, really - joyful!) alignment of the staff, the clients and the board behind the group's powerful vision and values was palpable.

Most importantly, though, at the time of this writing (three years since the new Executive Director was hired), the progress the organization has made in the community has stymied those who had written them off as a "dinosaur whose days were numbered" under the leadership of the former director.

At the other end of the Executive Transition spectrum is the Food Bank described in Chapter 6, whose board saw its job as putting on the brakes against the community-focused approaches of its visionary Executive Director.

The Food Bank board immediately focused its Executive Search on finding a more businesslike Executive Director. In striking the words "a passion for social justice" from the job description, they noted that such wording was little more than "touchy feely mumbo-jumbo."

Not surprisingly, the board hired a certified public accountant whose experience was entirely in the for-profit business world.

The new ED lasted only 18 months, during which time he managed to alienate both the staff and the community. In that short time, key staff left in droves. The organization went from being the pride of the community to being a lamentable reminder of what could have been.

Our list of examples goes on and on. From just these few, however, it is clear that a board that is Governing for What Matters is, first and foremost, conscious. The board is conscious of the power it has, in every decision, to change lives, to make a difference - to create the future of its community.

Boards that are Governing for What Matters do not let circumstances decide their end goals. Instead, they deliberately and consciously overcome obstacles, to achieve the community's highest aspirations and dreams. And they do so with consciousness, in every decision they make.

Chapter 25
Governing for What Matters:
A Celebration of What Is Possible

Pollyanna Principle #6 notes that people will go where systems lead them. In summing up this section on Governance, the most salient observation is that the framework of Governing for What Matters is truly a celebration of what is possible.

The Power of Simple

One of the most exciting aspects of this governance framework is that it eliminates the sense that governance is a spiraling series of complications within complications.

Governing for What Matters makes it simple for boards to hold themselves accountable for creating the future we all want for our communities and our world. Within that community context, it is then easy for a board to stay conscious of everything for which a board is legally accountable as well.

Simple steps, and not a lot of them. Simple guidelines. And a simple mandate: Aim first at the visionary results you want for your community, and then see everything else from that context.

If we expect the work of Community Benefit Organizations to create a better future for our communities, this framework makes it easy for the volunteer leaders of those organizations to do the job well.

Vision and Values as "Touchy-Feely Mumbo-Jumbo" vs. The Most Realistic Thing There Is

We all know the stories of the successful go-getter, who, on his deathbed, wishes he had scrapped all the meaningless "doings" of his life, and spent more time with the people he loved.

Truly, this is a tough concept to get across to those who have been bred into the culture of means over ends - money over love or peace or health.

In our experience, the level of resistance in addressing the issues of Vision and Values is directly related to the level of "sophistication" of the group doing the work. The board of a small, community-based grassroots organization will be far more willing to discuss and then base their work upon Vision and Values than the board of a hospital or a foundation.

We have often laughed that the more powerful the board members at the table, the more likely it is that the words *Vision* and *Values* will turn those grown adults into eight-year-old boys being forced to dance with girls at a school social. One can just picture them saying, "Values - Yuck! Eeeewwww!"

But repeatedly, we see that returning to Vision and Values is the only way an organization will ever get beyond aiming at the means ("Our goal is to be financially sustainable" or "Our goal is to finally solve this internal problem") and instead focus on what can be accomplished for and with the community ("Our goal is to create an extraordinary future for our community, and that focus will help us build strength in all areas.").

The striking difference between two of the stories told in previous chapters show this clearly. During the executive transition at the Food Bank, the mere mention of the words "social justice" threw the board into a tizzy. One could easily envision the reaction of those eight-year-old boys at the school dance.

However, at another poverty-focused organization - St. Vincent de Paul in Phoenix - the board made clear that decisions would be based entirely on its vision, its mission and especially its values. From the perspective of the eight-year-old boys, the board at St. Vincent de Paul had grown up.

And yet our society tells us that is backwards. It instructs that the "realistic" approach (i.e. focusing on day-to-day means) is the "grown up" approach. The rest - vision and values - is relegated to the daydreams of youth.

With a nod to both Aristotle and the Buddha, before we are "what we repeatedly do," first "we are what we think." When a board's thinking and being is guided, first and foremost, by What Matters Most, anything is possible.

Without those shared values and that shared vision aiming groups at what is possible, however, organizational dysfunction is destined to occur.

These topics are not irrelevant. They are not "touchy feely mumbo-jumbo."

They are, in fact, What Matters Most.

In the suburbs of a large metropolitan city, three like-kind organizations, each with high-powered boards, merged to form a single, strong organization. The merger was focused entirely on merging the "doing" part of the work - both their mission work and the back-office work. Board members were proud of their ability to complete the merger in a way that streamlined operations, making the work more efficient and creating economies of scale.

With no focus on the "thinking and being" that would guide that day-to-day work, however, there still is no "single organization" in reality, a full two years after the merger has been completed on paper. Instead, there is bickering and dissent. There is childishness and passive aggressiveness. There is no agreement by the merged boards nor the merged staff on what criteria will guide decisions, on what emphasis takes precedence.

In coaching the ED behind the scenes, we are devising ways to raise the issues of vision and values without anyone being the wiser - using different words, with the same intent. Here is what the ED has realized in this process:

> "If I tell the board they need to focus on Vision and Values, they will tell me that stuff is irrelevant and will politely refuse to participate. But clearly it is the piece that is missing. We merged the inner workings of these organizations. We never focused them on the shared vision and values of what we wanted to accomplish for the community and how we would do that work."

Creating the Future vs. Problem-Solving

When a consultant is called in to assist with an organizational issue, it is not unusual to find that issue is not new - it has been a problem for a long time.

It is also not unusual for organizations to have attempted to "fix" that issue previously. They may have created a plan, or had an intervention. They may have even had a change of staff / board members, and somehow the problem remains.

Problem-solving approaches cannot solve large, seemingly intractable problems. For the reasons stated in Chapter 7, problem-solving in such settings repeatedly fails to work. Yet, frustrated because they both acknowledge the problem and want it eliminated, groups keep trying to find solutions by aiming directly at that problem.

As we have seen in many of these examples, the solution was to look beyond the problem and beyond the elimination of the problem. The solution was to aim at what was positive, energizing and possible.

> At the Recovery Organization, the Executive Director had been a sore spot for years. Various interventions had all failed. It was not until the board was inspired by what was possible, and given a simple system for implementing what was possible, that they were able to seamlessly take action.

> At the Public Broadcast Group, fiefdoms had become simply the way things were. Team-building had been attempted and had failed. By bringing the whole organization together, however, and focusing them beyond the day-to-day and out towards what was possible for the community - the reason they were all there - the walls came down, and the factions were inspired to WANT to work together.

This simple framework, powerfully focused on Vision, Mission and Values, allowed for success where previous direct interventions had failed. It did so by focusing on what was possible, rather than what was wrong.

Governance as a Low Expectation System vs. Governing for What is Possible

Lastly, the success of Governing for What Matters comes from its expectations. Because our expectations become our work, and our work becomes our results, aiming organizational leaders at high expectations has a profound effect on everything an organization can be and do. But it has a further effect: creating highly functional, energized and engaged boards.

As noted throughout this text, current governance systems and current "Best Practices" focus boards almost exclusively on their accountability for the means - the combination of Legal Oversight, Operational Oversight and Board Mechanics.

Talk about low expectations! Leaders and experts in this sector have higher expectations for blighted neighborhoods and struggling nations than their expectations for the boards that are supposed to be leading the charge to address those issues.

Consultants, funders and other experts talk about boards as one might talk about juvenile delinquents. *They won't do what we tell them to do! Look how badly they are messing everything up! We have tried everything, but clearly they are beyond hope...*

As happens throughout all aspects of daily life, low expectations for a group's performance lead to prescriptive solutions - the creation of rules. There will be considerably more rules and hurdles, and those rules and hurdles will be far more ongoing, for example, for a low-income person receiving assistance than for a wealthy person receiving a bank loan. These rules all have to do with our expectations.

That is precisely what current governance systems have done for boards. Governance experts have been asked to create rules, sets of stricter and stricter guidelines, legal ramifications, legislative oversight. These standards are what governance experts have come to call "Best Practice."

A true Governance system with a "Big G" will show boards how to lead, guide and make decisions aimed at the potential our communities have for being healthy, vibrant, resilient, humane places to live. Such Governance in no way negates a board's Legal Oversight and Operational Oversight roles; it instead more sensibly aligns that work behind the board's most important role - Leadership. That is what it means to Govern for What Matters Most.

At that point, when a board is governing from those high expectations, Governance is truly a celebration of what is possible.

Program Development & Sustainability

How the
Pollyanna Principles
Create Programs that will
Create the Future

Chapter 26:
Developing and Sustaining Strong Programs

Imagine what is possible when the act of developing and sustaining programs simultaneously builds strong, sustainable communities!

When the assumptions and expectations at the core of how our programs are developed and sustained is focused beyond program sustainability and instead aims outwards at community sustainability, possibilities open up that had previously been "hiding in plain sight."

Our programs become stronger and more effective. Our communities become stronger. And as an added bonus, the work is more fun.

What Builds Strength and Sustainability?

Before focusing on developing strong, sustainable programs, it will be helpful to clarify: What is *sustainability*? What do we expect from sustainability? If we want more significant improvement in our communities, what might we change about our expectations of sustainability, so the very act of sustaining strong programs builds community improvement?

Most organizational sustainability efforts are focused on building financial strength. The word *sustainability* may therefore suggest such expectations as these:

- Ongoing cash flow
- Not being dependent upon grants or other single source of funds
- An endowment
- A large pool of donors
- Diverse funding sources

Because "we are what we think," however, if we change our assumptions and expectations about sustainability, our approaches will change as well. To change those assumptions, let's consider a different question: *"What sustains us in our personal lives?"*

In workshops, here are some of the replies elicited by that question:

- Family
- Friends
- Laughter
- Faith
- Beauty
- Good food
- A sense of purpose
- Generosity
- Fun

As folks add to that list, the mood in the room becomes more and more relaxed. People are smiling, then laughing as they suggest the things that make their lives whole. "Coffee! Golf! Chocolate!"

In our real lives, we may need money to *survive*, but to *thrive*, we need more.

Things are not much different for the programs that help build our communities. To *survive*, they need dollars. To *thrive*, they need something more essential, more authentic than just money.

Like an individual, when an organization has those more essential pieces in place, financial survival is a part of the sustainability picture, but not the whole picture, and not even the largest part. Even more like an individual, when an organization has all those other pieces in place, "survival" has a way of taking care of itself.

To develop strong, sustainable programs, then, will require that we move our expectations away from merely "financial strength." It will require that we aim where the Pollyanna Principles guide us to aim - at what is possible. Once we reach for what is possible, the very act of developing and sustaining our programs will be creating the future of our communities.

What Builds a Sustainable House?

If we were not building programs, but were instead building a house, what would it take to ensure that house would be strong and sustainable, for years to come?

Obviously, the house will first need a strong foundation. It will need solid framing to support strong walls. It will need a good roof, to keep out water; a strong finish to protect exposed wood from the elements; good plumbing, so a leak cannot wreak havoc.

In other words, a sustainable house needs an infrastructure that is strong in all ways. A strong foundation with shoddy framing and a leaky roof will not provide a sustainable house.

If that house is to remain strong, however, it will need more than just solid infrastructure. The strongest fortress will eventually turn to rubble if it is not cared for. To remain strong, that house will need ongoing human attention.

From there, the house will obviously require some money to sustain it. There are, in fact, some houses that are almost entirely sustained by money, such as a model home on a construction site. Such a house may be structurally sound, but it certainly is not a home. The moment the money goes away, that house will quickly fall into disrepair, as its purpose was only to be a temporary showpiece. Therefore, the final piece in considering what creates sustainability for a house is the purpose of the house itself.

To thrive long into the future, therefore, a house will require the interwoven pieces of strong infrastructure, people who care and regularly attend to the house, dollars for ongoing support, all guided by a clearly understood purpose - that the house will be a home for a long, long time.

Building Program Strength and Sustainability

As it is with a house, Community Benefit Programs that are built upon the interrelationship of those four components will be poised to thrive.

Rather than considering program strength and community strength as separate (and perhaps competing) interests, when we develop programs upon those pillars, the very act of developing and sustaining our programs allows us to be the change we want to see in our communities.

Addressing the four issues that simultaneously build strong, sustainable programs AND strong communities will therefore require four components:

1) Purpose:	Focus on the program's vision for the difference it will make in the community.
2) Infrastructure:	Build program infrastructure to be as strong and sustainable as possible.
3) Human Interaction:	Create an engaged web of people who care about supporting the program in all ways.
4) Money:	Raise necessary funds in ways that continue to align with the change you want to see in your community.

The following chapters will review each of these puzzle pieces, putting the Pollyanna Principles into action to simultaneously build strong program and strong communities.

Chapter 27:
A Sense of Purpose:
Shared Vision for the Community

In the discussion of Vision-Based Community Impact Planning, it was noted that our collective vision for success in our communities is the point at which we all agree. Only the most sinister of comic book villains wants our communities to be dirty, sickly, ugly, crime-ridden places to live.

That same overarching sense of purpose that guides planning for the end results we want to see will also be the key to success in developing and sustaining programs. If we do not start the discussion by locking our sights on the visionary end results we want to achieve for our communities, it becomes far too easy to focus on the means - our programs - and lose sight of the reason behind those programs.

Put simply, it's not about your organization; it's about the community.

By setting our sights on a larger purpose than just organizational survival, and maintaining that Community-Driven focus, all three of the other steps in the program development process change along with that change of focus. That overarching vision guides how we build infrastructure, how we build an engaged web of caring individuals, and how we raise money.

It all comes back to holding ourselves accountable for accomplishing our vision for the future of our community. Because everyone wants his/her community to be a healthy, vibrant place to live, vision starts and ends every conversation at the point where we all agree. This is the critical starting point, then, for ensuring that the way we develop and sustain our programs is aligned behind the change we want to see in our communities.

This is quite different from the starting point when we are focused solely on financial sustainability. For example, an arts donor may not be inclined to consider a financial gift to a non-arts organization.

However, that arts donor does indeed have an interest in ensuring her community is healthy and vibrant in all ways. Because of that, the arts donor will be happy to share all the other resources that can strengthen your program - her wisdom, her ideas, her experience, her connections, and all sorts of other resources that will be discussed in upcoming chapters. She will be happy to share those things, because she shares a concern about that central purpose - making her community a healthy, vibrant, resilient, humane place to live.

Chapter 28:
Developing Programs Upon Shared Community Resources

Traditionally, the steps to creating a new program can be whittled down to these:

1. Identify need / get an idea / work through an idea during a planning session

2. Determine the components to building that program

3. Budget those components

4. Raise money

5. Get started!

This approach assumes that virtually all aspects of the program will be built and run primarily by the organization itself. The approach fits the Business Model roots of Community Benefit work, discussed in Chapter 3, which envisions programs in the image of independent small businesses. This assumption is so ingrained in our thinking that we do not even consider there might be a completely different way to build a program.

Imagine, then, that all aspects of a program are not run by a single organization. Imagine instead that each program is built as a tightly woven fabric, with each thread being an aspect of the program that may be run by someone other than your organization.

That is what it looks like when we build the infrastructure of our programs upon a base of Shared Community Resources.

Building programs upon a core of shared community resources creates functionally collaborative programs from the inside out. Such an approach weaves community ownership of the effort into the very fiber of the program.

Such a tightly woven fabric is not easily torn apart. If a single thread unravels, the entire fabric does not disintegrate - the rest of the threads continue to sustain the fabric's wholeness. And because each of those threads is in reality a member of your community, you are building community engagement directly into the heart of your program. This will be a program the community would not let die, because it is theirs - not yours.

What that means is that we veer from the Program Development steps noted above. Rather than determining what the program needs and then budgeting those needs, a different thought process will be employed.

First, we will consider every functional component of the program - not line items, but the actual question of "Who needs to do what? And then what?" As each of those functions is considered, we will then ask, "Is someone in our community already doing that function? And if so, can we partner with them?"

The best way to describe how this approach works is to show what it looks like when a program is built collaboratively from the inside out, with an infrastructure comprised entirely of shared community resources.

Building the World's First Diaper Bank

In 1994, as our consulting firm's way of giving back to the community at holiday time, we held a community-wide Diaper Drive, collecting disposable diapers for 2 organizations close to our hearts - a crisis nursery and a low-income neighborhood center.

We sent out some press releases, and we asked a local radio station to sit in front of our office, to collect diapers from folks on their way to work. Through these efforts, we collected 20,000 diapers, and Tucson's December Diaper Drive immediately became an annual event.

Year after year, the Diaper Drive grew, as we shared what we learned about the need - a need that was going completely unmet. None of the federal safety net programs provided diapers - not Food Stamps, not Medicare, not the Women Infants and Children (WIC) program. Diapers are expensive, costing the average family $100 per month, whether those diapers are for babies or adults. With the average social security benefit hovering around $850 per month, and take-home pay at minimum wage being virtually the same amount, diapers took a back seat to rent, utilities and other survival necessities in many homes.

Diapers were at the root of so many issues. A mom who could not afford to leave the required package of disposable diapers with her child at the daycare center could not leave her child there, and therefore could not work. An elderly person who could not afford supplies would become more and more isolated, staying home alone from the fear of embarrassment. A young disabled person seeking education or work opportunities would be able to do neither without incontinence supplies. The list went on and on.

In the fifth year of running the December Diaper Drive, we collected 300,000 diapers for thirty agencies. We had requests for over two million.

In addition to the daunting fact that our volunteer efforts had not even scratched the surface of our community's unmet need, the consultants in us realized that if something were to happen to us (like the very real possibility that we might want to get back to our consulting work!), all the work we had done to raise both diapers and awareness of those critical issues would vanish.

The only way for that work to continue would be to turn our small personal philanthropy into an official Diaper Bank.

The year was 1999. After researching to learn how others had built Diaper Banks, we realized there were no other Diaper Banks.

We were about to build the first one.

Mapping Out the Diaper Bank's Functions

Having seen so many organizations exist in survival mode year after year, we wanted to find a way for this new organization to be strong from the start and have the best chances for remaining strong. We were lucky - building a first-of-its-kind organization gave us permission to experiment. What could we do to build strength into the very core of the organization?

We began by listing all the functions it would take to collect and distribute the diapers our community needed. What would this new entity actually do in the day-to-day? How would the Diaper Bank function?

Here is some of what we listed:

> Individuals would collect diapers in their homes, schools, workplaces and places of worship. If they were collecting at home, they would bring those diapers to designated drop-off locations. If they were collecting them outside the home, they would either bring the diapers to the Diaper Bank, or request that we pick them up.

> The diapers would have to be counted and sorted by size. They would need to be stored. When the diapers were needed, someone would then have to take those diapers off the shelf, making sure the inventory count reflected that reduction.

Those actions, when mapped out, looked like this:

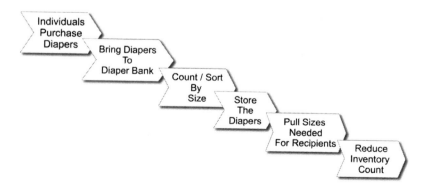

Each of the functions needed for the Diaper Bank's work was mapped out in a similar way. How dollars might come in, and how actions would flow once that happened (up to and including mailing thank you notes). How accounting and regulatory filings would be done. How the "issues awareness" campaign would work.

For every one of those functions, we then asked, "Is someone already doing this? If so, can we partner with them?"

It is important to note that we were not asking, "Does anyone already have this program?" Instead, we were looking at all the small functional components that would combine to create the program - each of those individual labeled arrows on the previous page. Was someone already doing one of those functions? If so, we wanted to know.

The Diaper Bank: A Functional Collaboration of Shared Community Resources

In considering the various functions that would be part of the operations of the Diaper Bank, the following were just some of those functional components.

- Tax exemption

- Board of Directors (governance)

- Bookkeeping

- Case management

- Warehousing (functions such as receiving, sorting, inventorying, storing, and distributing the diapers)

- Transportation (moving the diapers from one place to another)

The following pages detail just some of what we found when we asked, "Who is already doing that work?"

Tax Exemption, Bookkeeping and a Board of Directors

In our quest to learn as much as we could about how to build the Diaper Bank (more about that on page 238), we were introduced to Jannie Cox, CEO of Carondelet Foundation - the financial support arm for three local Catholic hospitals.

Jannie knew the Diaper Drive from its publicity over the years. She also knew our vision and mission were aligned with the mission of the hospitals - building a healthy community. During that very first conversation, Jannie suggested that Carondelet Foundation act as the Diaper Bank's fiscal sponsor during its initial years.

Fiscal sponsors are charitable organizations that extend their tax-exemption to groups whose missions are aligned with their own. In his 2005 paper, **How Fiscal Sponsorship Nurtures Nonprofits**, Third Sector New England's director, Jonathan Spack, further describes fiscal sponsorship as follows:

> "Although sponsored programs are not completely independent - they are legally part of the sponsor organization - they nevertheless retain programmatic autonomy and often have separate advisory boards making their strategic decisions. They are responsible for their own fund-raising, and they absorb any shortfall and retain any surplus."

With Carondelet Foundation as the Diaper Bank's fiscal sponsor, our work fell under the umbrella of their tax exemption, and under the ultimate accountability of their board of directors. While we controlled the Diaper Bank's day-to-day operational decisions, we were required to consult with Carondelet Foundation on major issues.

For their part, Carondelet Foundation handled the accounting for the Diaper Bank's funds, with the exception of a small operating account, whose reconciled bank statement and financial records would be reported to the foundation monthly. In addition to that financial reporting, the Diaper Bank would make at least an annual presentation to the Carondelet Foundation board of directors, to show how this effort was furthering their mission.

What a blessing for our fledgling effort! Anyone who has built a new program knows it is hard enough to just focus on developing the "program" side of that work. The added work of building a board, filing appropriate government paperwork, understanding tax-related issues such as which donors must be provided with which types of receipts - it can all seem overwhelming. In fact, it is precisely because of the enormity of ALL the work related to start-up that so many new organizations fall short on the administrative side.

But this new organization did not have to worry about any of that! We could just get on with doing the work of fulfilling our mission, knowing there was a knowledgeable, accountable entity watching to be sure we did not falter.

Truly the best gift was the ability to tap into the incredible wisdom and counsel of Jannie Cox, a veteran in fundraising and overall administration of community organizations. Rather than viewing Carondelet's oversight as a threat to our decision-making sovereignty, we cherished the ability to engage Jannie's wisdom when any major decisions had to be made.[1]

By the time the Diaper Bank left its nest at Carondelet Foundation, it was ready to do so. We had time to work the bugs out of the Diaper Bank's operational side, which then allowed time for more thoughtfully and cautiously setting up internal systems, including building our own board.

From the offices of Carondelet Foundation, to the businesses of each of their board members, to the corridors of their hospitals (whose staff worked to raise diapers during the December Diaper Drive), each of those individual threads became part of the interwoven fabric that created shared ownership of the Diaper Bank's infrastructure.

---

1 There was no more humbling experience for these two consultants than starting and operating a community organization, with full time, day-to-day responsibility for its success or failure. We recommend it to any consultant who has never been in those shoes.

Case Management

The issue of case management brought us founders into a state of panic. Imagine non-social-workers considering such questions as, "How will we decide who qualifies to receive diapers and who does not? How many case managers will we need? How many need to be bilingual?" And so on.

The answer became clear when we asked, "Who is already working with the people who need the diapers?" Our Diaper Drives themselves had started out providing diapers to existing agencies, as our private philanthropic gift. That is what we would continue to do.

The moment the decision was made, the benefits became clear. First, the families who would ultimately use the diapers already spend a good portion of their lives qualifying for this service or that - for Food Stamps or healthcare or the myriad individual services that require filling out more paperwork. Did we really want to be one more place they would have to fill out forms?

We also knew that if people needed diapers, they likely needed other things as well - housing, job assistance, food, etc. By working with other organizations, and requiring that the diapers be part of case management (and not simply distributed without such intervention), we were assured the diapers would be part of a more comprehensive effort to help individuals care for their families.

That was our intent. As it was with our fiscal sponsorship, though, we had no idea that this was only a small fraction of the reward of sharing what the community already had to offer.

First, there were mission-related rewards. For example, individuals who were not receiving any assistance for themselves often would seek help for their baby. The Diaper Bank became a de facto referral service, helping individuals find not only diapers, but other assistance as well. In this way, the Diaper Bank's infrastructure, in and of itself, was helping to further our mission!

Then, from the standpoint of building a strong infrastructure, the rewards were all about the 75 agencies who started out simply receiving diapers for their clients, but quickly became true partners in our work.

Over the years, those partner agencies have provided hundreds of volunteers for Diaper Bank events, sometimes even having their volunteer coordinator find volunteers when our need was large. The agencies, who receive the diapers at no cost, often provide cash donations to the Diaper Bank; one organization is so grateful, they send a check and a thank you note every few months. We certainly never expected to receive volunteers and cash donations from those agencies!

Then there is the reward that comes from the fact that the Diaper Bank's mission has become the collective mission of all 75 agencies it serves. The Diaper Bank's mission is to assist a mother who is trying to kick a drug habit. Its mission is to help an elderly person escape being homebound from the fear of embarrassment that accompanies incontinence. The mission is to help a mom leave her child at daycare, where she is required to bring a package of disposable diapers, so she can go to work to support her family. The Diaper Bank has 75 missions. That is possible because it has a singular vision - that overriding purpose - to create a future where our community does not need those 75 agencies, nor the Diaper Bank itself.

That synergy could never have happened if the Diaper Bank had not chosen to share this function with others in the community. That sharing of the workload added not only those 75 agencies as threads to our fabric, but all their volunteers and clients as well. Through that sharing of resources and that shared sense of ownership of the mission and the vision, the infrastructure of the Diaper Bank became stronger. At the same time, those other organizations were able to benefit from the strengths the Diaper Bank had to share.

Warehousing

With an annual community-wide need for two million diapers for babies, the elderly, and individuals of all ages with disabilities - it was clear: We were going into the warehousing business.

We priced out what the work would cost to do ourselves. First, there were the expenses for rent, utilities and insurance for the warehouse itself, as well as the cost for warehousing accoutrements such as racks and a forklift. Add to that the personnel-related expenses for an experienced warehouse person, and the total estimated cost approached $60,000 per year.

With the help of our local United Way, we broadcast-faxed a Request for Proposals to all the organizations in the Tucson metro area. (Clearly that dates this effort - a broadcast fax!)

The RFP told a bit about the Diaper Bank's plans, describing the need for space, equipment and staff. Then we noted the following:

> "If you are considering charging market rents, please don't bother. We can just as easily go to the market and rent a space. We are seeking a partner, not a landlord."

We expected a handful of proposals from the Food Bank, Salvation Army, Goodwill and the like. What we did not anticipate was the abundance of unused capacity our community had hiding in plain sight.

The highest bid we received was $30,000 - half our budget estimate. The lowest bid was $6,000, from a counseling agency that had a 2,000 square foot garage they were using just to store old junk. We had no idea either of these organizations had such resources lying unused.

We did site visits, and the winner became instantly clear. Tetra Corporation (now Beacon Group) had been providing vocational training for people with disabilities in our community for 40 years. Their warehouse was huge, with space that could easily be designated for the diapers. They already had racks and forklifts.

Our excitement came from watching how alive the place was, with clients of varying ability working on a whole range of projects. We learned that Tetra intended to use the diapers to train the developmentally disabled with warehousing skills. The synergy was almost too good to be true.

The total cost? $15,000 per year.

As it was with the issue of case management, Tetra/Beacon and the Diaper Bank have always seen themselves as having the same vision - making a positive difference in people's lives. During speaking gigs, we could not tell the story of the Diaper Bank without telling the story of Tetra / Beacon Group. As we would share their mission, and talk about how well they carry out that mission, every speaking gig for us became a speaking gig for them, too.

Through the ongoing partnership with the Beacon Group and its clients and supporters, those threads added significantly more strength to the fabric of the Diaper Bank's infrastructure. And because of the synergy of mission, the overriding purpose of the work was strengthened as well.

Transportation

During the first December Diaper Drive in 1994, we collected 20,000 diapers. By Year 5, an individual school might collect that amount, and it was not unusual to have 50 schools collecting diapers. During December, coordinating volunteers to pick up those diapers became a job unto itself.

Again, we asked, "Who in the community is already doing this portion of the work?" Once again, the answer became clear. One year, a plumbing company came to the rescue. (The irony of a plumbing truck hauling diapers was not lost on either them or us!) Another year, a courier service lent its support.

During another year, a newspaper delivery company stepped up to help. In addition to using their drivers and trucks for moving those diapers, they offered the assistance of their dispatcher. "Just have the schools call our dispatcher, and she will arrange the pick-up directly."

No worries about insurance. No hassles. These were not "nonprofit" organizations, but for-profit companies, whose owners were proud to be able to use what they already had to make such a huge difference.

Small business owners so often wish they could do more, but believe they have little to offer, simply because they are thinking only about giving cash. These companies were able to give something the Diaper Bank desperately needed, with virtually no additional cost to their businesses at all, simply by sharing resources they took for granted.

The plumbing company, the courier service, and the newspaper delivery company all felt they were part of something bigger. They started showing up at Diaper Collection events to help out. They sent checks now and then. They saw themselves as partners in the Diaper Bank's goals.

These business owners and their employees became additional threads in the fabric of the Diaper Bank's tightly woven infrastructure.

The Job of the Diaper Bank

There were many more partnerships the Diaper Bank created, all by asking, "Who is already doing that portion of the work?" Some, like our warehousing partner, were community organizations. Some were businesses, the most significant of which was our radio partner, Tucson's 94.9 MIXfm, the group that, as of this writing, still spends all of December, every year, engaging our community in the issues related to poverty and crisis.

With all this effort to share resources, the role of the Diaper Bank became clear:

1. Engage the community in creating a better future, raising awareness of the issues that put people into poverty and crisis, towards the end goal of increased compassion and social justice.

2. Coordinate all the functional partners to ensure a smooth-running operation; and

3. Galvanize the community to collect all those diapers

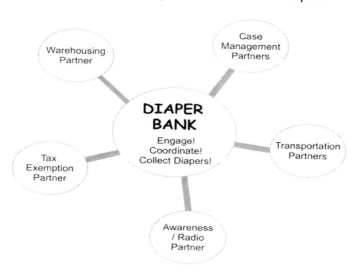

In the first few years of its operation, the Diaper Bank distributed almost 1 million diapers per year to 30,000 individuals, through its 75 partner agencies.

At the same time, the Diaper Bank ran a year-round intensive public awareness campaign about the issues related to poverty and crisis, including radio, television, billboards and intensive public speaking efforts. Throughout the year, the Diaper Bank worked to more deeply engage both individuals and groups in those issues.

The total annual cost for that entire effort - both the diaper collection / distribution program and the public awareness program combined - was under $100,000, a fraction of what it would have cost had the Diaper Bank been built to stand alone.

Building Infrastructure Strength

Developing the infrastructure of the Diaper Bank by assembling community resources certainly took more forethought on the front end. But that forethought happened in 1999. As of this writing, the infrastructure of the Diaper Bank has changed little, except to broaden the base even further.

In that time, we co-founders have retired from the board, leaving our "child" to grow up on its own, without the ongoing care and feeding (or some might say interference!) of its founders. We have therefore had plenty of opportunity to observe, both close up and at a distance, the effects of this shared infrastructure on both this original Diaper Bank, and its sister organization, the Valley of the Sun Community Diaper Bank, 125 miles up the road in the Phoenix metro area. (Read more about the Valley of the Sun Diaper Bank in Chapter 31.)

It is clear that the results both Diaper Banks have achieved have been due, in large part, to their collaborative infrastructure. It is also obvious that the collaborative nature of their infrastructure has been the key to their survival, as both the Tucson and Phoenix organizations have faced the same issues any new and growing effort might face (including and particularly the departure of their founders from the day-to-day leadership of the organization). The shared infrastructure of the Diaper Banks has allowed both organizations to keep providing service. When growing pains would strike, one by one, all their partners pitched in to ensure that both organizations survived and thrived.

That is because both Diaper Banks are owned by and deeply embedded within their communities, in every way imaginable. Both were built by engaging resources the community already had - resources that were just waiting to be tapped. As Dan Duncan, Senior Vice President of External Relations at Tucson's United Way put it, "You couldn't kill the Diaper Bank now if you wanted to. The community wouldn't let you."

Chapter 29:
The Pollyanna Principles in Action: Sharing Resources

Pollyanna Principle #6 notes that people will go where systems lead them. Where are programs aimed if their infrastructure is built by assembling existing community resources?

> **Pollyanna Principle #1:**
> We accomplish what we hold ourselves accountable for.
>
> **Pollyanna Principle #2:**
> Each and every one of us is creating the future, every day, whether we do so consciously or not.

It is rare to see the actual nuts and bolts of an organization's operational infrastructure actually modeling what the vision, mission and values might look like in practice. But the collaborative infrastructure of the Diaper Bank does far more than just reduce costs and build program resilience in the face of adversity. By building engagement into the very DNA of the program, the infrastructure is testimony to the fact that it is indeed possible to align an organization's sustainability behind the ultimate end result of building community sustainability.

By weaving the threads of ownership of the Diaper Bank throughout the community, the infrastructure of the Diaper Bank simultaneously spreads ownership of the issues as well. All those partners become advocates for the vision and the mission. By engaging as many of the community's human and other resources in its vision for the community, the program and the community are simultaneously strengthened, not just in the short term, but in the long term.

> **Pollyanna Principle #3:**
> Everyone and everything is interconnected and interdependent, whether we acknowledge that or not.

When we focus on our mutual strengths, as organizations and individuals, we engage the power we have together that we do not have separately. This is the exact opposite of "competitive advantage." When other Community Benefit Organizations donate money to the Diaper Bank and provide volunteers for Diaper Bank events, competition is replaced with collective power. When the Diaper Bank uses its public relations moments to tout the work being done by a partner organization, collective power triumphs over competitive advantage.

This is turf-free collaboration. Unlike top-down collaboration that asks us to share credit, money and authority (some of the most difficult things for us humans to share), this is collaboration that asks others to share what they are absolutely willing to share - the things they have just laying around, the work they are already doing.

These are collaborations that build connection and trust, based on the little things. It is not two separate organizations, joining together at the point of decision-making. It is instead reminiscent of the old fable of Stone Soup, where everyone in the community brought a bit of this or that, and Presto! We not only have a GREAT soup, but we all get to dine together when it is done!

> **Pollyanna Principle #4:**
> "Being the change we want to see" means walking the talk of our values.

The Values Statement at the Diaper Bank includes the following:

> The best decision will be the decision that provides the best end result for the highest number of our partners, the clients they serve, the issues they address, and the future of our community.

All parties to any decision will be treated with respect, dignity, compassion, grace, integrity, honesty and humanity.

We can accomplish significant change if the whole community works together, focusing ALL the community's varied resources towards improving our community's quality of life. All the community must share ownership of our problems and our solutions.

In addition to walking its talk in its actions, the Diaper Bank's infrastructure is actually a living model of what it looks like when community comes together to address common goals. By its very infrastructure, the Diaper Bank is being the change it wants to see in its community.

> **Pollyanna Principle #5:**
> Strength builds upon our strengths, not our weaknesses.

Clearly, the Diaper Bank's infrastructure is built upon the community's existing strengths. Just as clearly, that mass of individual strengths builds resilience into the very core of the effort. It builds the interlocking strength of a tightly woven fabric.

The current modus operandi of building free-standing "we must do it all ourselves" programs is the opposite of such resilience and strength. When a program relies on one entity for its survival, that single tenuous thread can easily collapse under stress - or simply blow away.

That is just the opposite of the Diaper Bank's infrastructure, constructed by tightly weaving together thousands of strong individual threads, building each area of program strength upon the strengths of others. Building programs around a functionally collaborative infrastructure builds financial strength as well, simply because it requires considerably less financial resources to operate.

Peel back the layers, and there is even more strength. There is the strength in realizing the abundance of community capacity that exists in every community, large or small, cosmopolitan or remotely rural. Regardless of size or location of a community, one can always find an empty storefront, a truck, a group of moms - some resource, hiding in plain sight, waiting to be tapped.

Then there is the strength such a program builds among the individuals who are giving. Instead of feeling inadequate ("We would love to help, but we do not have enough cash to make any significant difference..."), this engaged system for building programs celebrates the assets, resources and gifts we DO have as individuals.

In case after case, the things that made a huge difference to the Diaper Bank - for example, having full access to trucks for a whole month - were easy for those partners to share. That allowed those partners to feel strong, as if they mattered, because, of course, they did.

By providing their unique part, each party felt a sense of connection with the whole. Each party felt it was *their* Diaper Bank, *their* mission. The roots of ownership of the mission spread with each new partner, and that sense of connection became one more strength to build upon.

It all comes down to the fact that building program strength is not about money. It is about the strength of the shared vision for a better community, and the strength of engaged relationships, built on that shared vision. That is the tightly woven fabric that keeps the Diaper Bank strong. It is what keeps individual participants feeling positive about the difference they are making by giving what they have.

Finally, and most importantly, by engaging the existing assets and resources within a community, we build strength into the community itself.

Pollyanna Principle #6:
Individuals will go where systems lead them.

Considering the questions raised about systems in Chapter 12, building programs on a base of shared community resources creates systems that are both self-perpetuating and inspirational. The self-perpetuating part of the equation comes from the simplicity of the approach. Building on shared resources is simple to envision, implement and maintain.

In addition, building upon shared resources is an inspirational approach, providing community members with a concrete way to give what they have, to feel good about sharing that, and to know that they are doing something significant in creating change in their community.

The system is also inspiring from the perspective of the program, moving the program away from a sense of scarcity and aloneness, and moving towards the sense of abundance that comes from our interconnectedness.

Most importantly, this is a system that is aligned behind the collective power we all have to achieve something wonderful for our communities - to aim for a vision and achieve it together.

Chapter 30:
Community Engagement

Imagine what your community would look like if everyone was inspired to what is possible! Imagine what your programs would look like if they were built upon the community's wisdom and ideas - if they were sustained by the community's passion!

The previous chapter shows that our communities are rich in resources, hiding in plain sight and waiting to be engaged to improve the quality of life in our communities. Sitting at the top of that list of resources are a community's human resources.

When we engage the people who live in our communities to further the vision, mission and values at the heart of our work, everyone becomes energized. When "Community Engagement" moves beyond a list of activities, however, and becomes a way of being, that energy itself can transform a community.

Along the way, that engagement will build and sustain your programs. But those strong programs are not the goal of such engagement; they are simply a fabulous by-product. The ultimate goal of Community Engagement is just that - an engaged community.

With an engaged community, there is no limit to what is possible.

Community Engagement is Friendship

Community Engagement is the process of building relationships with community members who will work side-by-side with you as an ongoing partner, to make the community a better place to live. Considered from the perspective of that two-way relationship, Community Engagement is the organizational equivalent of friendship.

> My best friend knows me better than I know myself sometimes. She knows my history, my background. She knows what I am passionate about, my dreams. She shares information she thinks will help with my work, and she shares stories she thinks I will enjoy. She asks for my advice about her life, and shares her own advice about my life. The more open and honest I am in my friendship with her, the more joy the relationship brings.

> My best friend will help me out when times are tough, and she gives me some of the best presents I have ever received. And I do the same for her.

That is friendship.

When we are talking about Community Engagement, therefore, we are not using the word Friend as it is commonly used in Community Benefit work - as a euphemism for "donor". We are not talking about the transactional act of "friendraising" as a precursor to asking someone for money - the watchword that "fundraising is about relationship building," which suggests that we get to know people simply so we can eventually ask them to give dollars to the cause. We are not suggesting that we determine how much value someone has to the organization based on how much money they can provide.

Instead Community Engagement is about the kinds of honest, supportive two-way relationships that make our personal lives strong.

Just as it requires engaged people to sustain the infrastructure of a house, Community Engagement sets the stage for building and then sustaining great programs, towards the end goal of building and sustaining great communities.

By deeply engaging community members in every aspect of a program, the program will be better able to weather life's storms. Everything you do will be infused with a higher level of energy and effectiveness. That engagement is not just uplifting for your program; it is uplifting for everyone involved.

Just like friendship.

Nemawashi

In western culture, projects are typically proposed, developed, then unveiled. With the culture of rugged individualism in our veins, a project will sink or swim on the merits of the individual group proposing and developing that effort.

Traditional Japanese culture does not exalt the individual as we do in the west - just the opposite. The proverb, "The nail that sticks up gets hammered down" better describes the Japanese cultural views on individualism.

The more important factor in that culture is therefore not glory for the individual who came up with the idea or project, but the success that accompanies a group's embracing that effort.

The concept of Nemawashi goes to the heart of that cultural importance of consensus. Put simply, Nemawashi is the process of laying the groundwork for consensus from the very genesis of an effort, working out the bugs, finding out what the obstacles and barriers will be, learning about alternative approaches. With that groundwork laid ahead of time, when the effort IS ready to be unveiled, it has unanimous support, and is built with the input of many great minds, rather than just one or two. The industrial successes for which the Japanese became known in the latter part of the 20th Century are often credited in great part to the Nemawashi process.

Nemawashi happens informally and quietly. It can look messy to outsiders, as it is non-linear (and if we westerners are anything, it is linear!). It takes a great deal more time in the beginning, but efforts are far more likely to succeed in the long term when that groundwork is done well beforehand.

Chapter 31:
Community Engagement in Practice

When all an organization's efforts are seen through the lens of Community Engagement, the first step in any effort is to ask, "How could this effort be enhanced by engaging others?"

The benefits of such an approach are immediately obvious. More wisdom to build upon. Not having to be the "expert" but being able to be part of a whole group of "experts." Replacing a sense of us-and-them with a sense of shared ownership of that effort. Dozens of committed, caring friends, to help build and maintain the effort, advocating for that work in all sorts of ways. And ultimately, the benefit of more widespread impact in our communities.

The best way to share how this happens is to show what it looks like when we assume programs will be stronger if they are built by the kind of engagement that simultaneously strengthens our communities.

Community Engagement in Practice
Engaging Everyone: Building the Diaper Bank

Our first experience with the possibilities inherent in Community Engagement came when we set out to build the Diaper Bank.

As we began to consider how to build this new entity, we knew we wanted the effort to have long-term impact in changing our community. We wanted it to build on the successes we had created in our annual Diaper Drives. We wanted it to be owned by everyone, as that was the road to changing hearts and minds, and thereby changing our community.

But we had no idea what that meant we needed to do.

As consultants, though, we knew where to find those answers. We listed everyone whose lives had been touched by our annual Diaper Drives, and we set out to do our homework, to find the answers to our questions.

Through a process we have come to call Community Sleuthing[1], we met with anyone who would meet with us. We asked them a lot of questions, just like any good sleuth would do. We asked for their ideas, their wisdom, and their experience. We engaged them.

We spoke with philanthropists, social service providers and the actual recipients of the diapers. We met with teachers and students; with people who had donated diapers year after year, and with our congressman.

We met with the people we knew. They connected us to the people they knew.

---

1 Community Sleuthing - our own version of the Nemawashi process - is described in detail in *FriendRaising: Community Engagement Strategies for Boards Who Hate Fundraising but Love Making Friends.*

We asked the same questions of everyone.

How to build the diaper bank? How to run it?

How to address the big picture issues of poverty, seniors issues, disability, and everything in between?

What had they seen work well? What had they seen work horribly?

Who else should we talk with?

We asked and asked and asked. Through that process of engagement, everything about the way we had thought we were going to build the Diaper Bank changed.

The Diaper Bank's Results

As our first concerted effort to use this approach, the results of engaging the community to build the Diaper Bank surpassed our wildest expectations, accomplishing far more than we could have ever accomplished on our own.

Most critically, the approach of building the Diaper Bank on a foundation of shared resources grew directly from our engagement efforts. One by one, community leaders from all walks of life asked, "Do we really need another organization? There is so much duplication already. Yes, we know no one is distributing diapers - but does it have to be a separate organization?"

Those conversations allowed us to explore with all those smart individuals what was truly unique about the Diaper Bank, vs. what could, in fact, be shared. The uniqueness of the Diaper Bank was first its overarching *vision* - to create a community where we did not assume crisis and poverty would always be part of life.

The uniqueness also came from the Diaper Bank's *mission*. Obviously no one was collecting and distributing diapers, but neither was anyone telling the stories of all those other organizations as one big story, showing how everything affected everything else.

All this came from our discussions with our fellow community members. From those conversations, we also came to agree that there had to be a way to more effectively share resources. Had it not been for engaging the ideas, wisdom and experience of our community's leaders, the Diaper Bank's collaborative infrastructure would never even have been considered.

If it were not for our engagement activities, it also never would have occurred to us to consider a fiscal sponsorship. In fact, the paperwork for acquiring the Diaper Bank's own tax exempt status had been sitting on my desk during all those "sleuthing" conversations, waiting to be filled out and sent to the IRS. By engaging a fundraising colleague, he introduced us to Jannie at Carondelet Foundation. By asking for Jannie's experience and ideas, the Diaper Bank found a home, entirely at Jannie's suggestion.

We were still in our engagement mode when it came time to create the Request for Proposals for the warehouse. So we used our meetings to ask how folks might handle the RFP process. Most suggested we send it to the Food Bank, the Salvation Army, and the other likely suspects. But one wise soul suggested, "Send it to everyone. You never know who has what." If it were not for that suggestion, we never would have found the perfect warehousing partner in Tetra / Beacon Group.

The list of results goes on. From our engagement efforts, we learned more about the issues in our community. We learned how food banking works - the closest thing to what we would be doing. We learned who was already doing what in our community. We were introduced to people it might have otherwise taken eons to get to know, simply because we were not asking for anything more than their wisdom and ideas.

Engaging Another Community to Build a Second Diaper Bank

Given all the wisdom and ideas we gained through our sleuthing activities, we had no idea when we opened the Diaper Bank's doors in 2000 how important that highly engaged approach would be to our next steps. Within only a few months of that opening, the Diaper Bank was receiving an ongoing stream of calls from groups across the nation and around the world, asking how they, too, could start a diaper bank.

Anxious to determine if the shared-resource model could be repli-cated, to share that approach with others who called for advice, we investigated the possibility of building another Diaper Bank in the same collaborative way. That led to our traveling 125 miles up the road to Phoenix.

The Phoenix metro area is home to approximately 3.5 million people, in a land mass that spreads for over 1,000 square miles. Engaging individuals in our hometown of Tucson had been relatively easy. Phoenix, however, is almost four times the size of Tucson, and we knew only a handful of people there.

Using the same approach that had built the Diaper Bank in Tucson, we got to work engaging the individuals we knew in Phoenix. For the most part, these were not movers and shakers - a dental consul-tant, an accountant, a banker, a human resources consultant. Because we knew that everyone cares about building a strong, healthy com-munity, we knew we would learn a great deal as we began our con-versations with the people we knew, asking them to connect us with others, and then with others again, all around that shared vision.

While Tucsonans already knew about the Diaper Drive, in Phoe-nix, the concept was brand new. Very much like the Nemawashi approach to building new programs, we announced nothing until we had engaged dozens and dozens of individuals in conversation. When we did announce the effort, inviting those who wanted to par-ticipate in building the Phoenix Diaper Bank to a community-wide meeting, seventy-five people showed up to help! From that group, fifty volunteers met for a year, putting the infrastructure in place to open the doors to the Valley of the Sun Community Diaper Bank.

In both Tucson and Phoenix, virtually every single person we engaged became a staunch supporter of the Diaper Bank. People shared their ideas, their perspectives, and their contacts. Those contacts then shared their own contacts. What started as "our idea" became theirs.

All these many years later, those same individuals are still engaged. They are still volunteering, still making connections, still donating dollars, and still sitting on the boards of both Diaper Banks.

All of that and more was the result of asking for something each of us has in abundance - our ideas, our experience, and our wisdom.

Community Engagement in Practice
Engaging Doctors: The Cancer Support Group

The Cancer Support Group provides non-medical support (counseling, recreational activities, etc.) to people with cancer. Despite the program's success, and despite the fact that all its programs are free, the group was having trouble getting doctors to refer their patients.

Here is the approach they had been using for "Physician Outreach":

- Make an appointment
- Tell their story to the doctor
- Ask them to refer their patients
- Leave some literature behind

Things began turning around immediately when instead of being on the nonprofit equivalent of a sales call, the Cancer Support Group began asking and listening. Instead of doing "outreach," they began engaging the doctors in real conversations, seeking the doctors' wisdom, rather than doing all the talking and then hoping the doctors would do the right thing.

They did this by asking the questions to which they sorely needed answers:

What would you need to know before you could refer someone to us?

What would put your mind at ease / encourage you to refer your patients? What might stop you from referring someone to us?

Do you have any suggestions for our program that you think might help your own patients - maybe things you aren't seeing anywhere else and have always wished someone would do?

The reward was instantaneous. Doctors not only began referring their patients, but some of those doctors offered to form an advisory panel for the group. All it took was realizing that the doctors shared the vision of the Cancer Support Group. From there it was simply a matter of engaging their wisdom, their ideas, and their experience.

Community Engagement in Practice
Engaging Bilingual Volunteers: The Tax Credit Program

A primarily African American church in a low-income area provided a variety of services to assist people who lived in the surrounding neighborhoods. Those services relied on a large corps of volunteers, almost all of whom were members of the church's congregation. While few of those volunteers spoke Spanish, many of the individuals who needed the group's services spoke *only* Spanish.

This became critical in the church's Earned Income Tax Credit program, a program that helps low-income families get significant tax refunds. While the group had volunteer accountants to help fill in the tax forms, none spoke Spanish.

Instead of putting the word out that the group needed bilingual volunteer accountants, the group's director changed their intake process. She began asking the clients themselves, "What languages do you speak?"

Sure enough, the group found that some of the clients receiving their services were bilingual in English and Spanish. Now instead of simply being "recipients of the service," they became "volunteer interpreters" who just happened to also be getting their taxes done! They were able to improve the program and turn their "clients" into "partners," simply by engaging the wisdom of the people who were using their services.

Community Engagement in Practice
Engaging Young People: The Foundation

"Diversity and Inclusion" have become hot topics at many organizations. While a great deal of that focus has been placed on provider organizations, more and more foundations are looking internally, realizing that their own boards and staff often fail to reflect the diverse communities in which they provide funding.

The answer to diversity has, to date, been a prettied-up version of tokenism. I say "prettied-up" because of the unspoken assumption that tokenism for a good cause is somehow ok. But looking around at a board filled with all white faces (for example), noting, "We need faces of color at the table," and then heading out to find one of each of the various races and ethnic groups in town - well, there is no other word for that than tokenism. If we are going to model the behaviors we want to see in the world, that is not a great start!

The opposite of tokenism is true engagement. When organizations honestly engage the populations they are working to impact, the need for tokenism vanishes.

One of the best examples of this is a small family foundation called Every Voice in Action.

The mission of the Every Voice in Action Foundation is to ignite and support *Youth Voice*, "infusing the community with the unique perspectives of young people."

Realizing they needed to more deeply engage young people in every aspect of their work, Every Voice in Action developed the Youth Crew - a group of high school and college students that is directly responsible for granting $50,000 annually to youth-related efforts.

Every year, a new Youth Crew learns about philanthropy and learns about the community's issues. The Youth Crew then considers potential focus areas for grants. They write and issue the Request for Proposals, and they review those proposals. *Then the Youth Crew makes the final decisions on who gets funding!*

No tokenism; true engagement. While the issue of "inclusion" is certainly addressed, the strongest benefit is that the efforts of the Foundation create more impact in the community in the short term (via the project) and in the long term (via the hands-on education and empowerment they are providing to young people).

All this is a result of the decision by Every Voice in Action to be an engaged organization - to always be engaging the wisdom, the ideas and the experience of the population they intend to impact.

Chapter 32:
The Pollyanna Principles in Action:
Community Engagement

Pollyanna Principle #6 notes that people will go where systems lead them. Where do systems built around Community Engagement aim the work of Community Benefit Organizations?

Pollyanna Principle #1:
We accomplish what we hold ourselves accountable for.

Pollyanna Principle #2:
Each and every one of us is creating the future, every day, whether we do so consciously or not.

If anything is evident in all these stories, it is that Community Engagement extends accountability beyond just the four walls of an organization. If we want our whole community to become a force for change, with each and every member of our community holding him/herself accountable for creating a better future, the two-way exchange of Community Engagement accomplishes that.

This became infinitely clear as we built the Diaper Bank in Phoenix - a community where we started out knowing virtually no one, and where, within just one year, fifty people became committed enough to work for months on end, to make the Diaper Bank a reality. By engaging those individuals in what was possible for their community, they held themselves accountable for accomplishing that.

When the doctors assisting the Cancer Support Group were engaged in real dialogue, those doctors began holding themselves accountable. Their formation of an advisory group is evidence of that heightened sense of responsibility for making a difference.

There is no better example of a group holding itself accountable for the difference it intended to make in its community than Every Voice in Action's Youth Crew. First, the young people themselves are being taught how they can hold themselves accountable and act upon that accountability, to create community change. Secondly, though, the foundation is eschewing the top-down, "we-know-best" philanthropy of days past, in favor of a truly engaged philanthropy, working with the population they serve, and creating end results no single one of those parties could have achieved on their own.

Community Engagement transforms "people who care" into people who are holding themselves accountable, taking ownership of the issues a program is addressing. That is what it means to build an engaged community.

With Community Engagement, then, the means do not merely align behind visionary community end results. The means - building an engaged community - are themselves visionary end results!

Pollyanna Principle #3:
Everyone and everything is interconnected and interdependent, whether we acknowledge that or not.

Pollyanna Principle #4:
"Being the change we want to see" means walking the talk of our values.

Pollyanna Principle #5:
Strength builds upon our strengths, not our weaknesses.

In our initial Community Engagement work to build the Diaper Bank in Phoenix, one comment seemed to arise, almost verbatim, in virtually every one of those meetings: "What you are suggesting may work in Tucson. But Tucson is smaller, more cohesive. The organizations in Phoenix simply will not work together."

This comment occurred in almost every meeting we had, regardless of whether we were meeting with business people or funders or agency representatives themselves. It got to the point where my part-ner, Dimitri, and I had to stifle laughter when someone mentioned this "fact," as we had begun placing bets on how long it might take before we would hear those words!

The facts, however, consistently contradicted this assumption. Given the opportunity to engage themselves in an effort that often required long hours of meetings as well as a hefty dose of physical labor - physically handling hundreds of thousands of diapers - the people who built the Valley Diaper Bank took on those tasks joyfully.

Why joyfully? Because working together on something a whole group cares about feels good. The higher spirit in us humans craves those connections. When our work is aligned with the flow of our interconnectedness, we tap into the spirit that is already there, wait-ing for us to bring it out. That sense of something bigger than each of us becomes yet another strength upon which to build. What was formerly a "chore" becomes a task met with enthusiasm.

The flip side of connectedness and cooperation is competition. In Phoenix, the representatives of 50 organizations who were often positioned as competitors built the Diaper Bank together. During that process, they shared what might otherwise have been considered "trade secrets." They shared data.

They even shared diapers! One participant announced that they had just received a donation of far more Size 3 diapers than they could use. Did anyone need the remainder?

Engagement turns us all into partners, chipping in together to make a difference. It requires that we walk a talk of shared values, model-ing the behaviors we hope to inspire in others, as that is the only way the end result will come to pass. Every Voice in Action is the most obvious example of what it looks like when an effort is walking its talk through engagement. However, the truth is all these efforts put higher values into practice than we often see in traditional "nonprof-it" work. Each of them was being the change they wanted to see in their communities.

It is a lot easier to insulate ourselves from walking our talk when we are not connecting in a meaningful way with those who might point out our inconsistencies. The more honestly we are engaging with the community we serve, learning and working with them side by side, the more we can build upon the values we all share, to create the future we all want.

Engagement leverages the sense of connection / commitment to something we all care about, building individual strength, organizational strength, and community strength all at the same time. In the end, that spirit of interconnectedness and cooperation not only feels terrific; it is the only practical, vision-based road to turning our communities' highest aspirations into reality.

Chapter 33:
From Developing Programs to Sustaining Them

We have seen that it is not only possible, but immensely practical to build programs whose means align behind the visionary end results we are holding ourselves accountable for creating for our communities. We have seen that such alignment seeks ways to work cooperatively, to walk the talk of our values, to build upon all our communities' strengths.

We have seen the power of a shared vision, the power of building upon all our communities' shared resources, and the power of engaging community members in the core of our work.

From here, the question becomes, "How do we sustain it now that we have built it?"

The approach to resource development described on the following pages will address that question. But by this point, you are probably already noting that sustainability is automatically built into the core of a program's infrastructure when that program is developed by engaging all the existing assets and resources in the community.

Chapter 34:
Asset-Based Resource Development

To create more significant, long-term, visionary community change, the discussion of financial sustainability cannot be about generating cash for the shortfall; it must be about building financial stability for the long haul.

In part, Community-Driven organizations will address the issue of financial sustainability by changing the amount of funding that is needed, building support into the very infrastructure of the organization. An engaged organization, built on a base of shared resources, will not only require less cash, but it will generate cash support as a direct result of its level of engagement.

But what about the rest of the cash needs of the organization? For years, it has seemed the only way to generate cash flow has been to undertake tactics that divert an organization's time / attention / energy away from the actual work of providing the mission - time spent writing grant proposals, preparing for events, etc. Sadly, though, the result in most organizations is not a sense of sustainability; it is a sense of fear, weakness and scarcity.

Rather than diverting an organization's time and attention away from its mission, imagine doing resource development work in a way that fully aligns behind that mission! Rather than engendering a sense of scarcity, imagine using a model that creates a sense of interconnectedness and strength!

Having aligned the development of programs behind the change we want to see in our communities, it is exciting to imagine a model for resource development that would be guided by our accountability for creating the future.

Building on What We Have

There is a model for doing precisely what Community Benefit Organizations need. This model has been proven over time as one of the most successful sustainability models that has ever existed. It provides resources to accomplish what needs to be accomplished, without having to spend inordinate amounts of effort to generate those resources. It sustains when times are bad, as well as when times are good. And it is entirely aimed at accountability for the future.

It is the model upon which wealthy people make their money, sustain their lifestyles, and generate sufficient wealth to leave to their heirs.

Bill Gates, Warren Buffet, and Oprah Winfrey do not make their money from their "day jobs." If Bill and Warren and Oprah stopped going to work tomorrow, their income would not diminish by any noticeable degree.

The significant incomes of these wealthy individuals does not come from what they DO. It comes from what they HAVE. What they HAVE makes their money for them.

In considering the behaviors of wealthy individuals, one notices something profound: for the most part, wealthy individuals do not see each other as competitors, but as compadres. The recent announcement by Warren Buffet that the bulk of his estate will be donated to Bill Gates's foundation is just one of many such examples.

This makes perfect sense for individuals whose wealth is not predicated on what they do, but on what they have, because they already have plenty. Other wealthy people are not a threat, because these individuals already own whatever it is that is generating their income.

If an organization's income is generated by what the organization has, rather than from what it does, could the organization perhaps stop having to exert so much energy and attention to bring in that income?

That is the thinking at the heart of an Asset-Based approach to Resource Development.

Asset-Based Resource Development in Practice

The thought process in creating an Asset-Based Resource Development Plan is simple:

1. Identify the assets / resources an organization has access to
2. Determine how those assets / resources can be activated to generate more revenue and/or other resources

Identifying Our Assets

As is easily seen from the shared resources upon which the Diaper Banks were built, Community Benefit Organizations have tremendous assets and resources upon which to build.

In creating an Asset-Based Resource Development plan, a group will therefore identify the following:

- Physical Assets and Resources
- Program / Mission Assets and Resources
- Human Assets and Resources
- Community Assets and Resources

Physical Assets and Resources: What You Have

Physical assets and resources are the easiest to identify. They are, in essence, your stuff. The building or office or room you occupy. The parking lot. Your equipment - the copy machine, the computers. Physical assets and resources are all the physical things you have and use. Unlike the balance sheet, where an asset refers to something you own outright, in this more general use of the word, if you have legal right to use something (a leased car, a rented office), it is a resource you might be able to build upon.

A theater that rents its space when it is not producing performances is a good example of using a physical resource to generate revenue. An organization located near an arena, that sells parking spaces to event attendees when the office is closed, is another good example of a purely physical asset generating revenue. Leasing space on an organization's property for a cell phone tower is another example of using what you already have to generate money. And of course, the Diaper Bank's need for warehousing assistance allowed Tetra / Beacon - the organization with whom they contracted for that work - to generate cash flow from the space, racks, forklifts, etc. they already had.

Virtually none of these revenue generators requires a huge outpouring of up front cash or effort to raise that money. While the theater may have to clean up after the event, that expense would be factored into its rental price - it is not money they have to spend out of pocket, in the hopes of raising money. The same held true for the expenses incurred by the Beacon Group in warehousing the Diaper Bank's diapers - those costs were covered by the fee they charged the Diaper Bank. Similarly, while a volunteer may have to stand in the parking lot for an hour or two collecting parking fees, this is a minor amount of work compared to other fundraising efforts.

Program / Mission Resources: What You Do

If physical resources are what you have, mission resources are what you do. This does not necessarily mean charging for an organization's services, or charging more if you already charge. What it does mean is that the operational flow of your mission is a resource unto itself, and that mission work may be able to generate additional revenue, simply by virtue of the work you are doing.

The easiest way to find creative ways to generate revenue from the work you are already doing is to flow-chart that work. Start at the beginning - perhaps when a patron first walks in the door. Ask, "What happens first? Then what happens? Then what?"

Where do the participants hear about you? Then how do they contact you? What happens when they arrive? And then what?

Movie theaters do this well. They know you will first buy your ticket. Then you will head into the theater. Then you will sit for an hour of more, watching the movie.

Hey - if they're just sitting, we could sell them popcorn! And voila! Popcorn sales often generate more money than movie tickets nowadays.

An art cinema capitalized on the fact that rather than arriving together, most of their patrons would meet others at the theater. They created an outdoor seating area, and started selling beer, wine and pizza, transforming what had been just "going to the movies" into a "whole evening at the theater."

What happens in the flow of your programs? Are there people waiting (perhaps in a hospital), who might want some entertainment? Are there people coming for classes, who might buy books or other educational materials? How can the flow of activities surrounding what you do generate more revenue?

Human Assets and Resources: Who You Know

A group's human assets and resources include all the lives the effort touches. The list may begin with the board, staff, and volunteers. It may then expand to donors, program participants, sponsors, vendors, and foundations. Then there are the lives touched by all those people's lives, and so on.

People are always amazed at how many lives their efforts touch, and at how many people each board member and each staff person knows. Part of living such connected lives is that we all know a lot of people who could help our efforts in many many ways.

While organizations often bemoan the fact that they do not have access to lots of wealthy individuals (a scarcity mindset), when an organization builds its resource development efforts upon a base of the people they already know, they are almost always surprised at the results.

Community Assets and Resources: What Everyone Else Has and Does

Community assets and resources are the same assets and resources, used in exactly the same way, as was described in the chapters on Program Development. For a more traditional program - one that has not been built around shared community resources - considering community resources in their Resource Development Plan allows the group to rethink its program retroactively, to begin tapping community resources to address a portion of their project for which they would otherwise have to raise cash.

The use of community assets and resources in this way is one of the reasons we stopped calling this approach Asset-Based FUND Development, and began using the term RESOURCE Development instead. It is a reminder that money is just one of many tools Community Benefit Organizations use to accomplish their goals.

Because the approach to leveraging community resources was covered so extensively in the prior chapters, the examples on the following pages will focus on ways to leverage the remaining three types of assets - Physical, Mission and Human.

Chapter 35:
How Can Our Assets Generate Sustainable Revenues?

Like Community Engagement, Asset-Based Resource Development is not a specific tactic or strategy, but a way of thinking and being. It is the mindset that says, "Before we choose which tactics to use, we will identify what we have already to work with. We will then choose tactics that build upon those assets."

For each group, the specific strategies and tactics will be different. No matter how similar their mission is to another group, every group will have a different set of assets with which to work, different constraints, and different opportunities.

The similarity is that all groups have assets and resources they have not engaged. Those assets and resources are often hiding in plain sight, just waiting to be activated. In addition, depending on the group, those assets can often generate significant, sustainable income, with barely any additional work.

Warning:
The strategies that arise from an Asset-Based approach to resource development are not a quick fix. They are instead a foundation to build upon, to create long-term, sustainable sources of income.

These approaches do not negate using traditional fundraising tactics. Identifying and activating an organization's assets is simply an additional step between "identifying our needs" and "seeking funds." This new step might reduce the amount of money the group needs to raise - or the amount of work required to raise it. Most likely, it will generate new ideas about how to generate needed resources.

The stories on the following pages show how to build an ever-broadening base from which an organization can generate its own resources, built upon what the organization already has and what it is already doing. These approaches simultaneously strengthen the mission and build engaged support, aligning the means behind the organization's desired end results - community improvement.

Chapter 36:
The Environmental Group

The Environmental Group provides environmental education to both students and tourists at a field station along the coast of Mexico. In 1998 when we were working with them, their annual budget was the equivalent of $200,000 U.S. dollars.

Their Assets and Resources

Going through our interviews with the Environmental Group, we asked our questions about the flow of the program. We toured the facility, noting all their physical assets and resources. We talked about the lives they touched - among them, the people who came through the facility for various purposes throughout the year.

The more the group shared, the more it became obvious that they had so much to work with - an abundance of opportunities for creating revenue streams, at just about every turn.

Here is some of what we learned about the flow of their student-related program:

- Groups of American students were bussed to the field station, dropped off, and picked up several days later.
- The groups were high school and college aged.
- They were fed three meals a day, and they slept in sleeping bags in the field station dormitory.
- They spent the day on the beach doing research.
- At night, they would roam the beach, sit around the campfire, lay around and read, and just relax.
- The schools - or in some cases, the parents - paid a fixed fee per student for that experience.
- The students loved being there. Years later, some students were still telling stories of their experience at the Environmental Group.

This is what we learned about program flow regarding the tourists who would visit the site:

- Tourists arrived at the facility on large tour busses, as one stop in their tour of the community.

- They were toured around the facility with a guide from the Environmental Group.

- The guides gave a one-hour lesson on the region's sensitive ecosystem, mixing in stories of local lore to illustrate their points.

- The tourists loved the tour. They frequently lingered to ask questions before getting back on the bus. The Environmental Group was the most engaging part of their whole day.

- The tour busses paid a fixed rate per person to the facility. The tourists were charged nothing additional once they arrived at the gates of the Environmental Group.

As we toured the facility to check out the group's physical resources, our inquiries about the Gift Shop were met with this response:

"Don't ask. It was the brainchild of a board member, who figured the tourists would buy T-shirts. But the tourists don't want our stuff; they want the local trinkets. And high school and college kids can't afford the T-shirts. They just have a few bucks with them. The Gift Shop has been a sink hole."

Building on What They Had

Where the Environmental Group saw only teenagers with no money, there was, in fact, opportunity. Perhaps because we both had teenaged kids at the time, my business partner, Dimitri, and I knew there was indeed something for which teenagers would always part with their money - food!

We recommended they add snacks and bottled water to the shopping list when they went shopping for supplies. We recommended they add sunscreen and disposable cameras.

Similarly, where the Environmental Group saw tourists who had already paid a fixed fee and would pay no more, there was also opportunity. Our recommendations for the tourists were again based on this captive audience, and again, took virtually no additional work.

Start the tour asking if anyone wanted to purchase a disposable camera or sunscreen prior to beginning.

Then end the tour by passing the hat and funneling folks into the gift shop. "We are so pleased you were here. We want you to know that we exist solely on donations from individuals like you. If you feel you have learned something today, we hope you will put a dollar or two in the donation bin. And if you feel like you learned more than a dollar's worth, we hope you will add to that!"

Now for the most critical piece of information about the assets the Environmental Group was about to activate. The number of individuals who came through their facility each year - both tourists and students - was staggering.

All told, between the students and the tourists, approximately 10,000 individuals visited the facility each year. The tour busses alone brought hundreds of tourists to the Environmental Group, sometimes as often as daily, every week throughout the year. The students were not as numerous, but they stayed longer - multiple days to eat multiple snacks.

If the Environmental Group averaged $2.00 worth of bottled water, sunscreen or donations from each of those individuals, they would gross 10% of their $200,000 budget with virtually no extra work!

The Environmental Group: More Assets, More Options

Obviously the critical issue at the Environmental Group was their long-term vision. Not surprisingly, that vision included not only preservation of the region's sensitive ecosystem, but creating widespread passion for the region, to aide in those preservation efforts. Their mission, therefore, included expanding knowledge and familiarity with the region, to help generate the passion that would generate preservation.

It was truly a blessing to be able to be part of the work this group was doing. This was not just because of their mission and vision; it was, to be perfectly honest, because this was a beautiful place to be!

The Environmental Group's director spent a great deal of time touring us through the whole ecosystem, letting us experience it first hand - the sand on our toes, the search for various critters, the exploration of local sites. We learned that this is something she and her staff would often do for tourists and friends who showed interest in the local terrain.

That became another asset to leverage.

By transforming casual tours into for-pay educational excursions, they were simultaneously advancing their mission and vision, generating additional revenue from work they were already doing.

* *

In considering these approaches to resource development, a number of things become clear.

First, little additional effort was required.

Unlike a gala or other event, as the mission was served better (more kids coming to the field station, more tourists learning about the area), the more money the organization would bring in.

These efforts took no special expertise, and did not require charging more for what they did - the schools and the tour bus companies ended up paying nothing more for the services they received.

The approaches did not require aggressive fundraising - nothing more than asking for a dollar or two from visitors to whom they were already giving a presentation.

What these approaches required was that the Environmental Group look differently at the assets they had hiding in plain sight; to see those assets for what they were; and to set them in motion to generate cash flow.

By leveraging their physical assets (the local environment, their facility, their gift shop), their human assets (the tourists, the students, the staff) and their mission assets (everything they did as part of their mission), those assets could be relied upon to generate a significant part of their budget, year after year, with little additional effort.

Most important, though, these efforts all aligned behind their mission, simultaneously strengthening the community as they built resources.

Chapter 37:
Kids in Recovery

Kids in Recovery was a theater program focused on teens and substance abuse. The program had the combined results of keeping kids sober who were already in recovery; encouraging kids who were using drugs to get help; and preventing teens from getting into drugs in the first place.

The program did all this by assembling small groups of young people who were in various stages of recovery themselves, and assisting them in creating a script about each of their lives - how they had each gotten involved with and addicted to drugs, and how they had eventually overcome their addiction. These were the honest stories of their lives, given a bit of dramatic flair by the organization's founder and artistic director.

From there, the group became a theater ensemble, performing the very play that interwove all their stories. The plays were performed at high schools and churches all over the city. The audiences were all the same - room upon room filled with teenagers who were indistinguishable from the kids performing on the stage.

At the end of each performance, the teenaged performers would step out of their on-stage role, and give the statement we have all come to recognize as the first statement of recovery: "I am Maria, and I am an alcoholic." "I am Johnny, and I am an addict." And so on. As I type the words, I picture these young kids, on the stage, confessing their souls, and my eyes still well up.

After their bows, the young performers would sit at the edge of the stage, legs dangling, as they answered questions from the audience. Because they had just bared their souls, the teenaged audience was just as honest in their questions. "When you stopped using, did you lose your friends?" "Did your parents really not know?" "How bad was it in jail?"

The success rate for Kids in Recovery was considerably higher than other programs, because everything about the program was honest, and kids can spot a phony a mile away. Talk about the need to walk their talk in everything they did!

As we examined all the assets this organization had, the list filled page after page. Their work was successful. They were in the schools. They were working with recovering kids themselves. They had access to schools-full of young people. The list went on and on and on.

Natural partners emerged. Someone might choose to underwrite a single event in a single location - for example, an active member of a church might pay to have the group perform for their youth group.

Or a company that offers healthy snacks might sponsor a whole year's worth of events, for the exposure and name recognition.

Natural partners among Community Benefit Organizations arose as well, including those who were doing high-dollar anti-smoking or anti-drunk-driving ad campaigns. These were organizations who were already paying for advertising. Many of the kids who were acting out their lives had been smokers as well as drug users. Many of them had driven while intoxicated or been with others who were driving while high. These were points that could be easily woven into the stories they were telling, without in any way compromising the integrity of those stories.

By combining their human assets (the audiences) with their mission assets (the subject matter, the theatrical experience), Kids in Recovery could base a whole new revenue stream on the assets and resources they already had.

Chapter 38:
The Hospice

In teaching Asset-Based Resource Development at one of our workshops, we asked for a volunteer from the participants - someone we could put through the paces, to show how the process works. A woman who had been sitting eagerly in the front row shot her hand up as if she were in the studio audience of a game show.

She looked absolutely forlorn. "We have nothing. No one donates to us. We are in the middle of nowhere." She just about dared us to find a single asset in her sea of scarcity.

Her organization was a hospice in a remote, rural area. They had been in existence for 20 years. We asked our questions, learning about how the group accomplished its mission, caring for both the individuals living at the hospice, and their families.

"What contact do you have with the family after that person passes away?"

"Oh they send us these amazing cards, thanking us for making their loved one's last days comfortable."

"And then what?"

Uncertain silence and shuffling of her feet. "I'm not sure what you mean."

"After they send the note, what do you do?"

"We file it in the drawer."

"And how many of these do you think you have filed away in all those 20 years?"

You can probably guess how the story ends. There were 2,000 names in that drawer. Two thousand families who had loved what the organization had done during their loved ones' final days. Two thousand.

At the mention of that number, the buzzing around the room could have powered a small town. We just stood back and encouraged the group, "Tell her what she can do," and the ideas flew. The woman wrote to me months later to say that the session had changed everything for her, and that they had begun a program to gently and nurturingly follow up with the people whose lives they had so profoundly touched.

If you are thinking this is an extreme example, you are only partially correct. Yes, it is extreme. But this particular mis-step - not realizing the immensity of the human assets sitting right under an organization's nose - happens with every single group we work with. Yes, it happens with folks who are not sophisticated and perhaps do not have access to top fundraising counsel. But it also happens with people who should know better. It happens to organizations with full development staffs. It happens to organizations with highly connected boards. While this particular example may be extreme, it is not unusual.

To prove that point, I will go no farther than to revisit the organizations we examined in the chapters on Community Impact Planning.

At the Recovery Organization, between the board and their group of supportive volunteers, the organization could boast some of the community's most influential individuals. Many of those individuals had sons and daughters with substance abuse problems, who had been helped by the organization. Yet it had never occurred to this group of elite men and women to take a friend to lunch to tell them about the organization's work - even though their friends in fact knew of the success their sons and daughters had there!

Then one day, the board president arrived at a board meeting almost giggling. She showed the group a $1,000 check. "I was at lunch, and I was telling my friend how excited I am about all our new programs and all the work the board is doing. She just took out her wallet and wrote this check!" Among this group of some of the most connected, influential and public personalities in town - individuals who themselves were used to writing large checks for causes in which they believed - it had never occurred to them to consider what might happen if they shared their passion with their friends.

Moving from boards to development staff, consider the Public Broadcast Group. Between their radio and television audiences, their membership support included tens of thousands of individuals who had signed up during a pledge drive, writing annual checks to the station to support the programming they enjoyed. But aside from sending form letter after form letter, asking for more money, the development staff had no contact - none - with any but the very highest dollar donors.

The woman at the hospice is not as unusual as we might think. We all have a tendency to look beyond the assets that are right before our eyes, staring out towards that imaginary place where we believe the grass is greener. But especially when it comes to our human assets and resources, what we are ignoring is a veritable mountain of possibilities, looming enormously right in front of us - an asset that is almost screaming to be tapped.

Chapter 39:
The Pollyanna Principles in Action:
Asset-Based Resource Development

Pollyanna Principle #6 notes that people will go where systems lead them. Where are we aimed if we base our Resource Development efforts on what we already have?

> **Pollyanna Principle #1:**
> We accomplish what we hold ourselves accountable for.
>
> **Pollyanna Principle #2:**
> Each and every one of us is creating the future, every day, whether we do so consciously or not.

Perhaps one of the most exciting things about Asset-Based Resource Development is its direct tie to the vision and mission of the group doing the work. The more the group aims at its vision and mission, the more money comes in. There is no more direct link between "accountability for creating the future" and "resource development" than that.

If the Environmental Group teaches more people, more people will be spending money on snacks, more people will be donating when they pass the hat, more people will be going on excursions. The mission will be enhanced as the dollars are enhanced, and the community will receive more benefit from the organization's work.

The same will happen for Kids in Recovery. The more people watching (and being transformed by) the performances, the more sponsors will pay for those "eyeballs." The value increases to the sponsor as the value increases to the community.

The hospice group is in the same situation - the more compassionate and nurturing they are to those in their care, the more likely it is the family will want to thank them later with a gift.

It all comes back to the methods wealthy individuals use to generate their income. The more their assets grow, the more money they make, without having to work extra hard to make that happen. The assets build upon themselves.

And when the strongest assets are a group's vision, mission and values, having those assets grow strengthens our communities in the course of generating revenues.

Pollyanna Principle #3:
Everyone and everything is interconnected and interdependent, whether we acknowledge that or not.

Pollyanna Principle #4:
"Being the change we want to see" means walking the talk of our values.

Pollyanna Principle #5:
Strength builds upon our strengths, not our weaknesses.

Asset-Based Resource Development brings every one of the Pollyanna Principles about "means" to life.

None of the examples in this section require competing with other organizations, and in the case of Kids in Recovery, their sponsorship by anti-tobacco and anti-drunk-driving groups actually engaged cooperative relationships with other organizations.

Engaging all the lives an organization touches to help in all kinds of ways - the organization's human assets and resources - builds on the interconnectedness discussed in the chapters on Engagement.

As for building on our strengths, I have learned to anticipate the joy I see each time I facilitate this work with a group. "We had no idea we had so much to work with!" is always the response - always.

Just as it is with wealthy people, when we build our resources upon our assets, that very act builds the assets themselves. Each of the assets noted in this section is strengthened by using it for the cause.

This all comes back to being the change these organizations wish to see in the world. All these strategies align means behind ends, allowing the organization to proudly walk its talk.

These approaches are inspiring. They are simple to implement, requiring no special skills because groups are just doing what they already do, working with what they already have. While it may take a facilitator to help an organization realize all it does have to work with, it does not take a specialist to implement that work or keep it going.

Chapter 40:
Strong Programs:
A Celebration of What is Possible

I do a lot of keynote addresses, to a wide range of audiences in a wide range of communities. When I suggest that organizations can develop and sustain programs in a way that is engaging, inspiring, and cooperative, the response in the eyes of audience members is always the same. "Oh great," they are thinking, "another one of those Age-Of-Aquarius throwbacks who believe if we all hold hands and sing Kumbaya, all will be well."

The proof, however, is in the results.

The groups we have worked with over the years may have had vastly different missions, in vastly differing locations, with vastly different sets of people at the helm. But each of those groups shared the culturally reinforced belief that scarcity is the only reality. Each group began the work wearing blinders, unable to see the abundance of resources that was hiding in plain sight. And each group exclaimed, at some point during our work together, "I cannot believe all we have to work with! I cannot believe we never realized this!"

That abundance was the reality all along.

It is possible to create practical, easy-to-use systems for program development and sustainability that are collaborative and cooperative not just in their mechanics, but in their spirit. It is possible to create systems for building and sustaining programs that not only aligns means behind Community-Driven end results, but that actually improve our communities by the very act of building and sustaining those programs.

These systems work because this sector is not about money but about making our communities healthy, vibrant, compassionate places to live. They work because passionate people enjoy working with others who are passionate about the same cause.

It all comes back to that very first step - focusing on the vision we all share for making our communities extraordinary places to live.

Chapter 41:
Conclusion: The Pollyanna Principles and Individual Organizations

If the frameworks and systems described in Part 3 show anything about governance, planning, and the developing and sustaining of programs, it is that Community Benefit Organizations do not have to settle for "business as usual." There are indeed practical systems and frameworks for creating the visionary end results we all want to see in our communities.

We do not have to always be reacting, either to internal or external circumstances. We do not have to compete with those who want the same results we want. We do not have to be mired in the day-to-day, to the exclusion of the future we are creating.

We can aim at and create positive, affirming, visionary results. We can do so in the way boards govern, in the way organizations plan, in the way programs are developed and in the way they are sustained.

It is all possible. It is all practical.

We therefore hope you will see the examples in this section as just that - examples. I have shared them, not to show *the* way, but to show one way of putting the Pollyanna Principles into practice to improve the quality of life in our communities and our world. Having worked with others who have been focused on community change, we know there are other models and frameworks, all of which also provide practical means for creating visionary community results.

In concluding this section, I therefore extend the invitation to those working in the Community Benefit Sector to develop dozens more frameworks and systems, to align all the internal work organizations do behind the end result of accomplishing visionary improvement in our communities.

From there, the next step is to ensure that these frameworks, aligned behind the Pollyanna Principles and aimed at creating visionary community change, become the norm of how Community Benefit Organizations do their work.

Part 4

Creating the Path to the Future We Want

The Pollyanna Principles
in Action for
Whole Communities

Chapter 42:
Using the Pollyanna Principles
to Build Extraordinary Communities

When the systems used by an individual organization are rooted in the Pollyanna Principles, things change. They change internally and externally, and that change occurs almost instantly.

Imagine, then, the power of leveraging that change out to more and more groups - into entire communities.

That is what happens when the Pollyanna Principles are at the root of work done by funders, by capacity building groups, by associations and coalitions - by all the groups that affect not just one organization, but multiple organizations and communities.

One of the pleasant surprises we have found as we have expanded our work from individual organizations out towards larger community-focused spheres is that there is no need to create all new systems for this larger work. Because the systems we developed for individual organizations are community-focused, the same frameworks and systems work just as well when adapted to larger community efforts.

Therefore, the following chapters will not introduce new tools, but will tell the stories of how the systems and approaches described in the previous chapters have been used to bring community members together to build a healthy, vibrant future.

In the first set of stories, we will examine two different approaches for bringing people together for the purpose of furthering community benefit. In the second set of stories, we will see what is possible when we consider collaborative approaches to some of the most competitive work in the sector - funding and capacity building.

From these stories of success, we see that what appears to be impossible is, in fact, infinitely possible when we change the assumptions and expectations that guide our work. The power of each of these efforts was therefore rooted first in their thoughts, and only then in their actions.

When we change the way we see things, things change.

Chapter 43:
Convening for Community Results:
The Family Financial Security Summit

Having seen how Vision-Based Community Impact Planning makes visionary change practical and doable for individual organizations, would it not be equally practical for an entire region, state or country to consciously create its own future?

Numerous issues and assumptions arise when we expand planning efforts beyond a single organization. First there is the assumption that people will not agree - that organizations will not agree, that rural and urban interests will not agree, that various factions will not agree.

Then, if a group can build consensus, there is the assumption that it will take forever to do so. It is not uncommon to hear comments such as, "We tried to engage everyone in the community about an issue a few years back. It took so long that by the time the process was done, everyone had become tired of both the issue and the process."

It is indeed possible to forge consensus and to do so quickly. The story of the Family Financial Security Summit in Reno, Nevada showcases one such effort.

Back Story

The United Way of Northern Nevada and the Sierra has a knack for getting to the heart of what makes an effort effective. When it came to the goal of ensuring families in Reno were financially secure, it was therefore no surprise to us that their first step focused on engaging the community to plan that effort.

The idea of a summit - a gathering of great minds - seemed like a good first step. But that idea led to more questions than answers.

As this was to be a summit focused on "Family Financial Security," the group's first thought was that attendees would primarily be experts from Northern Nevada's financial sector. The more we focused the group on the desired end result, however, it quickly became apparent that one could only expect families to be "financially secure" if many non-financial conditions were also in place - and more to the point, that financial security was only one part of being "secure" overall.

Other issues arose in the discussion. What about education? What about health? What about a family's basic needs such as food and shelter? What about faith? From that discussion, the United Way decided to invite community leaders whose work was touched in any way by the issue of Family Financial Security.

That decision led to more questions - including the question of engaging the "real people" whose lives the Summit would be discussing. This was not a simple step for United Way - not because they did not see the importance, but because they are not a direct provider of services, and therefore do not have direct contact with such individuals. This led to United Way encouraging the groups they invited to then invite their own program participants.

With those participant-related decisions made, the next set of decisions revolved around the format for the day's work. A common approach to these sorts of events is to begin with a presentation regarding the current state of affairs, to set the stage for dialogue about possible solutions to the problems enumerated in the opening presentations. Because United Way of America has identified three areas that build Family Financial Security - increasing income, building savings, and gaining / sustaining assets - it was assumed the post-presentation discussion would be framed around those topics.

This raised several issues, not the least of which was that the group had already decided to expand the issues beyond the narrow discussion of financial matters.

More importantly, though, if Reno's United Way wanted the result of this summit to be an effective effort to build family stability, it had to tether its discussion to that stability, rather than tethering it to the instability that would be the subject of the morning presentations.

Lastly, if the framework for the discussion was so significantly predetermined without the input of all the attendees, those participants would not own the discussion, nor feel a commitment to move forward on the results at the end of the day. Instead, they would be joining a discussion that would have clearly started without them. "Here are the issues we are considering starting with. Does anyone have any other ideas?"

For the day to truly be effective, the participants could not feel they were attending someone else's event - the event had to be theirs. They needed to own the goals the effort would aim to achieve, and then own the path towards realizing those goals. That ownership would inspire them to take action and to sustain that action.

The result of these opening discussions was a one-day event at which one hundred community members from all walks of life drafted a workable multi-disciplinary plan to begin creating the future for Northern Nevada families.

Preparing for the Event

In preparing for the day of the Summit, several steps were taken. First, the United Way's CEO and President, Karen Barsell, engaged community leaders to discuss what might be accomplished during such a summit, what issues might be addressed, and how the event might accomplish that. In other words, she used Community Sleuthing to engage folks from across the community, to generate interest and ownership in the day's events.

As we prepared for the logistics of the program, several other steps were taken. The first was to make sure the room was set up for the kinds of engaged dialogue that would lead to success. Attendees would be gathering from the breadth and depth of a highly diverse region. At one extreme, the region included the urban area of Reno, with its economy dependent in large part upon casinos and tourism. At the other extreme were rural communities with tiny populations and little economic base.

That does not tell the whole story, however, because in some of those remote communities, the populations themselves were diverse.

Some families lived in abject poverty. Others were very wealthy, having migrated from elsewhere in the country to take advantage of Nevada's favorable tax structure.

All this needed to be taken into account if we were to encourage great dialogue. That meant ensuring that each table was comprised of individuals with diverse backgrounds and interests.

Lastly, the largest key to success would be a small army of facilitators, who could help move the discussion along. The day before the event, therefore, we met with the individuals who had been recruited to do that work.

The individuals in that group had not volunteered because they knew this work and wanted to be part of it. On the contrary, these individuals were all there out of a sense of loyalty to the United Way staff person who had asked for their help. None of them knew a thing about the approaches they were about to be asked to facilitate. We had ninety minutes to teach them not only the logistics of what they would be doing, but the theory and reasoning behind those steps.

With the wisdom that comes from past experience, we knew that these volunteers might enter the arena skeptical, but that they would be converted the moment they watched the attendees engage.

With these logistical pieces in place, we were excited to get moving, to make visionary community change practical in Northern Nevada.

The Family Financial Security Summit

The Family Financial Security Summit took place in July of 2008. A snapshot of that month shows a time when sharp increases in U.S. mortgage foreclosures blanketed the news media, the canary in the coal mine of impending economic doom. There was a general understanding that bad news was going to continue to get far, far worse.

As a result, the topic of Family Financial Security had a far stronger sense of urgency than it had when Karen and I first began planning the event earlier in the year.

At the strong urging of many of the participants who had been consulted about planning the event, the morning indeed began with a presentation - a grounding in statistics about the current situation, presented by a representative of the Federal Reserve Bank. The statistics were then made real in stories told by the Executive Director of the region's Consumer Credit Counseling Service, who shared the stories of middle class people who thought they had life in order, only to find the walls crashing in.

As could have been predicted, that hour of overwhelmingly horrible stories was a sobering start to a day that was intended to reach for what was possible. We knew the natural tendency would have been for the group to immediately dive in to brainstorm quick solutions. It was therefore critical to quickly move beyond today's reality, to tether the group's planning to the future they would be aiming to create together. From there, they would address today's problems on the way to creating that future.

We started by asking the group to set aside the doom and gloom stories they had just experienced, and to instead focus on the blank slate before them - the future of their region. We explained that the rest of the day would be spent creating that future. We reassured the group that we would not be ignoring the present, that we would simply be putting that "present reality" into perspective within the context of creating something positive and powerful. We promised we would end the day where we had started it, with today's reality.

Then we held our breath and dove in.

Creating the Future for Family Financial Security in Northern Nevada

The first questions the group addressed were the community-focused Phase 1 questions in the Community Impact Planning process.

With one hundred people in the room, it was likely there were one hundred different images of what it might look like if a family were financially stable. The first question helped ensure the group had a sense of the whole picture, rather than just the piece each individual was envisioning. That step created immediate consensus, while anchoring the planning in that vision of success.

To that end, rather than simply ask what success would look like in general, the question focused on a "real" family, asking the participants to describe what life would look like if the family was financially secure.

The Medina Family

Mom and Dad
Joe Medina - age 40
Teresa Medina - age 35

The Medina Children
Joey Jr. - age 9
Sandra - age 7
Ricky - age 1

Joe's Parents
Abe and Estella are both over 70

The group then addressed the following questions regarding the fictional Medina family:

If this family is financially secure, what does life look like for each family member?
What does life look like now?
What will life look like as each of these individuals age?
As the kids become teenagers, then head to college?
As Joe and Teresa plan for their own future?
As Abe and Estella plan for their future?

Question 1 - The Vision for Success

The following provides some of what the group came up with, as each table discussed what life would look like for the Medina family if they were financially secure.

Joe and Teresa:
Employed with secure jobs. Health benefits and life insurance. Home ownership with minimal debt. Involved in their community. Able to take an annual vacation. Involved with their kids' activities and schools.

The Children:
Basic physical needs are met. Savings account for each child. The children feel they are a valued part of the family. Financial education at home and in school. Loving, nurturing environment. Clothes are not second-hand. Healthy social circle. Interactive conversations between all three generations. Access to higher education.

Abe and Estella:
Retired / do not have to keep working. Own their home with no debt. Good health, and healthcare needs are met. A financial plan and assets to pass to their heirs. Multiple sources of income - investments, social security, pension. Able to live independently and self-supported. Socially active, involved. Quality time with family. Social network and family support.

Family Overall:
Intergenerational support. Common interests, enjoying family time together (vacations, recreation). They see money as a tool, not the goal. Open communications. Income adequate to assist the family to achieve long term goals. Helping others. Personal security, not just financial security. Strong connection with schools and community. Strong support system. Ongoing learning. Living in a safe, friendly neighborhood. Feel a sense of connectedness, belonging. Material, intellectual and spiritual needs are met.

From this review, it is easy to see that the question's focus on financial security did not limit the discussions. The groups quickly expanded that focus to all the other aspects of a stable, secure life. Even at this early point in the day, financial security was already being identified as only a part of the picture.

Question 2 - Reverse Engineering to Change Community Conditions

From the lively discussions about what stability in the Medina family would look like, the next set of questions began to lay the groundwork for that stability to become reality for this fictional Northern Nevada family. By marching backwards through the cause-and-effect of time, the group would determine what community conditions would lead to the Medina Family living in the picture the group had created for them.

The questions they addressed included the following:

- For families like Joe and Teresa's to be financially secure, what conditions must be in place in our community? What must our community have or be?

- For families like Joe and Teresa's to be financially secure, what assumptions and expectations must change about our community? What assumptions and expectations must change about families? Whose assumptions and expectations?

- For families like Joe and Teresa's to be financially secure, we must have a community where everyone thinks _____ is important. (or) where the culture is _____. (or) where the emphasis is _____.

The sheets with their responses covered every inch of the walls of the meeting space, rising ten feet high on all four walls. Condensed, the list of community conditions the group enumerated covered the following broad topics:

Education	Better education systems overall, better access to education for everyone
Financial Literacy	Education programs re: building assets and building savings
Infrastructure	Access to transportation including public transit; Flexible-hour services such as daycare, banking; More community centers with more services
Healthcare	Improved access; cultural and language competence among providers
Income	Livable Wages; diversified job opportunities
Cultural / Values	More collective responsibility to each other; attitudinal commitment to building strong families; "We are in this together."
Intergenerational Focus	Support for seniors to age in place; services balance needs across all generations
Economy	Strong economy overall; strong businesses; economic diversity
Basic Needs	Social safety net for individuals / families who are in need now; more community support for those services
Taxes	Cultural shift away from "taxes are bad"; must be able to pay for services our community needs
Quality of Life	Stronger community infrastructure for parks, community gathering places, art; more opportunities to connect as a community, as neighbors; sense of connectedness / block parties / front porch

Time to Reflect

In wrapping up Question 2, we asked the groups to pause. "What stood out for you in these discussions?" Busy people are rarely encouraged to reflect and learn together, and it is not always comfortable at first. In truth, while many of the attendees could not wait to respond, for many more, it was everything they could do to keep from rolling their eyes and asking, "Can't we please just get on with it already?"

Whenever we ask people to stop and reflect, though, regardless of that initial reaction, their responses always surprise not just us, but themselves.

To the group's credit, they shared and they listened. The most common theme was that despite the encouragement to invite them, "real everyday people" were not in the room, and yet this was all about them.

This observation on the part of the participants is evidence again of the power of self-inspiration over the prescriptive approach of the *shoulds*. While it had been suggested that "regular people" be engaged to participate in the Summit, that suggestion was not a priority until the participants had time to reflect and come to that conclusion on their own. By realizing it themselves, they owned it and would be more likely to act upon it.

Another theme had to do with the layers of assumptions we all tend to make about those who need help. The best example came from the discussion of the Medina family. In creating the Medinas, we intentionally chose both a surname and individual names that might or might not be Latino.

As a result, some groups immediately dove in to address the issues they thought this Latino family would be facing, talking about cultural competence and immigration issues. Others said, "Wow - it never occurred to us the family might be Latino!" It was a good object lesson for the attendees, many of whom work in fields related to social work, about the degree to which we unconsciously make assumptions about "people in need."

Finally, after everyone else had shared their thoughts, Reno Police Officer Patrick O'Bryan took the microphone. Suddenly, even those who were not entirely at ease sharing their observations were silent, waiting to hear from this uniformed officer, firearm holstered at his hip.

Officer O'Bryan uttered just three words: "Are you comfortable?"

He then paused for what felt like forever, looking around the room. Finally, he continued, "Because if you're comfortable, then nothing will change. To change our community, we need to step outside our comfort zone. So are we willing to be uncomfortable?"

The room lit up. Skepticism melted away. The entire group was suddenly ready to take steps to create the future they had envisioned.

Question 3: - Creating the Future in Small, Doable Bites

With a strong foundation in the thinking that would guide the plan, the rest of the day was spent energetically tackling the "doing" part. First the group consolidated the "community conditions" they had listed into major themes, so the rest of the day could be spent determining first steps in addressing each of those areas.

Some of those were the kinds of themes one might expect to arise at a Summit on Family Financial Security - education, healthcare, financial matters, basic needs, jobs.

But then there were themes that spoke of a different kind of stability. Quality of life, emotional and spiritual health, community connectedness. Added to that was the surprising topic of Tax Reform - surprising not because the issue was raised, but because so many people chose to gather under that banner to begin drafting a plan of action.

By the end of the day, individuals were taking ownership of the issues that had arisen, and many groups had already determined first steps towards creating a better future for the people of Northern Nevada. By the next morning, one group had already reserved the County Commissioners Chambers as a meeting place for further discussion and presentations.

However, the best part of these events is always the same, and it never gets old: watching skeptics become believers. At the end of the day, one of the leaders from the business community approached to thank us. "I confess I was skeptical about our work this morning - all that vision stuff. After the opening session with all the data, I thought we could just brainstorm some ideas and get started."

He continued, "But seeing where we have ended up, it is clear we never could have gotten anywhere close to these results if 'today' had been the starting point. We really did have to start at the future to accomplish what we did in such a short amount of time."

Family Financial Security Summit - The Results

At the time of this writing, almost six months have passed since the Summit, certainly not time to measure any significant community change. One thing certainly has changed, though - the level of engagement by Summit participants who committed to help bring to pass the vision of a community where families are financially secure.

Six months later, three of the eight groups are actively meeting. Another two groups are just getting their start, anxious to get moving, and just needing a bit of guidance to find a direction. One of the groups has so many projects at so many differing stages of implementation, and so many new committee members each time they meet, it is hard to keep track.

Most exciting is that the participants have all indicated the desire to come back together for a second Summit, to report progress and keep moving forward.

By assuming and expecting that the participants would quickly find a shared vision for their region, they did so. We assumed the participants would all work excitedly together, that they would build on each other's knowledge and ideas, that they would find shared values and would energetically move from "thinking" to "doing."

Those assumptions created our expectations about the Summit's potential. Those expectations created the Summit's participant list, its format, and ultimately, its results.

Chapter 44:
Convening for Community Results: The Learning Community

For ten years, the leaders of a healthcare foundation believed they had been funding and supporting healthcare. As if struck by a thunderbolt, the leaders of the foundation came to the realization that what they had instead been funding was "sick care" - a clinic here, a prevention effort there.

That singular revelation led to question upon question. What would it look like to aim their work at creating health, rather than treating or preventing illness? Where would one begin, if the real goal was to build a healthy, resilient community?

And most importantly, how can a small foundation, whose grants are in the thousands of dollars (not the millions) make such a difference?

One thing is for certain: It would require scaling up *The 3 Statements* to guide every part of that effort. This is a story of leadership beyond the board room, though. It is a story of community leadership.

It is the story of St. Luke's Health Initiatives' *Health in a New Key* effort.

The Back Story

In the United States, when a tax exempt, public benefit organization is sold to a for-profit company, the proceeds from that sale must be reinvested in the community for a similar purpose as was being provided by the original tax exempt organization. This is commonly accomplished by placing the proceeds from that sale into a charitable trust, to be used to benefit the community.

Given the privatization of healthcare in the U.S., in virtually every large community (and many small communities), a formerly tax exempt hospital has been sold to a private, for-profit company. As a result, many communities now have at least one "health conversion foundation," whose purpose is to ensure the proceeds from those transactions continue to provide health benefits to the community. St. Luke's Health Initiatives (SLHI) is such a foundation, originating from the sale of St. Luke's Health System in 1995.

Roger Hughes is the foundation's Executive Director. Ask anyone who knows Roger, or who has had even one conversation with him, and you will hear the word visionary. Roger's background is eclectic - a professional musician who has never stopped recording; a PhD futurist; a professional career in health and science philanthropy.

Under Roger's leadership, St. Luke's Health Initiatives has gained a reputation for the creative pursuit of dramatic impact in the area of health policy. In every effort undertaken by SLHI, intellectual curiosity and bold creativity combine with a contagious and realistic optimism to generate success after success.

SLHI goes where no one has gone before. They get stuff done. And they do it all with less money in the bank than virtually any other major foundation in the Phoenix, Arizona area.

In 2003, Arizona State University Professors Alex Zautra (Psychology) and John Hall (Public Policy) met with Roger to explore what it might take to build a healthy, resilient community. SLHI's initial funding to ASU's Resilience Solutions Group grew into a partnership that has continued to inform the work the foundation does.

Health in a New Key

The tenth anniversary of SLHI's existence as a foundation was approaching. How to celebrate? Not the types to host a self-congratulatory gala or other such event, SLHI instead decided to launch an initiative around resilience. Merging Roger's musical and healthcare interests, they called the initiative Health in a New Key.[1]

---

1 For considerably more information about this well-researched and powerful concept, visit www.SLHI.org

Health in a New Key launched with a special grant round, an experiment to see what would happen if, through their grant process, SLHI encouraged both exploratory and long-term efforts to build community health and resilience. The exploratory grants were small - $10,000 to $15,000 apiece for five organizations, for one-year efforts to put a toe into the resilience wading pool. The long-term grants were $50,000 per year for five years, going to four large-scale efforts.

The request for proposals for both the exploratory and long-term grants required that applicants use a vision-based, strength-based, interconnected approach to their projects - an approach that mirrored the Pollyanna Principles in every way.

When SLHI announced the grant round, inviting interested parties to attend a briefing, approximately two hundred showed up. We all knew the reality - if you offer money, people will show up. The SLHI staff confided to us at that meeting, however, that they did not anticipate they would receive many qualified proposals once the groups learned how much their approaches would need to change to get these monies. They anticipated seeing a lot of the same old proposals, couched in the language of resilience.

They were wrong. Of the eighty proposals they received, only a handful were truly off the mark. Had they had enough funding, SLHI would have funded many more of those requests.

The Health in a New Key Learning Community

When the SLHI staff members were initially pondering the possibility of doing a more innovative grant round, they also started exploring the possibility of leveraging their impact by creating a Learning Community - a Community of Practice around the issue of community health and resilience. Such an effort would allow people to share their experiences and learn from each other, as they infused their work with new approaches based on new assumptions.

The questions at the heart of the Learning Community were these:

> As those groups change *what they think*, how will that change *what they do*?

> How can they learn from one another in that process, to create considerably more learning together than any one of them could accomplish on their own?

> What new wisdom might come from this shared learning, that might then be shared with the community at large?

Having been part of some of the conversations that had brought SLHI to this point, when it came to the Learning Community, they asked for our help. "We know what this looks like at 30,000 feet," they told us. "How can we make it work on the ground?" How could they translate lofty concepts into practical steps?

Our first recommendation was that they not limit the Learning Community only to grantees. If everyone and everything is interconnected, and if SLHI intended to walk its talk, to build strength upon strength towards its overarching vision, the sensible approach would be the most inclusive approach possible.

That recommendation came from our observation of the Learning Community trend among innovative funders around the country. While creating such Learning Communities has been an admirable step, we had been (and continue to be) consistently dismayed that these funder-initiated Learning Communities are, almost without exception, only for grantees.

If the goal is widespread community impact; and if individuals have self-selected, showing their commitment to creating that impact by submitting a proposal; and if there is limited (if any) extra cost to include non-grantees in such a learning process - then is it not arbitrary, exclusionary and just plain counter-intuitive to exclude those individuals from these forward-thinking initiatives?

The ultimate goal of the Learning Community for Health in a New Key was to leverage learning to the broader community, to expand resilience thinking throughout the community, and make it the norm.

Given the surprising number of grant applicants who had provided worthy proposals, SLHI determined that it made no sense to limit the Learning Community just to the nine who had been chosen to receive funding.

From there, the focus of this large group would be simultaneously simple and incredibly complex - a focus on the vision, mission and values at the heart of the Health in a New Key effort.

The vision had been clearly stated from the outset - a healthy, resilient community.

The mission, too, had been clear - bring together a group that could explore and discover what must change in practice to accomplish that vision. How will programs need to change if they are to aim at creating a healthy, resilient community? And how will the internal work of their organizations have to change, to accomplish those end results?

The values that would guide the process would stem from the work of the Resilience Solutions Group. They would be rooted in the factors that had been found to be evident in both resilient individuals and resilient communities.

Those factors included the need to connect and build trust, the need to build on strengths. The group's work would therefore be integrally guided by those factors as the core values of its work. When there were tough decisions to be made, we would all defer to those resilience indicators as our guide.[1]

In November of 2005, the grant recipients were about to be announced. The kick-off event was planned. The Health in a New Key initiative had begun.

---

1 For more on the work of the Resilience Solutions Group, head to http://www.asu.edu/resilience/

Forming a Community

The kick-off event for the Learning Community in late 2005 included a workshop led by Jody Kretzmann, co-founder of the Asset-Based Community Development Institute at Illinois's Northwestern University. Most of the participants did not know each other before that November day. By focusing them immediately upon their strengths as individuals and as a group, Jody had them energized from the start.

From there, the group adjourned until January, vowing to start the New Year with that visionary question: How do we build a healthy, resilient community?

The group quickly found a pattern that worked for their sessions.

During the first part of the meeting, group members would share what they had learned, been puzzled by, been excited or surprised by, as they ventured forth to do their work in new ways.

The second part of the meeting was a learning experience of some sort - a presentation, a facilitated dialogue. The topic might have to do with learning about a particular aspect of resilience, or it might have to do with getting past a quandary the group had encountered - some of what was shared in the first part of the meeting. Always the choice of topic came from the group.

And then the meeting would wrap up during lunch, with a discussion of what the group wanted to learn next, what they wanted the next meeting to focus on. Each meeting built upon the last, as the learning built upon itself.

At all the Learning Community meetings, SLHI staff was present. They were not present as "the funder, keeping an eye on the process from above." They were instead present as participants, partners, learning alongside the other participants as equals. Everyone in the room was learning new ways of doing and being, and to their credit, that included SLHI.

The group met every two months, each meeting lasting four hours. Four hours may seem like a lot of time, but if the group is learning together - learning new topics, learning about each other, becoming a community themselves - that cannot be done in quick bursts. After the group became more and more active, participants noted that they aggressively guarded the dates of those meetings. They did not want to miss a one.

Participants came from the breadth of the community. Some were agency representatives - executive directors, program managers and case workers. Some were academics - professors who were doing community work as the practical application of a research effort.

And some were community residents. The long-term resident of what had become a low-income area. The woman with schizophrenia who was now working inside the mental health system to create strength-based / interconnected efforts to engage the mentally ill in their own treatment.

Along the way, the learning was infused with the connections they all brought. Mirroring the vision-based, values-based, strength-based approaches they were learning, the group had itself become a microcosm of a healthy, resilient, engaged community.

The Meetings: Part 1 - Working with New Systems

Aristotle is right - we are, of course, what we repeatedly do. But when "what we do" includes new ways of thinking and being, it is not always easy to override our old habits, to maintain our new ways of "doing."

Adding to that difficulty are all the people we encounter who are not comfortable with new ways of thinking and working. Sometimes it is just not easy to keep doing what we want to do, despite best intentions.

Having a safe place for sharing those practical considerations is therefore a vital part of success when we are entering new terrain. (This is why such groups are often called Communities of Practice - they are indeed communities, but they are focused on a practice - something we do, rather than something we are simply studying in theory.)

The following is a sampling of the frustrations the group shared throughout their first year of basing their work on the Vision, Mission and Values of building a healthy, resilient place to live.

Bureaucracy Frustrations: How do we address the conflict between trying to engage the community in a meaningful way, and the rules and bureaucratic layers that serve as an impediment to that engagement?

Rethinking Everything: Re-thinking how we do our work means re-thinking language, re-thinking how we listen, re-thinking what it means to have control vs. give control away, rethinking the balance between organizational culture and societal culture.

More Frustration: The feeling that we are sometimes moving two steps forward and one step back.

Funders: The lament at having to deal with funders who "don't get it." One participant finally noted, "If the current way of funding isn't working, then why doesn't this group do something about it?" And participants volunteered to meet together to determine what steps they would begin taking towards that end.

Maintaining Momentum: While it is not difficult to bring folks together when an effort is new, how to maintain momentum for ongoing project maintenance after the first steps are done or the first major effort has been a success?

Succession Planning in Collaborations: What to do when a collaborative partner leaves the group? What to do when the board members of one of the partner groups rotate off the board, and the new board members don't think the partnership has value? What to do when an individual participant in a collaborative effort has a new boss who doesn't see the value of the time her employee is spending on that partnership?

Internal Succession Planning: How to do succession planning for keeping a vision-based, resilience-based, strength-based approach internally within the participants' own organizations? "If we leave, does this approach leave with us?"

The group also shared success stories:

A hospital was planning a Child Safety Seat program. Instead of creating the program and announcing it to the community, they engaged community members to create the teaching messages for the program.

The "Little Sister" of one of the participants was an 18 year old single mom, frustrated at how difficult the system makes it to succeed. The Health in a New Key participant began encouraging her to turn her frustration into a strength, from which the "Little Sister" began getting involved in politics.

One group had had little luck connecting with school principals to get their program into the schools. When they realized they already had relationships with many of the teachers, they began engaging those teachers, relying on them to approach the principals (bottom up). The program is now in the very schools that would not return their calls.

Another group changed their entire annual retreat to focus on what was working well, rather than focusing on what was not working. Their plan for the year then built upon those strengths.

Then there were employment stories. One group changed its approach to personnel management, aiming away from problem-solving, and looking instead at each employee's goals (vision) and strengths. "The change in attitude and morale has been immediate!"

And then, there were the "aha" moments.

A substance abuse organization realized, "We track individuals while they are in treatment and shortly after they leave, but not when they are out there, being successful, when they could help inform our own work! So this year, after our alumni dinner for program graduates, we re-engaged with all those graduates, to see if they would help us build our own efforts. Now we are building our own internal work upon the very assets we helped our clients find in the first place!"

Another "aha" moment had to do with language and labels. One group, whose project was related to the Seriously Mentally Ill population, realized they had been using the term "Seriously Mentally Ill" because that is the terminology used within the Mental Health System. Outside the system, though, folks hear the words "Seriously Mentally Ill" and they panic! How serious is "seriously" mentally ill? Am I safe around him/her? The Learning Community participants realized they needed to avoid labels, and instead use the listener's own frame of reference to tell a different story.

This particular "aha" moment drew considerable discussion. Professionals in all fields tend to fall victim to using shorthand and jargon, even when talking with those who are not practitioners in that particular field. Those hearing the words often envision something very different from what the jargon means to the person using it.

And so, immediately after the mental health folks told their story, another participant told of her own language revelation, when talking about getting assistance for "People on Disability." The group realized the huge difference in public perception when we talk about someone "being on Disability" vs. talking about some-one who has a disability vs. simply telling that person's story with no labels at all. The Learning Community then considered all the other labels they use - Low-Income Families, The Unin-sured.

And finally, there were those whose projects themselves were already, in that first year, seeing successes beyond even their own dreams.

The group working with the "Seriously Mentally Ill" shared that a participant in that work - a young woman with schizophrenia who had many obvious strengths - had been so encouraged by her participation in that project, that she had formed an organiza-tion to assist at-risk youth with meaningful community service (rather than the mundane work typically encountered by those who are sentenced to community service).

While these are all small stories, they indicate a change of focus from problem-solving to aiming at proactive, visionary end results. They indicate means that are built on strengths, connections, engagement, and values, all of which can change systems. And they indicate a change in those systems themselves - moving from a problem-based approach for personnel management to a vision based / strength-based approach, as just one example.

These changes all occurred within just the first year of this effort. Imagine what the conversations will be like in Years 4 and 5!

The Meetings: Part 2 - Learning New Systems

While the first portion of each meeting was dedicated to sharing the participants' own wisdom and experience, another portion of those meetings was dedicated to learning new ways of thinking and being. As the group focused on Vision, Mission and Values through the lens of Community Health and Resilience, there was always something new to learn.

The topics covered in this first year of meetings just scratched the surface. Some were presented by outside experts - The Frameworks Institute, The Arizona State University Resilience Solutions Group, Kids at Hope. Some were facilitated as exploratory dialogue among the participants themselves.

- Vision-based approaches to planning
- Language and frameworks
- Resilience in Individuals and Communities
- How we bring resilience into our internal (non-program) work
- Asset-based approaches to resource development
- The difference between "at risk" and "at hope" approaches

The conversations after these sessions were notable - not just because they were intensive and enlightening for the participants, but because, more often than not, they moved the thinking of the presenter forward as well. When a group's purpose is to constantly be moving the discussion forward, learning and applying what they learn, and then reflecting on what worked / didn't work, to try again and learn more - well that cannot help but move everyone's learning forward, including those doing the teaching!

Here are just some of the questions raised during the learning portion of these sessions:

- What would the community look like if it were fully resilient? What indicators might measure that?
- How do we shift community culture? How do we change cultural values?

- How can we be less "Us-and-Them" and become more inclusive in all our work? How do we overcome the challenges to being inclusive with those we are already interacting with?

Over the course of that first year, Dimitri and I looked forward to every meeting as if it were Christmas morning. And we left every meeting as if it had indeed been the best Christmas ever, talking about it for days afterward.

We were not alone. Participants confessed that they had indeed attended that first meeting because the funder had invited them. "But now? I wouldn't miss these meetings for anything!"

People arrived happy to see each other. They left feeling encouraged, exalted. As one participant left a particularly thought-provoking and inspiring session, he was smiling as wide as I had ever seen anyone smile. "We just keep setting the bar higher and higher," he told us. "And we just keep clearing it!"

Effects of this Project on the Funder Who Started It

The Learning Community quickly became a source of energy and encouragement through the simple act of sharing the group's collective experience and wisdom. By mid-year, they had begun meeting at each other's facilities, touring and learning from each other on each of their home turfs. They built friendship and trust. They began adding others to the group to both expand the conversation and further leverage the impact of the group.

There was another side to this effort, though. That was the effect of this process on the funder who had initiated it in the first place. Participating in this process created as much, if not more, impact on SLHI than on any of the other individual participants.

First, there were the changes to SLHI's entire grant process. What had begun as a one-time approach to a one-time grant cycle has become the year-round modus operandi at SLHI. Their grant process is now based on the mutual nurturing of ideas, on strength and interconnection. The process is defining results through the lens of resiliency and health - through the vision SLHI has for the future of the community - rather than on problem-solving.

Secondly, a big issue that arose during this initial year revolved around the organizational infrastructure that would be required within individual *organizations*, if this effort was to effect significant *community* change. Those doing that work - Community Benefit Organizations of all shapes and sizes - would need technical assistance in these new approaches. However, there are few consultants who know how to work in this way. By the end of the first year, therefore, SLHI had begun convening another Learning Community - one for local consultants who wanted to explore doing vision-based, strength-based, resiliency-based consulting.

Numerous issues such as these arose during this first year of Health in a New Key's Learning Community. In each case, the end goal was always the driving force behind the decision. Will it bring us closer to building a healthy, resilient community, with strong efforts towards making that happen? Then those are the steps we must take.

Health in a New Key: Epilogue

With the excitement of Year 1 behind them, the Health in a New Key Learning Community worked together to decide what the participants wanted to accomplish in Year 2. This was another big change from what tends to be the norm for funders, as funders are accustomed to making many of these strategic decisions themselves, rather than asking the group and following the group's wishes.

As we have told the story of this Learning Community to groups of funders in our travels, they often comment about the individual decisions made by SLHI, noting the significance of each of those decisions. Changing their grant process to focus on vision, strength, connection, values. Including everyone in the Learning Community who wished to participate. Sitting at the table as participants and learners in the process, rather than guiding the process.

Having worked with SLHI for almost ten years now, in a variety of capacities, we have come to realize that it is not those individual decisions that make their work so successful. It is instead the vision and values that guide everything they do. And their mission? It is not "to provide funding for healthcare." It is to serve as a catalyst for creating a healthy, resilient place to live.

As a catalyst, there was no other choice in the minds of SLHI staff but to have the Learning Community choose its own path for Year 2. It was not a matter of control, but of aligning their actions behind their end goal of creating that visionary change.

When Vision, Mission and Values govern the work we do - whether that work is to govern an individual organization, or to lead a community-wide effort in a community of 4 million people - it becomes more and more evident that this approach is the only logical road to take.

Chapter 45:
The Pollyanna Principles in Action: Convening for Community Results

Pollyanna Principle #6 notes that people will go where systems lead them. The systems in this section are similar to the systems used in individual organizations - planning, governing, engaging. The results of using those systems is obviously magnified, as the scope of the projects is magnified. While we could have logically predicted that would occur in these larger settings, it is still exciting each time we experience the extent of those results.

> **Pollyanna Principle #1:**
> We accomplish what we hold ourselves accountable for.
>
> **Pollyanna Principle #2:**
> Each and every one of us is creating the future, every day, whether we do so consciously or not.

As has been mentioned throughout this book, the context of the larger vision for our communities is the point at which virtually all of us agree. However, when we talk about this topic with experts in the sector, we are often told stories that purport to disprove that sense of solidarity of vision. Here is an example, as told to us from the counseling world:

> "We were in a session with service providers, trying to create a collective vision for the service we provide. But after 2 hours, people were simply more entrenched in their positions. Those who believe service should be ongoing and free were on one side of the room, while those who believe in the fee-for-service approach were on the other side."

Upon close examination, however, it is clear that these groups were not discussing their vision for success in the community, but the more self-centered vision for their particular portion of the sector. The example above is not focusing on how the community would look, but how the services themselves would look.

The focus of both the Family Financial Security Summit and the Health in a New Key Learning Community were just the opposite of that narrow focus on "what we do." Both efforts first focused outward on the future they sought to create for their communities. They then focused on the cause-and-effect conditions in those communities. Only then did they address changes within the sector, the industry, an individual organization.

When we reach towards a vision for our communities, we find common ground. As happened with both the diverse groups described in this section, *the groups self-inspired to hold themselves accountable for bringing that visionary condition to reality.* That shared vision for the community became the assumption and the expectation upon which systems could be built for moving forward.

Clearly, though, the height of holding oneself accountable was seen in the challenge put forth by Reno Police Officer O'Bryan. "If you're comfortable, then nothing will change. To change our community, we need to step outside our comfort zone. So are we willing to be uncomfortable?"

As we saw from the businessman who approached us at the end of the Family Financial Security Summit, taking a vision-based approach to planning is itself sometimes a step outside the comfort zone. There is comfort in talking about today, with less comfort in considering the future we have the power to create.

When we think it is impossible to create social change, we stay inside the comfort zone and do not even try. But when we change our expectations - realizing that if something is not scientifically impossible, it is possible - we self-inspire to hold ourselves accountable for achieving what is possible. That is when we begin to see results.

> **Pollyanna Principle #3:**
> Everyone and everything is interconnected and interdependent,
> whether we acknowledge that or not.

If we were to condense the lessons of the Family Financial Security Summit and the Health in a New Key Learning Community into one word, that word would be "together." Clearly both efforts were focused on building something together that could not be built individually. In truth, though, that is one of the facts of community change that has been proven repeatedly since the dawn of the ages; that no one person or entity can create significant community (or regional, or national, or global) change without such an effort being far larger than just that one person or entity.

Each of these efforts ignored the narrowly defined niches and silos that often divide the various parts of this sector. The narrow definition of mission was ignored when St. Luke's Health Initiatives chose to include any effort that would somehow contribute to building a healthy community. A narrow focus on financial issues was eschewed at the Family Financial Security Summit, in favor of the more inclusive focus on what might cause stability in all its various forms.

When we assume we are separate, we build systems that reinforce that separateness. When we assume we are interconnected and interdependent, we build systems that reinforce those connections.

Because everyone and everything is, in fact, interconnected, and because we all want the same bright future for our communities, that collective power becomes just one more strength upon which to build the future we envision. Truly we are what we think!

Walking the talk is one thing when it is just your organization creating a values statement and adhering to it (or not). It is a whole different ball game when values are publicly on display through a group effort.

We saw the importance of discussing those values when the assembled individuals at the Family Financial Security Summit chose to focus so much of their time discussing issues such as quality of life and other matters of the spirit. We saw it as they openly took time to bare their souls a bit, to reflect on what they were thinking and learning during the process. We especially saw it in the values-based challenge to step outside the comfort zone - to walk the talk of the change they wanted to see in their communities.

Modeling the behaviors they want to see in others has been especially apparent in the Health in a New Key effort. Funders and consultants are both accustomed to being deferred to, accustomed to being in control. However, the Learning Community was intended to build upon the wisdom of each and every person in the group, allowing control to be owned by the group. Walking the talk therefore included both the explicit and implicit mandate to lead this group to self-leadership.

At the end of the Learning Community's first year, we met with the SLHI staff to determine the goals for Year 2. The questions raised during that discussion were not the kinds of questions funders often address: Who owns this effort? And from that, whose decision should it be to determine the goals for the upcoming year?

Yes, SLHI had provided grant funding to some of the participants. Yes, they funded our facilitating the group. They had also funded their own staff time, the meeting space, and importantly, they funded the food! (How can one expect an open gathering of minds and hearts without food?)

But did that make the effort "theirs?" Or did this effort that started out as theirs now belong to the group? And what did that mean?

As they returned to the values at the core of the effort, SLHI determined that Year 2's goals were not theirs to decide. As long as the effort continued to aim at the vision of a healthy, resilient community, the Learning Community participants themselves had to be the ones to determine the specifics of what they would accomplish that year.

Wow. The funder who had initiated and maintained the effort, and who was continuing to do so, was intentionally choosing not to micromanage the effort's next steps.

St. Luke's Health Initiatives had instigated this effort, and they were facilitating it. It had been their initial goals and their dollars that had started this effort. And they consciously decided to give up control over the group's immediate purpose, giving that control to the group itself. Their mission - to be a catalyst for community health - was being backed up by their values, all aimed at their vision for a healthy, resilient community.

The larger the effort, the more necessary it is to know one's values up front, and to lead by instituting systems that reinforce those values at every step.

Pollyanna Principle #5:
Strength builds upon our strengths, not our weaknesses.

When considering community assets and strengths, this sector tends to quickly acknowledge the "hard" assets one might find in the community, much like those that were engaged to build the Diaper Banks. Typically included in that list of assets are both physical assets (such as buildings) and human assets (for their volunteer capabilities, their connections, their overall desire to assist).

There are, however, considerable community strengths and assets that are often overlooked - assets that, when engaged, are perhaps the most powerful of all.

First, there are the multiple non-financial assets funders bring to our communities.

Ask funders what they bring to the table in changing their communities, and most will talk about their dollars. In truth, though, a funder's real strength comes from the other assets they posses - assets they frequently do not even realize they have.

Every funder, from Bill Gates to the smallest individual donor, has more power to convene and engage the community than they have money. While those dollars are absolutely needed, the convening and engagement are needed as well.

When funders invite, people show up. And given what we are all able to accomplish together that we could not accomplish alone, the power to convene is a funder's greatest strength - far greater than the influence of their dollars.

Another equally valuable hidden strength is the wisdom everyone in our communities can bring to the cause of building healthy, vibrant, humane places to live. Both the efforts described in this section are evidence of the value of that wisdom.

From the beginning, the goal of the Health in a New Key Learning Community was to build upon that wisdom, to enhance the efforts of each of the individual participants, enhancing their individual results. The further goal was to leverage that considerable asset to the community at large, to build new learning and even more wisdom.

During the Family Financial Security Summit, groups from the same organization were intentionally split up, and the traditionally more "powerful" players - funders, sponsors - were assigned to separate groups. The intent was, again, to provide as much opportunity for everyone to feel comfortable to share their knowledge, their experience, their wisdom. The energy that arose from that sharing was a significant strength from which to kick off the group's subsequent efforts.

When systems do not focus on one party as "the expert," then everyone can be the expert. They then find incredible strength in the expertise that is shared.

Chapter 46:
Cooperative Funding and Capacity Building

"Competition and scarcity as reality" is almost a given in the world of funders and grants. While funders lament that competition, they tell us they have no choice. "We certainly don't have enough money to fund everyone. If we don't use a competitive process, how would we decide who to fund?"

The issue of competition extends to capacity building as well. As much as the sector seems to agree that collaboration is a great way of doing community-focused work, they seem to equally agree that collaboration would be almost impossible in the area of capacity building. After all, if capacity building is about building organizational strength, isn't that, almost by definition, proprietary?

As you might expect by the time you have come this far in this book, the answer is that some of the most effective funding initiatives we have seen have eschewed competition altogether, finding ways to indeed fund everyone.

In addition, the most effective capacity building initiatives we have seen have been done as collaborative efforts. These approaches are not only more cost effective, but more effective overall in their results.

Non-competitive funding and collaborative capacity building are therefore more than simply *"not impossible."* They are systems for building a collective community strength that is far stronger than any one individual effort could achieve.

It is exciting to consider the kinds of exponential leaps forward our communities could make if such systems were the norm rather than the exception.

Funding Everyone:
Hospital Emergency Rooms
Community Health Endowment, Lincoln, Nebraska

Lincoln, Nebraska's healthcare foundation, the Community Health Endowment, formed as the result of the sale of Lincoln General Hospital. Unlike St. Luke's Health Initiatives, which had been a nonprofit hospital, Lincoln General had been owned by the city government. The resulting foundation has a fifteen person community-based board of trustees appointed by the Mayor of Lincoln, which is charged specifically with administering the funds. Knowing those funds belong not to a private endowment but to the people of Lincoln, the organization proactively and aggressively holds itself accountable to the community, both for fiscal transparency and to show it is creating impact with those dollars.

In 2003, Lori Seibel, President and CEO of the Community Health Endowment, was approached by one of the three area hospitals for funding to address the fact that an increasing number of residents were using the hospital's emergency room for their primary care. Because healthcare is expensive in the United States, and many individuals have neither health insurance nor, as a result, a primary care doctor, this has become a critical issue for every hospital across the U.S.

The result is an overload on the entire emergency system, including tremendously long wait times, overworked staffs, and the hospital's inability to receive payment for these visits - all due to the overwhelming number of emergency room visits for ailments that are not really emergencies. In addition, emergency room care is not conducive to providing continuity of care, resulting in poorer health outcomes for these patients.

When the funding request came in, Lori knew this was a critical issue. But she also knew what the result would be if the Community Health Endowment funded this request: The applicant hospital would "casework" those patients away, only to have them show up in the emergency departments of the other two area hospitals.

So Lori did what funders rarely do. She told the hospital that the Community Health Endowment would fund the project under one condition - that the project be a group effort of all the area hospitals, to find a community-wide solution. The Community Health Endowment would provide not only the funding, but the facilitation, the meeting space, and whatever other non-financial support would assist in making the project a success.

The Project: E.D. Connections

As noted throughout this book, successful collaborations rely on a spirit of cooperation, rather than the financial mechanism of collaboration. In Lori's words, it took a year of "dating and courtship" for the representatives of the hospitals to get to know each other, feel comfortable with each other, and build trust. "Writing the check was the easy part," Lori says of the $300,000 in funding provided by CHE over three years for E.D. Connections (E.D. for Emergency Department). The not-so-easy part kept the Community Health Endowment busy playing the roles of facilitator, mediator and troubleshooter. They brought the parties together, did research, and kept minutes of the proceedings.

By the end of the effort to get E.D. Connections off the ground, the hospitals were sharing records and personnel management, and sharing the effort to find a "Medical Home" for the non-emergency patients that were using their facilities. They defined a Medical Home as a doctor's office or clinic where the medical personnel consider the patient to be "their patient."

The goals for E.D. Connections were ambitious - a 50% reduction in costs related to 'non-emergency' Emergency Room care, and a 50% decrease in the number of visits. The actual results exceeded those goals significantly. Visits were down 65% *just in the first year*, and costs were reduced 63% - saving $600,000 *in that first year alone*. There has also been a significant impact on costs associated with ambulance and emergency medical services.

More importantly, 100% of those who were using the Emergency Room as their primary care now have a Medical Home - a doctor or clinic they can rely upon for those non-emergency matters. In addition, 100% of those individuals now have prescription assistance as well.

As E.D. Connections nears the end of the three-year funding provide by the Community Health Endowment, another indication of the project's success has occurred. The hospitals have jointly committed to financially support the continuation of E.D. Connections into the future and to pursue additional collaborations to address other pressing health issues.

"In the midst of a highly competitive healthcare environment, this is a true testament to the mighty power of collaboration," Lori told me. "But it is important to note that our role in this has not been the primary role. We took the time, and sometimes we took the lumps. But one thing we can't take is the credit for what was accomplished. That goes entirely to the partners who sat at the table. They had everything to gain and everything to lose, and they are the ones who made this happen."

As we have seen over and over, though, it took the ability of the funder to see through a different lens to make that all happen. When she did, it happened more quickly than anyone could have imagined.

Funding Everyone:
Collaborative Capacity Building
Technical Assistance Partnership
St. Luke's Health Initiatives, Phoenix, Arizona

If there is anything considered to be proprietary in the world of Community Benefit Organizations, it is "Capacity Building." Because Capacity Building is the term used for building the internal capacity of an organization, it is by definition, all about the "me" or "us" of building a strong organization.

Much of the work emphasized in Capacity Building is assumed to be competitive. Learning to raise money is obviously considered competitive, as is marketing - gaining the competitive advantage that tells a donor why he/she should give to your organization rather than another. Board development and volunteer management also have a competitive bent, as the "good ones" are frequently considered to be in short supply, and the demand for those "few good ones" is steep.

Capacity Building is therefore not typically seen as a group activity.

Unless, of course, the group spearheading the Capacity Building is St. Luke's Health Initiatives. Always a step ahead, the Technical Assistance Partnership at SLHI places most of its emphasis on the word "Partnership."

The Project: The Technical Assistance Partnership (TAP)
The Technical Assistance Partnership at SLHI has become a hallmark of how a foundation can leverage its dollars to create significant community impact, by funding everyone who applies.

Here's how it works:

Several times a year, SLHI announces a TAP Talk Meeting - a gathering of all organizations who are interested in getting technical assistance for any facet of their work. As long as their mission in some way addresses building a healthy community, groups are welcome to participate.

Attendees split off into groups based on what they want to learn. Those interested in planning might gather in one area; those interested in board development in another area; those interested in technology enhancement in another area; and so on.

The organizations in those groups become a team. Team members determine specifically what they want to accomplish, and SLHI provides a consultant or other professional to assist all of them together in gaining that expertise.

The results are staggering. Yes, organizations learn and grow, gaining the knowledge they would have gained had they hired a consultant on their own. But there is so much more! The TAP teams build on the knowledge and wisdom of the teammates, providing an ongoing source of support. SLHI reports that some of their TAP teams are still meeting regularly, years after SLHI stopped providing professional assistance. That happens because the participants find value not just in the professional guidance, but in each other.

The dollars invested in this program prove that funding everyone does not have to be pricey. In 2007, 150 individuals representing 128 organizations received capacity building assistance through participation on a TAP team. The total expense for that effort was $155,000, or $1,200 per organization. It does not take much to know that a grant of $1,200 per organization for capacity building would buy virtually nothing if it were doled out individually.

In a wonderful irony, by funding everyone, SLHI is able to accomplish more for $1,200 per organization than many funders are able to accomplish for ten times that amount.

But the money is not the whole story for TAP. The more important story has meaning far beyond the financial statements - the evidence that Capacity Building does not have to be a solitary act. In fact, TAP proves that Capacity Building can be far more effective when done as a group effort, where a Learning Community and group support are added to the benefit of just getting a consultant to get the job done.

Evaluation of the TAP project has been ongoing, as St. Luke's Health Initiatives measures the program's effectiveness year after year. But TAP participants do not need to see evidence as measured by SLHI. They know the impact the program has, and they tell their stories loud and clear, to anyone who will listen, repeatedly using the same words: *"We would not be nearly as effective if it weren't for TAP."*

Funding Everyone:
Collaborative Capacity Building and Collaborative Funding
Woods Charitable Fund and the
Lincoln Community Foundation, Lincoln, Nebraska

Some of the most innovative collaborative work we have seen as we have traveled across the U.S. has been in communities ranging from 250,000 to 500,000 in population. Lincoln, Nebraska, is one of those communities.

In addition to the Community Health Endowment's success in its group funding strategy, a partnership between Woods Charitable Fund and the Lincoln Community Foundation has proven to be another ground-breaker in the annals of funding capacity building.

First, the project was initiated by two funders, working together to see what might happen if they partnered on a project from its inception. While such collaboration is encouraged for on-the-ground provider organizations, the same collaboration is not common in the funding world. Typically, collaborations among funders begin when a proposed project needs more funding than one funder can (or wants to) provide, and generally occurs because that grantee has "shopped" the project to more than one funder. It is rare that funders initiate such a joint effort on their own.

The second intriguing aspect of this effort is that the foundations chose a Capacity Building initiative as the place to begin. Even more intriguing, they chose to create a Capacity Building Partnership, rather than fund individual Capacity Building efforts - another case of a group process aimed at accomplishing work that has, to date, been considered one-on-one work.

Lincoln's Capacity Building Partners
Deb Shoemaker of the Lincoln Community Foundation and
Pam Baker of Woods Charitable Fund are friends who had spent considerable time talking about the various issues facing their community. From those discussions, they decided to take a new idea to

their boards of directors: The two foundations would hand-pick five organizations, across disciplines, across organizational age and size, and across levels of "readiness." They would then provide joint funding and convening for the leaders of those five groups to learn together for two years.

While Pam and Deb identified some capacity issues based on their assessments of these organizations, it was up to the organizations themselves to determine what assistance they felt they needed. From there, Pam and Deb would work together, bringing in outside experts where necessary, to guide the various capacity building initiatives.

The group would meet every eight weeks, and the work would be intensive. After two years, they would see what happened.

Like the results St. Luke's Health Initiatives saw with the TAP program, the results of this effort have been noteworthy. The organizations stayed together and grew together, learning from each other as well as from the gathered experts. (In the interests of full disclosure, we were one of the groups of experts brought in to teach governance to the five organizations.) The organization initially considered to be the most "at risk" was the one that, in the end, became the shining example of how such an effort could help turn a group around.

At the end of the two years, the organizations asked the funders if they could have a third year to work specifically on fund development. Yes, they chose the most competitive of competitive work as the focus of their additional year of learning together!

Like the other two examples in this section, the funders saw their role as far more than just providing funding. Their primary role was as convener. As we have noted throughout this book, that role is one of the most community-effective and cost-effective roles a funder can undertake.

Chapter 47:
Funding and Capacity Building - The Pollyanna Principles in Action

At this point, you, the reader, can apply the Pollyanna Principles to do your own analysis of these efforts.

First, all parties began to hold themselves squarely accountable for Community-Driven results, quantitatively and qualitatively measuring outcomes. While it is easy to see in the hospital scenario that the results were aimed at the community, rather than any individual organization, the same community focus holds true in the arena of capacity building, an effort that traditionally has almost no focus outside an individual organization's four walls. Clearly these efforts built community capacity while building organizational capacity.

In addition, these efforts all held themselves accountable for aligning their means behind their desired end results. They built on their inherent connectedness as a significant strength, and then created strength-based approaches to build even higher. All three efforts walked their talk, with the funders learning alongside the participants. In the words of Lori Seibel of Lincoln's Community Health Endowment, "We learned along with them, grew with them, taking the time to let them help us be smarter."

Most importantly, all three efforts focused on challenging and changing systems that the sector has simply assumed to be "the way it is done." As a result of challenging those systems, more effective approaches emerged.

Funding everyone. Collective capacity building rather than individual capacity building. Funder-initiated collaborative funding. Using the power of convening to leverage the power of their dollars.

The difference is not just a tweak here or there; it is a different way of seeing and being. All four funders in these stories changed the way they saw reality, and with that, reality changed - for them as funders, for the participants in their projects, and for the communities they hold themselves accountable for serving.

Part 5

Creating the Path
to the
Future We Want

What's Next?

Chapter 48
What's Next

Individuals will go where systems lead them.

From our brief celebration of the dramatic difference that is possible when systems are built around the Pollyanna Principles - both systems for individual organizations and systems for larger efforts - one thing becomes clear: There is much work still to be done.

This section will therefore focus on the question, "What's next?"

What other systems might be explored, to ensure that the work of Community Benefit Organizations is aimed at and aligned behind creating an extraordinary future for our communities?

How can we create sector-wide infrastructure for encouraging, supporting and mobilizing the dramatic community improvement this sector is capable of achieving?

This section addresses the following two sets of issues:

- Recommendations for Community-Wide Infrastructure
- Recommendations for Further Experimentation

The suggestions in this section are not intended to be a comprehensive list. On the contrary, we hope these ideas will get your own creative juices flowing, to consider what other systems might assist the work of Community Benefit Organizations to improve their communities - to provide support to continue aiming in the direction we all want to go.

An in-depth consideration of each of these systems might require a book just for that purpose. The entries here are therefore intended as thought-starters, to encourage conversation and consideration of these important next steps in the ongoing evolution of Community Benefit work.

Chapter 49:
Community-Wide Infrastructure

My very wise friend, Mark Myers, read an early draft of *The Pollyanna Principles*. In one of our many conversations about the manuscript, as we focused on the issue of Community Infrastructure, Mark asked me, "What was the most important thing Thomas Edison invented?"

His answer: The electric utility.

"Edison invented all sorts of tools we still use today," Mark said. "But the most enduring and life-changing was the development of the infrastructure."

Our communities already have infrastructure for our basic needs - police and fire, roads, water, power, sewer. Beyond those basic needs, we have infrastructure for schools and libraries, for parks, for economic development activities.

Imagine the dramatic results we would see in our communities if there was also infrastructure for the work being done to improve our quality of life!

Systems that would strengthen the capacity of communities to constantly be striving for "extraordinary" would include Community Infrastructure for

- Convening

- Resource Sharing Systems

- Measurement / Evaluation

- Learning Communities / Communities of Practice

- Collaborative Funding of Issues

- Organizational Support

"Self-Supporting" Supports No One

Before diving in to enumerate the various systems our communities need for creating the path to community improvement, it is important to be firm about one thing: The notion that any of these systems should be self-supporting is both ridiculous and self-defeating.

We do not expect that Fire Protection or Police Protection or Libraries or Parks or Economic Development efforts will be self-supporting. We acknowledge that this infrastructure is simply what responsible communities provide for their citizens.

If what is stopping our communities from being considerably improved is a lack of community-wide infrastructure to support such efforts, then it is time we figure out *how we can* have such infrastructure, instead of reciting the various excuses for *why we can't.*

The ongoing drumbeat that such efforts somehow be self-supporting comes from the Culture of Can't. "We can't afford it. Where do you think the money will come from? We would love to, but there are other more pressing priorities right now."

If we need libraries and public schools, and we acknowledge that we would not want to live in a community that had neither, then we need to acknowledge that the same thinking applies to the infrastructure that will improve the quality of every single aspect of our lives. "Pay as you go" and "memberships" and other organizational survival mechanisms turn community infrastructure into just one more competitive, lose-lose game.

So walk the talk. Find the funding. And create infrastructure you would never let die - for everyone.

THAT is the Culture of CAN. That is creating our future. That is aligning our means behind the end results we want for our communities.

Community Infrastructure for Convening

If creating community improvement is reliant on developing a more cooperative environment, our communities will need infrastructure dedicated to convening and facilitating those efforts.

Most of us have seen great cooperative beginnings falter, simply because none of the individual participants could spare the kind of time required for the ongoing care and feeding of a group process. As a result, the very core of creating community change - bringing groups together to build trust and work together - has become entirely reliant on the good will and "not in the budget / on top of everything else I am already doing" volunteer work of one of the participating group members. As soon as day-to-day life intervenes, that "extra project" first begins to be postponed, and eventually fades to the land of "whatever happened to...?"

If cooperation is critical to creating the kind of community improvement organizations have the potential to create, then responsible community leaders will hold themselves accountable for developing systems that encourage and support that cooperative environment. Such infrastructure might include:

- Physical meeting / convening space
- Facilitators skilled in multi-organizational facilitation, for any groups who want to work together towards creating community change
- Education and skill-building in working cooperatively
- Technology for ongoing communication

Whether such systems are housed at a Community Foundation or a Nonprofit Resource Center, having reliable community systems for convening significantly improves the chances that *working together* will become "just the way our community does things."

Such systems are both mission-effective and cost-effective. They are rooted in interconnectedness rather than competition. They are built upon the strengths of all those participating. They are systems that allow community leaders to walk their talk, creating a cooperative, interconnected environment.

Community Infrastructure for Resource Sharing

To ensure programs can be built upon a base of shared resources, communities will need infrastructure to facilitate resource sharing.

Systems for sharing resources - co-locating, sharing information, etc. - have been a critical component to innovations in the field of technology, where participants realized early on that many brilliant minds learning together made everyone's efforts stronger. If such resource sharing can work in the highly competitive field of technology, imagine the impact among groups whose primary motivation is not competitive advantage, but community change!

Water cooler discussions, technology and other systems for sharing information and resources - these are the kinds of systems that eliminate much of the need for competition in the first place. Such infrastructure might include:

- Training in how to create programs based on shared resources
- Facilitation to assist with that task (and perhaps ongoing coaching, mentoring, guidance)
- Shared databases to identify who has what resources
- Assistance with community engagement guidance
- Convening / meeting space
- Incubator space for start-up efforts
- Co-location space for more mature, like-kind efforts
- Communications tools / technology for sharing of information
- Systems for facilitating fiscal sponsorship

Rather than making these components the responsibility of individual organizations who may or may not have the skills, the budget, or the time to make "sharing of resources" happen, responsible community leaders will create systems that make the sharing of resources "just the way things are done around here."

Such infrastructure is both mission-effective and cost-effective. It is one more step community leaders can take to hold themselves accountable for creating the future they want for their communities.

Community Infrastructure for Evaluation / Measurement

The issue of "evaluation" is addressed further in the next section re: the need for future experimentation and study. But regardless of how we measure or what we measure, one thing is certain: It is in the best interests of our communities to develop systems for community-wide measurement, towards the end goal of improving all of our work every day, to hone our skills and efforts to ensure we are improving our communities.

While program-level change - measuring the impact of an individual program on individual lives - is possible within an individual organization, measuring community change requires a shared commitment to why we are measuring in the first place - the future we want to ensure we are creating. It requires shared discussion of what is important, what indicators we, as whole communities, want to measure.

Imagine the benefits of such ongoing, systematized discussion, in and of itself!

The ability to move everyone forward together is an inspiring reason to have a community-wide repository for shared data - someone to gather the data, sort it, and make it available to those who need it.

It is also an inspiring reason to ensure everyone has the ability to collect that data, to be sure it is available to be shared! And as is commonly understood among organizations who struggle with such efforts, the ability to collect data in a meaningful way is currently not in place in many (most?) individual organizations.

The record keeping, analysis, investigation and overall documentation / reporting required to measure well (or, to be honest, even to measure poorly) can be staggering, especially for a small organization. If it is important to measure, not for the sake of individual organizations acquiring funding, but for the sake of whole communities holding themselves accountable for creating a better future for our world, then it will be critical that communities determine how such measurement can be better accomplished.

By making measurement and evaluation a community-wide function rather than solely an organizational function, such measurement will be elevated to its own highest potential - helping Community Benefit efforts accomplish more significant change. Rather than being used as a tool for organizational justification, evaluation and measurement will be used as tools for community change.

Whether such a function is housed at a Community Foundation or City Hall, a more institutionalized, community-wide system for measuring the effectiveness of efforts to improve conditions in our communities would be a big step towards ensuring we are making progress in creating the extraordinary future we all want.

Community Infrastructure for Learning Communities / Communities of Practice

Growing out of the theme of convening is the theme of building Learning Communities or Communities of Practice - two different terms for what is commonly the same type of effort.

Simply put, a Learning Community / Community of Practice is a group of individuals who learn from each other and with each other on an ongoing basis, with the goal of improving their work.

The value of creating community infrastructure for the ongoing facilitation of Learning Communities goes beyond adding to the individual knowledge of each member. That value also goes beyond the shared learning of all group members. As we saw with the Health in a New Key effort in Chapter 44, some of the most exciting results are the development of new wisdom, and the development of the kinds of deep trust that lead to strong, engaged partnerships.

Learning Communities / Communities of Practice are asset-builders. They build learning upon learning, and trust upon trust. They build wisdom upon the wisdom of those in the group, and then leverage that to create not only more and more wisdom, but to share that wisdom with those outside the immediate group.

As a result, Learning Communities are inspirational systems. These are wisdom-building systems that inspire participants to learn more, to bring new wisdom to the group, and to bring their questions in a spirit of trust and cooperation. In a Learning Community, everyone is learning together, teaching together, building higher together.

It therefore makes infinite sense that, in addition to community-wide infrastructure for convening in general, community leaders create infrastructure specifically for the development and convening of community-focused Learning Communities.

Community-Wide Learning Communities for Boards

Imagine this: In every community, the norm among Community Benefit Organizations is that boards are focused on creating extraordinary community results, and that they know how to lead and govern towards that. If that is the future we all want for boards, one of the conditions that must be in place is the ongoing convening of a community's board members, to learn together, share together, build trust together and focus together on the big picture.

It is not uncommon for communities to have some type of support system for Executive Directors. That might take the form of a monthly ED Brown Bag or Roundtable. But it is the rare community that has the infrastructure in place to provide that support for board members.

As a sector, we can continue to blame boards for all that is not working. Or we can realize that being the volunteer leader of an organization whose day-to-day work is dramatically different from the board member's own day-to-day work and experience requires ongoing learning, ongoing encouragement, and ongoing support.

A one-day workshop, or a single training, book or event will not develop the skills board members need to do their work.

Boards, organizations and communities would benefit tremendously from community-wide systems that provide a safe place, where board members from different boards with different missions could learn together and learn from each other. In such a Learning Community, high expectations for creating a visionary future could be re-inspired and supported with practical tools.

Most importantly, board members would finally have a place where they could talk honestly and openly about something they rarely get to discuss, especially with those from outside their own board: They could talk about what it means to govern.

Community Infrastructure for Collaborative Funding of Issues

Given the powerful impact of collaborative funding, it is in everyone's best interest that our communities develop infrastructure to facilitate and support collaborative funding, in all its various meanings.

In some communities, well-established Funder Roundtables meet monthly, with 30 different funding groups attending. Elsewhere, the number of regular participants is three or five. And in some communities, we are asked, "What do you mean, a Funders Group?"

Funder Groups have the potential to produce far too much community benefit for there not to be such infrastructure in every community. At the very least, such groups can meet regularly to get to know each other's priorities, each other's styles, each other's frustrations.

Beyond just networking and building trust, Funder Groups have the ability to explore community issues of common concern. They have the ability to learn together. They have the power to collaboratively fund efforts based on community-focused outcomes.

When we facilitate Funder Roundtable Discussions in the communities we visit, we ask funders, "Do you encourage collaboration among your grantees?" Their resounding answer is, of course, yes.

When we ask our follow up question, though - "Do you all collaborate yourselves, as funders?" - the answer is again resounding. "No."

Walking the talk. Modeling the behaviors we want to see. Being that change. Teaching by example.

If the only purpose for developing community infrastructure for funder collaboration was to have funders hold themselves accountable to the same standards they are expecting from their grantees, this would be a wise move.

However, the best reason for developing such systems goes beyond just walking the talk. The best reason has to do with the potential those funders have together, that none has individually. When funders aim their collective power at the long-term outcomes they want to see in their community, they are realizing the power of their interconnectedness and their shared strength.

And because individuals will go where systems lead them, creating community-wide systems that facilitate, support and encourage funder cooperation and collaboration simply makes sense.

Community Infrastructure for Organizational Support

I have mentioned throughout this book that the current system under which "Nonprofit" Resource Centers operate, at least in the U.S., is in need of reconsideration.

As we rework this critical infrastructure component, here is how that restructuring might look if the Pollyanna Principles were used to create truly Community-Driven management support organizations - Community Benefit Resource Centers.

- Leaders of Community Benefit Resource Centers would hold themselves accountable for creating the future of their communities - a future where Community Benefit efforts have the knowledge and support they need to do their work, because that work is what will make our communities extraordinary places to live. (Pollyanna Principles #1 & #2)

- Leaders of Community Benefit Resource Centers would ensure everyone is working together to make that infrastructure possible, because we all benefit from that infrastructure being there. A food bank recipient and an arts patron all benefit if the Community Benefit Sector is strong. The business community benefits. We all benefit. (Interconnectedness - Pollyanna Principle #3)

- Community Benefit Resource Centers would model the behaviors they want to see among the organizations they support, and throughout their communities. They would teach approaches that aim towards community improvement, rejecting those approaches that encourage competition, that encourage boards to aim at means over ends, etc. (Pollyanna Principle #4)

- Community Benefit Resource Centers would focus on their own measurable outcomes, again, walking the talk of what they are teaching. (Pollyanna Principle #4)

- Community Benefit Resource Centers would not have to go begging for funds. They would not have to use fundraising means that go counter to the end results of serving everyone (memberships), just to make ends meet. They would not be placed in scarcity mode by the very communities that rely on them for building a strong Community Benefit Sector. Community Benefit Resource Centers would instead be collaboratively built and would be maintained as an ongoing fixture in the community - considered as important to the ongoing health of the community as the library, the parks and recreation department, the community college. (Pollyanna Principle #5)

Such systems would pave the way for the Sector to become all it can become, and to be all it can be, on an ongoing basis.

"Nonprofit" Resource Centers are currently the sector's teachers. They are also often the equivalent of the sector's healthcare system - the part of the sector that keeps individual efforts strong and healthy.

The work of Community Benefit Organizations deserves the very best educational support, and the very best "healthcare" possible, on an ongoing basis. The investment in such infrastructure benefits everyone. Like the work of the public school system and the community economic development office, the work of Community Benefit Organizations improves the quality of life for everyone.

Summary - Community Infrastructure

When communities build infrastructure, they are creating the future of their communities.

Roads, power plants, utility lines, bridges, buildings - communities need that physical infrastructure now. But that infrastructure will also meet the community's physical needs tomorrow and the tomorrow after that.

Schools are about the future. Libraries are about the future. Yes, they create the intellectual infrastructure of our communities now, but they are really about building that intellectual infrastructure for tomorrow's citizens, and beyond.

Communities build business infrastructure both for today's needs and for building the future of those communities - economic development infrastructure, micro-lending infrastructure, small business assistance infrastructure.

Communities build recreational infrastructure as well - parks, ball fields and golf courses. We acknowledge that our current citizens need places to enjoy life and gather together, and that these are also critical components for the infrastructure of tomorrow.

The infrastructure described on the previous pages is the missing link in our communities - infrastructure for creating the social future of our communities.

Community Benefit Organizations do not compete because they want to. They do not struggle for organizational survival because they want to. Their boards do not "leave their brains at the door" because they want to. They do not "fail to work together" because they want to.

They do so because that is where the current systems have led them.

When communities find themselves in an endless cycle of patch-working old roads and schools and utility plants, they eventually realize, "We need to build what we *do* need, instead constantly trying to fix that old stuff."

The issue of having adequate infrastructure for the work of building extraordinary communities is precisely the same. It requires that we look beyond the individual problems and their symptoms-based "solutions" - that we look beyond the worn out prescriptive mandates that organizations "stop competing" and "start collaborating" and "get some board training."

The answer lies in building infrastructure - systems that will encourage and support the actions we do want, rather than fighting the ongoing battles against the symptoms we do not want. And the answer further lies in systems that will support affirming, vision-based, cooperative work, led by boards that are holding themselves accountable for achieving what is possible.

Unlike roads, schools and parks, the infrastructure components listed on the previous pages do not require a lot of money. What they require is that community leaders hold themselves accountable for creating the social future of their communities in the same way they hold themselves accountable for creating the physical, business, intellectual and recreational future of their communities.

Just as our community leaders want to see a well-educated, well-read population (school and library systems), with great jobs (economic development and business support systems), they can create infrastructure systems to support the kinds of community work that creates healthy, vibrant, humane places to live.

Building that infrastructure is an investment aimed at our highest potential to improve the quality of life in our communities, from the inside out, and from the bottom up. The investment itself is minuscule compared to the potential results.

We are creating the future. If we create that future with the current systems, we can be assured we will continue to experience (and be frustrated by) the same results (or lack thereof) that we currently see from this sector's work.

If, however, we build infrastructure to support cooperative, vision-based work in our communities, the sky really is the limit of what this sector's work could accomplish, in every community around the world.

Whether we choose to create such infrastructure or not, people will go where the systems lead them. The choice, as always, is up to us.

Chapter 50:
For Future Experimentation and Study

In developing the Community-Driven Institute, our vision has been nothing less than a healthy, compassionate, vibrant world. Our mission is therefore to ensure those working to create that healthy, compassionate, vibrant world have everything they need to get the job done.

Many conditions need to be in place for that reality to come to pass. Some of those conditions have been addressed in the section on community infrastructure. Some have been addressed by changing the assumptions and expectations behind the largest, most enveloping systems organizations use - governance, planning, program development and sustainability.

However, much remains to be done.

If, as a sector, we re-aim governance, there will still be a need to re-work management systems - systems that currently include a glass ceiling (and second-class organizational citizenship) for those whose primary focus is mission-related, rather than "management" focused.

If, as a sector, we restructure planning to aim at creating more visionary community change, current evaluation norms will still require that we measure what is often irrelevant data, for means-based reasons.

And if, sector-wide, boards refocus their own efforts, there will still remain siren song after siren song, calling them to the rocks of "means" over "ends."

Yes, there is considerable work still to be done, if the systems upon which our work relies are to all be aimed at ensuring strong, healthy, resilient efforts to make our communities extraordinary.

The following, then, are some of the areas where we have been considering what is possible and where we would love to see future experimentation and future study.

Broadening the Management Hierarchy

A young, caring person goes to college, gets a degree, and becomes a counselor at a mental health agency. Talented, bright, and compassionate, she makes a terrific counselor. She continues to study, taking every opportunity to advance her craft. She gets her Masters in Social Work, and eventually rises to Head Counselor in her division.

Devoted to making a difference in people's lives, she continues to bring new ideas and new vision to her division, always aiming the division at its potential to make that difference. She is promoted again, this time to Head of Clinical Services for the entire organization.

Suddenly her life is filled with management issues. She is encouraged to take Human Resources courses and financial management courses. She is encouraged to learn about budgeting. She spends hours in meetings about things that have nothing to do with patients, with the community, or with mental health.

Such is life in the Community Benefit Sector.

In many arts organizations, there are two separate career paths. One heads up the ladder on the "art" side of the organization; the other climbs up the "business" side of the house. While the system of "Artistic Director" and "Managing Director" is far from ideal - it is indeed a system fraught with tension and ongoing turnover - there is one thing to be said in its favor: It is a system that at least recognizes there are two sides of the house, and that the theater or symphony or dance company would indeed be nothing without a significant focus on the art - the mission.

Human service and other organizations have a long way to go in this area, as mission often seems wholly absent from the highest echelons of management. The "top floor" of non-arts organizations do not have anything remotely akin to the position of "Artistic Director." A role that might resemble a "Chief Mission Officer" simply does not exist.

If one remains dedicated to mission over management, there is indeed a glass ceiling limiting how far up the career ladder you will go. For organizations whose primary purpose is community benefit, that glass ceiling is a dangerous one, as mission, vision and values are so often divorced from the highest levels of decision-making.

Changing governance to focus first on mission, vision and values is a big step towards changing the balance between "business management" and "mission." Ultimately, however, for such change to have meaning throughout the organization, management systems must be reconsidered and restructured, to ensure the "top floor" of management includes at least as much emphasis on mission as it currently emphasizes the business side of the house.

Changing the Norm in Measurement

It is no secret that there is sector-wide dissatisfaction with the current state of program evaluation. The current focus on measuring short-term program effectiveness and accountability for funds is misdirected at best, and harmful at worst. Clearly there is a significant need to change the norms and expectations for measurement of individual programs.

The current norm in evaluation is scarcity-based. It is dollar-focused and attribution-focused (i.e. "If we collaborate, how can we prove our efforts were the ones that made the difference?"). Current approaches to program evaluation often feel downright punitive.

Current "evaluation" is routinely accused of measuring the wrong things. The image created by Distinguished Professor Joel Orosz on page 10 is haunting in its accuracy. "If we were to provide the typical one-year funding for a project to teach an infant to walk, we would declare the results marginal at best..."

As Chogyam Trungpa notes in Cutting through Spiritual Materialism (in a literary context that has nothing and everything to do with Community Benefit Organizations), "The basic problem we seem to be facing is that we are too involved with trying to prove something, which is connected with paranoia and a feeling of poverty. When you are trying to prove or get something, you are not open anymore, you have to check everything, and you have to arrange it "correctly." It is such a paranoid way to live and it really does not prove anything."

In our own work with Vision-Based Community Impact Planning, we have found that groups are relieved when they see that the small bite-sized goals in Phase 2 of the plan can be easily measured in the short term. But beyond measuring whether or not a short-term goal was accomplished, the only question that matters still remains unasked and thus unanswered: Are we changing the condition we hoped that "bite-sized goal" would change? Are we making any real difference at all?

The old adage is true: What gets measured indeed gets done. Imagine, then, what might "get done" if the norm in measurement (including measures of "organizational excellence") asked all programs to consider questions such as

- What is the change we are aiming for?
- How might we know if we are getting closer?
- How can we measure community health, wisdom, peace, beauty? Should we even try?
- What community benchmarks will help us determine if we are, in fact, building communities that are compassionate, resilient, connected?
- What indicators will show a community that feels spiritually whole and integrated?

Imagine that the norm in measurement is celebration and reflection! Imagine that the norm in measurement is an effort to determine what is working and not working, to determine progress towards both short-term and long-term goals. Imagine that the norm in measurement is that we learn from that measurement, and then apply what we learn to make things even better.

Imagine further that this is what was measured at every board meeting. Imagine a report, as common as the financial reports boards currently review, that reviewed progress on community-focused goals - progress on community change, progress on the difference the group seeks to make. Imagine such a report being the norm at every board meeting.

If we intend to hold ourselves accountable for creating the future of our communities, the next step must move beyond developing and using vision-based tools for planning. We must address the question of what and how we measure the effects of those plans, and how we make "measurement of our community end results and the difference we make in people's lives" the norm in measurement in the Community Benefit Sector.

Experimenting with the Day-to-Day of Board Work

From the tremendous results we have seen from our work with boards to date, we know there is more to be done, specifically regarding the ongoing sirens' songs that call boards away from a focus on ends, and out towards a focus on means.

As we work to focus the sector on its potential, we have looked to faith traditions for guidance in this area. I do not mean divine guidance (although that is always appreciated), but the guidance that comes from the thousands of years of tradition of the systems that remind us humans of our higher capacities.

There is a reason virtually every religion is focused around regular, often daily renewal and reminding practices - prayer, meditation. There is a reason such practices include, in virtually every religion, communal gathering under the guidance of a spiritual leader whose job it is to remind us of our potential to love each other, to treat each other with compassion.

Those who developed the world's faith systems learned a long long time ago that, left to our own devices, our hard-wired survival fears will override our humanity. As a result, in virtually every faith tradition, systems were developed to guard against the backsliding that stems from those reflexive behaviors. Those systems have included ongoing practice, the guidance of someone who has walked the same path and seen what is possible, and support from others who are practicing along with us.

What we would therefore encourage boards to do is nothing less than what every faith encourages us to do - set aside our fears and consciously choose the path that reflects our uniquely human potential to live together joyfully.

Regardless of the extent to which a board believes it is working from a vision-based mode, the tendency to react from means-based fear is overpoweringly strong.

The following are just some ideas intended to consciously counteract those tendencies.

Keeper of What Matters Most

One simple idea is to transform the role of "immediate past president" into the role of "Keeper of What Matters Most" - the organization's vision, mission and values.

The immediate past president is typically a seasoned board member, devoted to the cause. He or she has spent a year or two leading the board, having to be on top of his/her game at every board meeting, facilitating the discussion and leading the charge between meetings. Yet once their term is done, organizations tend to squander this incredible asset.

What better person to serve as Keeper of What Matters Most?

The job would require only that the "Keeper" listen to the board's discussions, and continually remind and guide that conversation back to the highest purpose of the organization. Because that higher potential is indeed the potential of this sector, the position of Keeper of What Matters Most would be the highest calling of board service. The impact of that position would be felt not only by the organization, but by the community overall.

Boards as Learning Communities

Years ago, as we began sharing the framework for Governing for What Matters publicly through our website, a specialist in Communities of Practice, Rosanna Tarsiero, sent me a note asking, "What if boards all considered themselves Communities of Practice - Learning Communities?" The thought has stuck in my mind since that time, and I credit Rosanna for suggesting it.

What if the culture of every board was a culture of learning? What if board members faced every issue with a spirit of curiosity? Imagine a board culture where board members expected to learn at every meeting - where they did not expect to "know the answer" to every issue raised, but to "learn the answer alongside everyone else at the board table, who is also learning."

The work being done by boards in this sector is new compared to the work of the business sector or the government sector. It is overpowering to consider the possibilities if every board of every organization saw its role as not only leading / governing the organization, but adding to the bigger discussion of what is possible, all the time.

Some steps in this area might include structuring time at every board meeting to focus on shared learning and reflection. It could be as simple as discussing topics that have arisen in past meetings, that the board did not feel it had enough time to explore. It might be as simple as having a time at every board meeting where board members share something they learned since the last meeting.

The point is that boards have the opportunity to experiment with being better learners. It is impossible to do that if the culture of a board encourages the volunteer non-professionals who lead the organization to pretend they know everything there is to know about that job. If instead boards embraced the opportunity to always be learning, the knowledge gained could be yet another powerful asset upon which to build.

If nothing else, board meetings would never be boring again!

Experimenting with Evaluation of Resource Development Efforts

When it comes to evaluating the results of Resource Development efforts, the experimenting is not so much the need to develop new approaches but to actually use any approach at all.

Perhaps every person reading this book could share a story of a fundraising effort that was marginally effective at best, but that was continued for years, regardless of its ineffectiveness. It usually takes the introduction of a new Executive Director to eliminate that sacred cow - often an annual event that, after factoring in staff time, actually loses money every year.

If the board is accountable for ensuring the organization has the means to accomplish visionary end results, squandering time and energy on less-than-effective fundraising systems is a luxury no organization can afford.

Therefore, as boards review budgets every year, having a universally recognized system for evaluating the effectiveness of each and every one of the organization's revenue-generating efforts would be a huge boon. Such systems would benefit individual organizations, the funders and donors who support those organizations, and ultimately would provide more benefit to our communities.

Experimenting with Cooperative Funding

Lastly, let's focus once more on the issue of cooperative funding. While the issue has been raised in various places throughout this book, the fact remains that there are few models of how such cooperative funding might work. That leaves significant room for exploring new approaches.

There are at least two broad categories of approaches to be explored. First, there is the category of funders coming together, to jointly provide funding, as well as non-cash support.

In addition there is the intriguing work that can be done by a single funder, to create non-competitive modes of funding, where everyone is funded - perhaps something akin to what Lincoln's Community Health Endowment did with the area hospitals, or what St. Luke's Health Initiatives has done with their Technical Assistance Partnership effort.

Throughout the young life of this burgeoning sector, it has proven to be true that "As funders lead, so goes the sector." The influence of institutional funders is often vastly disproportionate to their actual levels of funding. That influence has created the movement towards collaboration, towards the development of Nonprofit Resource Centers, towards measurement.

That influence could create the next wave of vision-based, interconnected, values-based, strength-based systems for leveraging funder dollars. Having shared the results of just a few such innovative efforts, it is clear that the potential results if such cooperative systems became the norm for funding would be truly breathtaking.

We encourage funders around the world to experiment to find more innovative funding mechanisms to accomplish that. We further encourage funders to form their own Learning Communities, to leverage what they are learning to others in the community, and to other funders around the country and around the globe.

Chapter 51:
The Future We Create

Here is the future we can begin to create right now.

A future where our home, this planet earth, is at peace. Where all peoples share this global home, perhaps first in an awkward truce, and then in true harmony.

A future where our planet is physically healthy, where rivers run clear and clean, where air is pure, where the animals that inhabit this planet (including we human animals) and the physical environment are living in balance.

A future where we value our collective potential and responsibility as much as we value our individual potential and responsibility. A future where the true meaning of humanity, in all its ability, is present.

Because we are creating the future with every action we take and every decision we make, we can choose, every day, whether that is where we will aim our work. From there, accomplishing such lofty goals is possible, simply because it is not impossible.

It is our greatest hope that you will use The Pollyanna Principles to find a million ways to achieve those visionary end results. It is our hope that you will explore and discover new approaches and systems to align means behind those visionary ends. That you will link arms with everyone who wishes to create such change - across disciplines, across silos, across the arbitrary lines that divide funders from providers from governments from businesses.

It is our hope that you will do so consciously, and that through those conscious efforts, the culture of our sector's work will change.

What is on the line is nothing less than the future of humanity. That is because we are creating the future, every day, whether we do so consciously or not.

The choice is ours.

What future will you create today?

Acknowledgments

It is with great joy and affection that I express my gratitude to the many individuals who gave a piece of themselves to make this book possible. In the six years and at least four separate incarnations of this book, it is hard to comprehend how many friends, colleagues and teachers are present in these pages.

Dan Duncan, Jannie Cox, and Cheryl and Larry Smith all shared their offices and homes to give me a place to write. Steve, Mary and Kate Cortopassi, for whom generosity seems far too weak a word - this final version of the book became real in your living room. How can I begin to thank you for that?

For painstakingly helping me think through what it meant to write this book, for gently cajoling, and for asking, "Are you sure you really want to say this?" I cannot begin to thank Debbie Stewart. Your friendship and your expertise are a blessing, Debbie!

Jane Garthson, Ginny Hildebrand, Bonnie Koenig, Ann Lucas, Ed Portnoy, Renata Rafferty, June Renzulli, Elizabeth Sadlon and Tracey Sisson assisted with various stages of peer review, lovingly guiding me back to what was important as I veered off track. Amanda Breeden, Mildred Clark, Kelli Johnson, Kathleen A. LeGried, David Mathe, Valerie Plomin, Jeri Slavin, and Karin Wandrei proofread every word, polishing the book as it went into the home stretch. Erin Tierney, your final review - and your undying belief in this book - were invaluable.

To the clients with whom Dimitri and I have been blessed to work, whose stories grace these pages, we have learned so much from you. And to our "children" - the Diaper Banks in Tucson and Phoenix - you make us proud, every day.

To participants on various online discussion lists - the Com-Prac / Communities of Practice list, the ARNOVA list, the EVAL-Talk list of the American Evaluation Association - you have stretched my thinking in so many ways. And my boundless gratitude goes to Steve Nill and every one of the participants on Charity Channel, where, for over ten years, it has felt like home.

Mark Myers and Joey Tanner Barbee - your incredible wisdom and insights pushed this book from "almost there" to "nailed it." Your encouragement to make the book a celebration of what is possible reminded me to see past the problems in the writing, and to aim at my vision for what the book could be. To have had each of you as a friend all these years, to encourage the best in me, is an honor I cannot imagine I deserve.

I must thank the incredible gang of seven who gathered in the desert in 100 degree June heat to focus on what is possible. You are my inspiration, my support, my kick-in-the-butt. To Rick Carter, who puts all this into practice and shows what is possible, every day. To Bonnie Koenig, for your no-BS practical wisdom and your experience around the world. To Tracey McConnell, for sharing right before our eyes how this work is changing you. To Bob Moore, for your enthusiasm at every major juncture on so many of our journeys. To Michael Kumer, for asking tough questions, for making us dig deep to get to the essence, and for sharing our work with anyone who will listen. To Elizabeth Sadlon for always cutting through to the right question and for being my favorite devil's advocate. And to Tracey Sisson, for showing us the pony and giving us new language. I cannot wait to see where the journey takes us next!

Then there are the people whose presence in my life simply makes each day livable. First, my undying thanks to the Tapiocans. You have had to endure hearing about this book for so long, I cannot believe you have not restricted me from ever mentioning it again. Here's to our growing old together, sharing horrible puns, photos of our dogs and kids, and celebrating every single thing life throws our way, till death do us part. Andrew, Bill, Jane, Jeane, Mari, Mark, Michael, Nathan, Renata and Sue - I love you all madly.

Nick Perona and Erin Tierney - no matter how many miles apart we are, you are always there for us. I don't know how to tell you what that means to both Dimitri and me, every day.

My mom and dad, Rose and Walter Gottlieb; my brother and sister-in-law, Marty Gottlieb and Jeri Slavin; and my nephews who always make me laugh - Walt, Zach and Sly. My "other family" - Dyan, Mito, and Derek. My best friends since 7th grade, Debbie Solomon and Ray Ranghelli. Your constant enthusiasm and support for our work means everything (even when you can't totally figure out what it is we do!).

Nanette Pageau surrounds me every day with more love than I could possibly deserve. My daughter, Lizzie Sam, makes me laugh and keeps me sane, and has endured hearing the words, "No really, the book is almost done" for six years now. You are both on every page here.

And to Dimitri Petropolis, my best friend and business partner, who turns what would have been "I" into "we" throughout the book - I cannot imagine being on this adventure with anyone else.

Lastly, there are teachers too many to name, who have given me a gift beyond what is contained in these pages - the gift of ongoing growth in all ways, a path I vow humbly to continue walking for as long as this life gives me the opportunity. Thank you for having walked this path before me.

To be surrounded by this many extraordinary people is something for which I am grateful every single day. I bow to each of you, for all you are and all you do, and for all we have ahead of us together.

About the Author

Hildy Gottlieb has been called "the most innovative and practical thinker in our sector." As President of the Community-Driven Institute, her ground-breaking work aims the Community Benefit Sector at its highest potential - creating the future of our world.

In 1998, after working for five years as consultants to community organizations, Hildy and her business partner (and best friend) Dimitri Petropolis had an epiphany - regardless of the quality of work done by their clients and other organizations, those organizations were not creating significant improvement to the quality of life in their communities.

This realization led to the development of the thought-processes and methodologies that became the Pollyanna Principles, and that laid the groundwork for the development of the Community-Driven Institute.

Hildy's credentials include teaching, writing and consulting in the Community Benefit Sector, as well as co-founding two community organizations - the world's first diaper bank in her adopted hometown of Tucson, Arizona, and a second diaper bank in the Phoenix area. Steeped in that in-the-trenches reality, Charity Channel CEO Stephen Nill has labeled Hildy "a practitioner's practitioner."

Hildy's numerous awards include a Points of Light Citation from President Bill Clinton. Her books have become industry standards, including her manual on Board Development, and her most popular work, "FriendRaising: Community Engagement Strategies for Boards Who Hate Fundraising But Love Making Friends."

Outside her work life, Hildy is the single mother of an adult daughter who continues to be her inspiration. Hildy credits her inspirational public speaking abilities to years of teaching Spanish and creative writing in her daughter's grade school classes.

INDEX

CPSIA information can be obtained at www.ICGtesting.com
Printed in the USA
242479LV00006BA/27/P

9 780981 892801